BEARING THE TORCH

BEARING THE TORCH

The University of Tennessee, 1794–2010

T. R. C. HUTTON

The University of Tennessee Press
Knoxville

LIBRARY OF CONGRESS CATALOGING-IN-PUBLICATION DATA
Names: Hutton, T. R. C., author.
Title: Bearing the torch : the University of Tennessee, 1794–2010 / T.R.C. Hutton.
Description: First edition. | Knoxville : The University of Tennessee Press, [2022] |
Includes bibliographical references and index. |
Summary: "The University of Tennessee has its origins in Blount College, founded in 1794
and named after territorial governor William Blount even before Tennessee was a state.
The last scholarly history of the university appeared in 1978, but this book presents a very
different treatment. It seeks nothing less than to be a social history of the university,
fully integrating historical context, and allowing the book's central 'character'—
the university itself—to emerge among historical themes and concerns. For example,
Hutton shows how the school's development was hampered in the early nineteenth century
by Jacksonian notions of laissez-faire, including exceedingly cheap state funding
(a theme that emerges often), how the school nearly disappeared as the Civil War raged
in a very divided region, how the university found creative ways to resist reconstruction,
how students embraced dramatic social changes during the Progressive era, and how in the
Cold War era the school became a successful research institution"—Provided by publisher.
Identifiers: LCCN 2022001411 (print) | LCCN 2022001412 (ebook) |
ISBN 9781621906872 (hardcover) | ISBN 9781621906896 (pdf) |
ISBN 9781621906902 (kindle edition)
Subjects: LCSH: University of Tennessee, Knoxville—History. |
State universities and colleges—Tennessee—History.
Classification: LCC LD5293 .H87 2022 (print) | LCC LD5293 (EBOOK) |
DDC 378.768/85—dc23/eng/20220223
LC record available at https://lccn.loc.gov/2022001411
LC ebook record available at https://lccn.loc.gov/2022001412

CONTENTS

ILLUSTRATIONS

ACKNOWLEDGMENTS

This book began as an idea discussed between former UT chancellor Jimmy Cheek and Department of History head Ernie Freeberg, who asked me if I would be interested in a unique research opportunity. I jumped at the opportunity for many reasons, including appreciation for their faith in a historian with only one book under his belt. Long-time university provost John Zomchick arranged for me a very generous course release, while Steve Smith, the dean of libraries, also became an early supporter of the book. Special thanks also go out to Prof. Amy Elias and the UT Humanities Center for a sponsorship that made this book possible.

The majority of my research was conducted at the spectacularly well-staffed Betsey B. Creekmore Special Collections in UT's Hodges Library. I am deeply grateful to Kris Bronstad, Becky Becker, Jennifer Beals, Laura Romans, Bill Eigelsbach, and especially my former students Bailey Culpepper and Grace Sloan for making my hours there pleasant and productive. Alesha Shumar, UT's university archivist, provided me with a wealth of photographs to select from for the book and shared her colossal knowledge of the school's history and its byzantine paper trail while also providing general guidance along the way. This book would have been an impossible undertaking without her help.

Michael Cohen, William "Doc" Hardy, and Ernie Freeberg each took time out of their busy professional schedules to look at chapters for me, while Bob Levy, Will Kuby, and an unnamed reader each read the entire package and gave me very helpful criticism. My copyeditors, Katie Hannah and Jon Boggs, saved me future blushes by fixing countless mistakes and omissions. Bea Burton constructed a thorough index.

Some of my most remarkable discoveries about UT in the eighteenth and ninteenth centuries were made with help from Trent Hanner at the Tennessee

Libraries & Archives in Nashville. I benefited immeasurably from research on the university's history carried out by Betsey Creekmore, Professor Donna Braquet, the late Professor Milton Klein, my friend Jack Neely, and my mentor Professor Emeritus Bruce Wheeler. I stand on the shoulders of some very good scholars. Special thanks also to Katherine Ballantyne and my former student Shelby Harper, who each shared their research on student life at UT in the mid-twentieth century.

Countless times I was asked who I'd like to publish with, and I was fortunate to end up with my first choice in the University of Tennessee Press. Scot Danforth, Tom Post, and Thomas Wells are good friends, and I enjoyed working with them immensely. Scot especially helped guide me as an author and showed tremendous patience when I didn't know what I was doing.

I was honored that UT's Vice Chancellor for Diversity & Engagement Tyvi Small asked me to use what I'd learned about UT history by serving on a research and advisory committee to study university place names. My subsequent work with Rev. Renee Kesler and Alesha Shumar was a tremendous pleasure, and I hope I was of some service.

My colleagues in the University of Tennessee Department of History were always a source of encouragement and helpful questions about their employer's history. Thanks to Ann Jefferson, Jason Dawsey, Dan Feller, Monica Black, Can Yüce, Matthew Gilles, Chad Black, Jeff Norrell, Marina Maccari, Lynn Sacco, Kristen Block, Tore Olsson, Luke Harlow, Pat Rutenberg, Rob Bland, Chris Magra, Brandon Winford, Nikki Eggers, Shellen Wu, Victor Petrov, Michael Lynch, Bill Mercer, Tess Evans, the late Josh Hodge, Max Matherne, Brittany Poe, and Laura Roesch. I'm acutely grateful to Shannen Dee Williams, Cynthia Tinker, and Julie Reed for their specific insights into subjects that pertained directly to UT's history over three centuries. By and large, the people who helped me most of all in our department were Kim Harrison, Mary Copeland Beckley, and Bernie Koprince, friends who happened to be an administrative staff who provided me with whatever practical assistance I needed. My colleagues in other departments, Amber Roessner, Mark Hulsether, and Martin Griffin, offered moral support and service as intellectual sounding boards. Thanks also for the support I received from my comrades in the United Campus Workers my entire time at the University of Tennessee, especially during the early days of the COVID-19 pandemic, when many of us were otherwise left to our own devices while teaching remotely.

Finally, a special thanks to the East Hall bunch, young scholars and artists who made my own first experience at a university (Appalachian State University in North Carolina, to be exact) decades ago monumental. Tay Hambrick, Tracy Hall, Phil Laton, Laurie Troutman Williams, Ian Williams, Bryan Thompson Timms, Beth Marshall, Matt Barton, Greg Deleruyelle, Jeremy DeWitt, Joanna Blitch, Scott Houston, Brandon Padgett, Alex Howard, Randall Wood, Katherine O'Neal, Steve Davis, and Anne Wright weren't involved in this book in any direct way, but they were my crew during my undergrad days. They helped me learn the value of ideas and the bravery to be creative, and each of them supported my goal of becoming a historian. Intellectually curious college students learn as much from their peers as they do their professors, more really, and I hope my students at UT had the same level of peer support I did from my friends.

INTRODUCTION

During the 2019–2020 school year, the University of Tennessee celebrated its bicenquasquigenary, or its 225th anniversary, as an institution of higher learning. Strictly speaking, Blount College was founded outside of the United States (i.e., two years before Tennessee statehood), at a time when higher education as we understand it in the twenty-first century did not exist. The school that began as Blount College in a Knoxville parsonage in 1794 has grown and changed with the times and, along the way, has survived trials that nearly proved fatal on more than one occasion. This is a history of the University of Tennessee, replete with anecdotes and vignettes of interest to anyone involved with the school, from the chancellor's office to the homes of Vols fans whose familiarity with the school is limited to the sports page. But it is also the life story of a school whose history reflects that of its state and its nation; this history exemplifies the relationship between education and American democracy. Politics is what one might call the natural condition of democracy, and far too many times, UT's mission has been hindered by politics in the state and on campus. The University of Tennessee's story has always been defined by inclusion and exclusion, and the school has triumphed when it practiced the former and failed when it took part in the latter. *Bearing the Torch* traces that ongoing process, detailing the University of Tennessee's contributions to what one of the school's past presidents called the "diffusion of knowledge among the people."

Even though many Tennesseans today could scarcely imagine the Volunteer State without its state university, its survival from the administration of George Washington to the present was hardly inevitable. It was the actions of women and men who cared about education. Blount College began as a relatively informal arrangement aimed at providing learning for the scions of wealthy (exclusively white) families living on Cherokee land well to the west of what was then considered the United States. UT began as an educational arrangement in the backcountry. It grew into a Southern university and one of the only Research One institutions in Appalachia, the whole time in the eastern section of a state that has always envisioned itself in three competing sections, known as "grand divisions."[1] A large part of UT's story is centered on the efforts of a school in the Tennessee River valley, halfway between the Great Smokies to the south and the Cumberland Plateau to the north, to convince Middle and West Tennessee that "Rocky Top" represents the entire state. Simultaneously, closer to home, the school has always had a fascinating symbiotic "town&gown" relationship with the city of Knoxville.

The University of Tennessee has become an opportunity for any and all students in an atmosphere where a college education seems less a luxury and more a necessity for those who wish to join or remain in the American middle class. Education always creates an elite unless it is available to everyone. UT's saga has been a constant search for the expansion of education to the greatest number possible. Who deserves to be educated? Women were not allowed as permanent students until late in the nineteenth century, and women's struggle for equality as educators on the campus continued for some time after that. African Americans asserted their rights to be students at the school for decades before the barricades of Jim Crow finally fell in the 1960s. Both before and after these major changes the school has seen other struggles for equality of education. Many times students have been leaders. Many times people in official authority have damaged the university's mission.

In the first quarter of the twenty-first century there is a sort of uniformity among American state universities that the University of Tennessee reflects. Today it is a state university among state universities, and a foot tour of campus would witness architecture and student life reminiscent of similar-sized schools all over the United States. The school once known as Blount College, East Tennessee College, East Tennessee University, and finally the University of Tennessee began as a relatively informal arrangement for the education of a small number of frontier youths during the last days of the eighteenth century, a rare privilege west of the Appalachians even in the last days of the Enlightenment. It eventually became an ongoing experiment in the democratization of higher learning, but only after generations of existence in a misogynist slave society followed by a century of Jim Crow. Over the course of centuries, the school came to resemble other state universities in many ways while also reflecting the conditions and history of Tennessee and southern Appalachia: from the Civil War to the New

Deal to the Civil Rights era, the University of Tennessee experienced American history in its own way.

The last book-length history of the University of Tennessee, *To Foster Knowledge: A History of the University of Tennessee, 1794–1970* (1984), came out as a part of a small spate of Southern university histories in the mid-1980s—although it had been in the works for nearly two decades as a collaboration between three historians.[2] Passage of time was not the only reason to succeed and update their work. The book remains an excellent documentary source (this book cites it multiple times) but parts of its prose have not aged well. The authors' references to "sexual deviance" among students, "oriental" instructors, and the popularity of music featuring "strange jungle beats" suggest a datedness that begs for a successor. Their facile reference to "idiocy of the 1960s" is a poor stand-in for the almost absolute absence of attention to the significance of the decade on this campus: Knoxville's Civil Rights movement (led primarily by students of nearby Knoxville College) and the desegregation of the student body and faculty.[3] These historians end on a sour note, and their disapproval of recent changes shines through. But most of those recent changes were movements toward equality, diversity, and democracy. And throughout, the strength of UT was always subject to the quality of its leadership, especially when students of the university decided to lead.

Many Tennesseans would be especially bewildered by *To Foster Knowledge's* dismissive statement on UT sports: "Games are still interesting, even if essentially irrelevant to the development, mental or physical, of the great mass of the student body."[4] It was as sure a thing in the 1980s that games on the UT campus were not irrelevant to the great mass of the student body even if not everybody played. Calling sports "irrelevant" at a campus like UT's would be akin to saying the same of its physical plant or food services. While sports do not contribute to intellectual growth, neither do courses and curricula designed only for career-building. Having sports teams with a national profile attracts students from out of state (in a decade of teaching there this author has had multiple students who were drawn by the Vols mystique from as far as New Jersey and California) and, even when the athletic department handled players' academics poorly on the whole, the Women's basketball team's unusually high academic standards always acted as palliative. Moreover, high-profile athletics acts as an ambassador to private-sector donors at a time when the state governments occasionally treat their universities with malevolent neglect. Even if athletics have been deleterious for the mission of schools like UT, their effects pale next to those of the war on public education that many politicians wage in the twenty-first century.

My most modest hope is that this book proves interesting to the students, alumni, and employees of the university (perhaps some of its "fans" might like it as well). But I also hope students of American educational history, with or without any connection to the University of Tennessee, will find some value in it. This history does not detail every single moment of the University of Tennessee's history, and some readers will find certain exemptions disappointing. Of course this is unavoidable for an institutional history of an institution that has earned the love and passion of millions in Knoxville or elsewhere. I hope whatever omissions readers find here will inspire further research into the school's history in the near future.

The history of the University of Tennessee is a story of complex interdependence among a countless number of people. No one on the campus does their job successfully without help from dozens—perhaps hundreds—of other people. Public higher education is no longer something available only to the privileged, but a four-year degree has never been as readily available as a high school diploma. Nevertheless, the operation of a university relies on the labor of women and men who perhaps never had a chance to go to college. With that in mind, I dedicate this book to the staff of the University of Tennessee, especially those who risked health and safety to keep the campus "on line" during the 2020 coronavirus outbreak. They made this book possible and they make this educator proud.

CHAPTER ONE
Slender Beginnings, 1790–1860

. . . .

"In America, more even than in Europe, there is but one society,
whether rich or poor, high or low, commercial or agricultural;
it is everywhere composed of the same elements. It has all been raised
or reduced to the same level of civilization. The man whom you left in
the streets of New York you find again in the solitude of the Far West;
the same dress, the same tone of mind, the same language,
the same amusements. No rustic simplicity, nothing characteristic
of the wilderness, nothing even like our villages. This peculiarity may
be easily explained. The portions of territory first and most fully
peopled have reached a high degree of civilization. Education has
been prodigally bestowed; the spirit of equality has tinged with
singular uniformity the domestic habits."

—ALEXIS DE TOCQUEVILLE—
A Fortnight in the Wilderness (1831)

The school that would one day become the University of Tennessee was originally named for one of the most notorious political schemers in American
history. Blount College was named in honor of William Blount in 1794, two years
before Tennessee became the sixteenth state. Blount had been a subordinate to
George Washington during the American Revolution, and later represented
North Carolina at the 1787 Constitutional Convention in Philadelphia. When
the school was founded Blount was in charge of the Southwest Territory, 43,000
square miles of land occupied by the Cherokee, Creek, Chickasaw, and Choctaw
nations, as well as nearly 36,000 newly arrived settlers from east of the Appalachians (of this population, just under 10 percent were enslaved). Within a few
years Blount, by then a US Senator, was subject to the first and last congressional
impeachment in American history for conspiring to help Britain seize control
of the Gulf Coast from Spain. Late in the previous decade, Blount had already

Blount College. Higher education in Knoxville began in a simple parsonage
on Gay Street with readings of Horace, Euclid, and the Bible.

made similar gestures *toward* Spain in the 1780s during the attempt to create
a new US state known as Franklin, but it had not damaged his reputation to
the same degree. Blount's impeachment did not pass, but he had already been
expelled from the Senate in 1797, and he returned to Knoxville where he soon
thereafter attempted to sabotage federal land negotiations with the Cherokee
Nation. When he died in 1800 from an epidemic that swept Knoxville, William
Blount was a national pariah and a terrible embarrassment to the newly formed
republic. But he remained extremely popular among the white settlers of Tennessee, particularly due to his belligerent attitude toward Indians, and Blount
College retained his name until 1807.[1]

Perhaps its rancorous namesake was appropriate since the school was, by the
transportation standards of the day, quite foreign to the United States. Blount
College was not the first institution of higher learning west of the Appalachians,
nor was it the first one founded in what would become Tennessee; the Presbyterian schools now known as Transylvania University and Tusculum College were
organized in the future states of Kentucky and Tennessee, respectively, in the early
1780s.[2] It was, however, the first American school with no official affiliation to a
religious denomination, with a charter instructing its trustees to "take effectual
care that students of all denominations may and shall be admitted to the equal

advantages of a liberal education," and "receive a like fair, generous and equal treatment during their residence therein." Euro-American settlers moving west brought with them an attachment to (almost entirely Protestant) Christianity, but in the eighteenth century no single denomination held an overwhelming majority. Presbyterians seemed to have a numerical advantage among the first white settlers, especially those of Scottish and Ulster ancestry. But they were soon joined by Methodists, Baptists, Moravians, and members of other sects, so that no one ecclesiastical body dominated. Although literacy was not uncommon, an educated clergy was a luxury for any denomination. Religion and learning were both intertwined and elusive, so settlers allowed their children to be taught by instructors from other denominations, and many of them had come west to avoid the hegemonic established churches on the Eastern Seaboard. Moreover, at the time of Blount College's founding, the Enlightenment was still in flower, and more than a few Americans were beginning to dissociate formal learning from any church. Early Knoxvillians were probably not yet prepared for a separation of religion and education, but they did hearken to the republicanism of Thomas Jefferson, the man who coined the phrase "separation of church and state" in 1802. For all of these reasons, the nonsectarian (but certainly not secular) Blount College was well suited to the desires of the Knoxville population.[3]

The school also related to another Jeffersonian fixation: the alleged inevitability of westward expansion. The school was built on land that had been claimed by Cherokee as late as 1791, and most of the white arrivals in Knoxville in the intervening years did so with the expectation of encroaching even further into Cherokee territory. The Cherokee Nation had had a varied, but often stable, diplomatic relationship with English-speaking peoples since early in the eighteenth century. They had intermarried with white settlers, and many people living in what would become Tennessee (a word derived from *Tanasi*, a Cherokee town that existed under what is now Tellico Lake in Monroe County) negotiated dual national identities. The American Revolution caused a wave of anti-Cherokee sentiment in the rebellious colonies because many Cherokee had a tacit alliance with the British dating to the Seven Years' War. American attacks on Cherokee towns radicalized many Cherokee, but ultimately led to the Nation's permanent decline in power in the Tennessee River valley. By the end of the 1790s, the Cherokee occupied only a small portion of what became the state of Tennessee. A century after its founding, Blount College was memorialized as a vanguard of civilization infiltrating an untamed wilderness, surrounded by "'endless leagues of leagues' of forests, haunted with wolves, bears and 'the hawk-eyed and wolf-hearted Indian.'..." In fact, the Cherokee had gone to greater lengths than virtually any other native nation to accommodate and adapt to Euro-American demands and, by the eighteenth century's end, their society had nearly as many claims to the trappings of so-called civilization as did those to whom they sacrificed their land on the Holston River. It was an irony that was probably lost on Blount College's exclusively white student body.[4]

The origins of higher learning in Tennessee trace back to the educational traditions of the Presbyterian Church and the Scottish Enlightenment, leavened with the "unifying and Americanizing force" that was the College of New Jersey (which would later become Princeton University).[5] Presbyterian missionary John Martin had taught and preached among the Overhill Cherokee as early as 1758, and two others founded the school that would become Tusculum in 1783. Blount College's founding headmaster and instructor, Pennsylvania-native Samuel Carrick, was a Presbyterian minister and former student of William Graham, a Princeton graduate known for having an unparalleled influence "over the literature and religion of Virginia," and other parts of the southern backcountry where his pupils preached. The territorial legislature appointed Carrick to the newly chartered school shortly after he preached to their assemblage.[6] Like other Presbyterians, he valued a classical education; rhetoric, logic, Greek, and Latin were taught alongside what was then called "natural and moral philosophy." Memorization of facts was stressed, and probably tested by "the humble and simple, old-school, tedious business of recitation."[7] Scriptural knowledge was probably balanced with "the distinctively Scottish philosophical formulation of the great neoclassical themes of order, proportion, and reason" propagated within the ivied walls of Princeton. Blount College almost came to a premature end in 1803 when a representative of Greeneville College (now Tusculum) convinced a member of the Blount board of trustees to throw support to Greeneville, some seventy miles away, with the expectation of the Knoxville school's eventual demise. Carrick defended his school's existence at a subsequent board meeting, and won support from fellow board member Archibald Roane. Roane happened to be Tennessee's governor at the time and probably wanted an institution of higher learning as close to Knoxville, then the state capital, as possible. Governor Roane was able to convince the board's majority to remain with Blount College regardless of its affiliation, and Greeneville College was left to its own devices in the sparsely populated areas east of Knoxville. The challenge against Carrick's school was not apparently a matter of Presbyterian doctrine, but rather a recognition that Tennessee's moneyed population could support only so many schools, and competition would ensue. Blount College was one step closer to breaking free from its unofficial Presbyterianism. Nevertheless, even after the school became

Presbyterian minister Samuel Carrick
was one of the first educators west of the
Appalachians. Blount College began in 1794
under his tutelage.

state supported later on, the Presbyterian dominance of its faculty remained notable.[8]

Blount College holds the distinction of being the first coeducational college in the United States. Barbara Blount (William Blount's daughter), Polly McClung, Jennie Armstrong, and Mattie and Kittie Kain were listed as students during the school's brief existence.[9] The most logical reason for their inclusion would be that an ad hoc arrangement was available to a small number of women from wealthy families; the arrangement lasted for such a short span of time that it is a picayune footnote to the history of Tennessee and American education, a small precedent that was not imitated for generations. It is unlikely that these women received instruction seated alongside their male classmates (for that matter, it is also unlikely that Carrick taught any of his students in the physical classroom environment familiar in our own time). Perhaps these women's education at Blount constituted little more than the tutorial education available to women of elite backgrounds further east. However, the most expansive interpretation of Blount's education of women emerges from the flash of republican radicalism in the 1790s combined with the modest loosening of gender roles produced by life west of the Appalachians with exposure to Cherokee customs (or, as a previous institutional history phrased it, "the circumstances of frontier life . . ."). It would be another three decades before North America's first truly coeducational institution, Ohio's Oberlin College, was founded in 1833, and it would be another half century after that before state and private schools in the South began to even consider following suit.[10] For that matter, other "frontier" schools like Kentucky's Transylvania College, did not follow suit even though they existed under similar material conditions (*sans* contact with the Cherokee). Women's education at Blount College was perhaps a *sui generis* historical anomaly that ceased no later than 1808, but its posterity refused to consider it meaningless. In 1892, when women were first admitted to the University of Tennessee, they honored the memory of Barbara Blount by naming a student-run literary magazine after her.[11]

Blount College was an elite institution for its time and place, in one nineteenth-century historian's words, "a classical Academy for the sons of the comparatively wealthy . . . coming therefore mainly from the leisure class, who desired an acquaintance with the polite arts."[12] It was understood that schooling under Carrick prepared the student for life as an informed citizen of a republic, and perhaps even an elected official or public servant. Books of any kind were a dear commodity even for the wealthy, and students probably came under Carrick's tutelage from a wide range of relative preparedness. In fifteen years of existence, Blount College conferred a degree on only one student, William E. Parker, who ended up fading into relative obscurity after graduating in 1806. Other Carrick students went on to have exceptional careers. Hugh Lawson White, Carrick's first student, became a US Senator and helped found Tennessee's Whig Party in 1836 (his 1836 presidential run scored him twenty-six electoral votes from Georgia and Tennessee). His pupil and protégé Isaac Anderson continued the East Tennessee Presbyterian legacy, founding a school in Blount County, short miles south of Knoxville.[13] Anderson's school, the Southern and Western Theological Seminary (later Maryville College) accepted free Black and Native American people, including Skah-tle-loh-skee, also known as John Ridge. Ridge later represented his nation in Washington DC and negotiated the terms for the treaty that led to Cherokee removal west of the Mississippi in the 1830s (John Ross, the future Principal Chief of the Cherokee Nation, may have also studied under Anderson). Clement Comer Clay, one of Carrick's later students, became Alabama's eighth governor and later represented the state as US Senator. In 1807 Congress granted the school 100,000 acres of land recently taken from the Cherokee by the Treaty of Tellico (1805) with a view toward making it, and one other school further west, publicly supported colleges. Carrick briefly remained as president of newly named East Tennessee College (hereafter ETC) until his unexpected death two years later. Without its president and only teacher, ETC closed its doors after less than two years of existence.[14]

East Tennessee College's board of trustees remained in existence, but for many years their collective efforts to reenergize their school came to naught. Much of the Cherokee land handed over to the United States in the Treaty of Tellico was occupied by white squatters, most of whom were unwilling to pay for land they had already applied their labor to for years—let alone for a distant school for a small number of wealthy elites. Unlike many other states, Tennessee had no property requirements for male suffrage (at least for men who could prove they had resided in the state for more than six months), and vote-conscious legislators were too skittish to press the issue. By 1820 the state managed to squeeze less than $9,000 out of the land grant for ETC even after the United States took the Cherokee land between the Little Tennessee and Hiwassee Rivers in the 1819 Calhoun Treaty. The Tennessee legislature's failure to secure the school what it had been promised remained a bone of contention for the next three decades, with the board of trustees invariably blaming the state government for inadequately doling the land revenues that had been promised by Congress in 1807 (the primacy of the Cherokee on said land was hardly, if at all, mentioned).[15] The board also attempted a lottery in 1810, trying to sell eleven thousand tickets for 3,405 prize purses ranging from $6 to $5,000. Hugh White, by this time a trustee, wrote to President James Madison and former president Jefferson asking them to buy tickets. The scheme was an absolute failure, ultimately yielding $450 and some unsolicited (but prescient) advice from the latter.[16] Jefferson demurred from buying a ticket, claiming he "made it a rule never to engage in a lottery or any other adventure of mere chance," but did offer advice on future construction for the moribund school.

> I consider the common plan followed in this country, but not in others, of making one large and expensive building, as unfortunately erroneous. It is infinitely better to erect a small and separate lodge for each separate professorship, with only a hall below for his class, and two chambers above for himself; joining these lodges by barracks for a certain portion of the students, opening into a covered way to give a dry communication between all the schools. The whole of these arranged around an open square of grass and trees, would make it, what it should be in fact, an academical village, instead of a large and common den of noise, of filth and of fetid air. It would afford that quiet retirement so friendly to study, and lessen the dangers of fire, infection and tumult. Every

professor would be the police officer of the students adjacent to his own lodge, which should include those of his own class of preference, and might be at the head of their table, if, as I suppose, it can be reconciled with the necessary economy to dine them in smaller and separate parties, rather than in a large and common mess.[17]

Jefferson's familiar vision of a college campus presaged the physical outlay of the slave-constructed campus he founded, the University of Virginia, nine years later.[18] But ETC's trustees did not take Jefferson's advice, nor could they duplicate his ambitions for what he called the "slender beginnings and progressive growth of our institutions."[19] The school's first decades were modest ones.

The following decade was a period of regression for Knoxville—and not entirely because of the loss of its college. The state capital moved west to Nashville in 1812 and stayed there until 1817 when it came back to Knoxville for two years before moving west yet again (after a few years in Murfreesboro, the state government settled permanently in Nashville). The War of 1812 increased Nashville's commercial importance and the national profile of its most famous resident, future president Andrew Jackson. After the war, Jackson engineered the purchase of Chickasaw land between the Tennessee and Mississippi Rivers in 1819, and the town of Memphis grew quickly as an entrepôt for what was becoming the cotton kingdom to its south. The trade in cotton and enslaved people turned Memphis into one of the largest cities in the slave states and, by 1860, among the fifty largest cities in the United States. The steam power era made life on the Cumberland and Mississippi Rivers vibrant, and Memphis and Nashville thrived in turn, but Knoxville shrank in relative size and influence rather quickly. The city on the Holston River was connected to the sprawling Tennessee, but the latter river's navigability was hampered by shoals and whirlpools.[20] When the *Atlas*, a small side-wheeler, arduously made it upstream to Knoxville in 1828 the town marked the rare accomplishment (and one that would rarely be repeated for nearly a century) with a citywide celebration. Missouri had become the twenty-fourth state in 1821, and Tennessee no longer bordered the western edge of the United States. As Tennessee went from being part of the Old Southwest to part of the Old South, Knoxville got short shrift, and the reopening of its college was not inevitable.[21] In turn, ETC was less of a priority to the state government than it ever had been, especially as other little country colleges sprung up elsewhere in Tennessee.

ETC reopened in 1820 as part of a two-school partnership with Hampden-Sydney Academy, a Knoxville boys' school, a temporary measure that gave the trustees time and resources to plan their school. They bought a steep forty acres west of Knoxville and just to the north of the Holston River known interchangeably as "College Hill" and "Barbara Hill" after Barbara Blount. A large central building (against Jefferson's advice) was completed on the hill's crest in 1828, surrounded by mulberry trees and native hardwoods. New faculty members came aboard, including Hugh Brown, a Knoxville newspaperman knowledgeable in Latin.[22] Samuel Carrick had begun teaching in his home until he was granted space in a house in central Knoxville. As of the 1820s, his school's successor, manicured and set off from the town by nearly half a mile, looked like something that might constitute a *campus*.[23]

ETC came into its own just as political tides were turning in the United States. Andrew Jackson, long the major domo of Tennessee's public affairs, was inaugurated president in 1829, and with that a new variety of firebrand politics grew in the United States. In the days of William Blount, it was understood that American society was, if not as hierarchical as the British they had rebelled against, at least slightly given to a deference based on wealth. The wealthy were expected to be publicly virtuous and accept leadership roles and, in turn, they demanded respect from their less fortunate neighbors. But the Jackson presidency signaled an electoral and cultural revolt against the "moneyed aristocracy," whom he believed conspired against the commonweal. From the days of the Revolution until just after the War of 1812, the word *democracy* was a source of fear for men like James Madison, and perhaps even William Blount and Samuel Carrick, but Jackson's supporters insisted that democracy was the goal of a republic.[24] Jackson was actually relatively unpopular around Knoxville (especially in his second presidential term), and it was in fact Hugh White who led opposition to him in Tennessee in the 1830s.[25] Nevertheless, the revolt against old eighteenth-century social structures was probably just as strong in eastern Tennessee as it was anywhere else.

Actual aristocracies were hard to come by in the upper South, but institutions like ETC were open to Jacksonian attacks simply because they taught the privileged at the expense of the taxpayer (as of 1821, the tuition was fifteen dollars per semester for study of "the dead languages" and another fifteen for students studying arts and sciences, but within two years it was reduced to general fee of ten dollars).[26] In an open attempt to score votes from the squatters on Cherokee land that had been granted to ETC, Knoxville lawyer Thomas Arnold made criticism of the school part of his platform for a congressional campaign in 1827, accusing ETC of building "palaces, with light houses of the sky on them (Center

College had a prominent open belfry), for the sons of a few great men to go up and star gaze," in place of common schools for poorer children. Knoxville physician and author John C. Gunn was incensed by the seeming physical symbolism of the new building on Barbara Hill. "Behold that great rotunda—that monument of folly—the college," Gunn wrote in 1829. "That building for the rich man's son— that building which closes its doors against the poor man's child . . . this temple of aristocracy." Gunn might not have been an advocate of public education for all (a concept popularized in the Northeast soon thereafter by Horace Mann, but still a distant prospect in Tennessee), but he definitely resented the fact that "the south-of-the-river people (i.e., squatters) paid drop by drop of sweat to erect this tomb of extravagance." It was a quintessentially Jacksonian complaint against a school that, as late as 1827, featured commencement orations in Latin, Greek, and French.[27] Perhaps as a gesture to changing times, in 1829 the board of trustees authorized tuition-free admission of "two young men from each county in East Tennessee" determined to be "from indigent circumstances," provided the new students were recommended as having "promising talents" and "good moral character."[28]

Others from the area felt the school should be *better* funded. In 1830 a speaker at a gathering of ETU alumni in Alabama excoriated "the venality and carelessness of the Legislature of Tennessee, and the prejudices of the people at large against education." Both the government and the electorate had, in recent years, "done all in their power to paralyze the State University, by cutting away and deteriorating its fund at every opportunity." The speaker hoped that, even as Tennessee purposefully made itself "one of the most illiterate of civilized people," by under-funding ETC, the same mistakes would not be repeated with the new "richly endowed and splendid institution, the University of Alabama," which opened its doors to students for the first time that following spring."[29]

Along with the flattening of pecuniary privilege, the other overwhelming Jacksonian impulse was accelerated Indian removal, a policy that directly affected ETC more than Doctor Gunn's protest. In 1835 a faction of the Cherokee Nation known as the Treaty Party signed the Treaty of New Echota, giving up land south of Tennessee's Hiwassee River, an area that the state of Tennessee organized into the Ocoee District (an area that makes up roughly six counties in what is now Tennessee's southeastern-most corner). The New Echota treaty symbolized a part of the Cherokees' relenting to what they considered an inevitable forced removal by the federal government. With the understanding that the land sales that followed 1806 had done little to help Tennessee schools, the legislature granted the Ocoee District land sales to be divided between ETC and a Nashville school.[30] In 1837, the vast majority of Cherokees still living in what was becoming part of

Tennessee were forcibly removed by the federal government. A year later, with most of the Ocoee land sold to white buyers, ETC recouped gains of more than $34,000 (allegedly less than a quarter of what the school was to have received from the earlier land sales). It was a rare moment of solvency for the school, one that had come at the expense of what would eventually be known as the "Trail of Tears."[31]

In 1834 ETC came under the leadership of Joseph Estabrook, the president who, according to one college history, made his school "accommodate [itself] to Jacksonian Democracy."[32] Since 1827 there had been two presidents, Presbyterian clergyman Charles Coffin and (for one apparently disappointing year) mathematician James Piper, both with connections to the old Blount College.[33] By all accounts, Coffin was an able and willing educator, but his tenure in office was dampened by criticisms like those from Thomas Arnold and John C. Gunn and a general inability to fund his impoverished school; Piper's time as president amounted to one year. Estabrook's arrival brought elements of the old mingled with shades of the new, and his eventual success was fortified by the windfall brought about by the Ocoee land sales. The native New Englander had once begun studying for the Presbyterian clergy at Princeton, but only after graduating from Dartmouth, one of the early nineteenth century's greater educational centers for science, engineering, and industrial arts. Estabrook was a much-needed arrival for a school and a town that had lost prominence since their respective foundings, and he was probably more hopeful for ETC's future than Coffin and Piper had been, especially since enrollment had increased, as had on-campus student boarding, which he believed by the end of 1835 to be "the main cause of our prosperity." "Should providence continue to bless our exertions we look forward to a large & highly reputable college," he crowed to a New England cousin in a Christmas Day letter. "Our requirements and course of study is same with Amherst and Yale."[34]

Under Estabrook, ETC adjusted its area of teaching to attract a broader array of students, not limited to those who aspired to law and politics. Classical education in Horace and Virgil was not abandoned, but it was supplemented with a greater emphasis on science and a more precise codification of the curriculum. English was added as a subject to make the school more attractive to prospective teachers on the primary level.[35] In so doing, Estabrook countered the criticisms from Arnold and Gunn by making the school a supporter of common schools—free public schools—at a time when they were much needed and newly funded in Tennessee.[36] At the 1838 commencement, Estabrook made clear his support for "popular education," and made it clear that schools like his were not to blame for education being too exclusively disseminated.

The diffusion of knowledge among the people is termed by orators and politicians the corner-stone of our political fabric. With few exceptions it is badly
laid, or rather, not laid at all; and, though, in some States it is a never failing
topic of panegyric, nothing effectual has been accomplished; the instances
are indeed few, where efficient, energetic action bears any proportion to its
acknowledged importance. So much talk without work may well lead us to
doubt the sincerity of some of the advocates; it is, nevertheless, a convenient
loop 'to hang a speech on,' and is admirably fitted to shew the affection of
the candidate for the 'dear people.' But I fear 'Common Schools' are too often
on the lips, while *office, office* [Estabrook's italics] only, is in the heart. Else,
why in the halls of legislation do we find this same advocate defeating every
enlightened and liberal plan, and sanctioning such only as will keep alive the
subject, without accomplishing the object.[37]

Even after the anti-aristocratic impulse of the late 1820s shepherded by Arnold
and Gunn, funding for and accessibility of common schools had failed to substantially increase. Estabrook pointed out the sad paradox of Jacksonian politics:
attacks on privilege coupled with parsimonious public spending amounted to
little in the way of noticeable improvements. Although Estabrook did note that
his home state of New Hampshire had some of the best common schools in the
nation, he left out mentioning the key difference between it and his adopted state,
which was plain when North and South were compared: the lack of infrastructure,
including common schools, in states where slavery was still the law of the land.[38]

Owing to its new status as a more general institution of higher learning, the
school was renamed East Tennessee University (ETU) in 1840.[39] The student
body increased prodigiously under Estabrook's leadership, reaching ninety-five
in the 1837–38 school year. So many classes were held (including a series notably
entitled "art of school teaching") that a class catalog was needed.[40] *University
Magazine*, founded in 1841, became the school's first student-run publication,
aided in its start by a Knoxville town newspaper. A newspaper advertisement from
1847 written by longtime board secretary D.A. Deadrick announced six faculty
members would begin the school year in mid-October with a $15 yearly tuition
($10 for the school's younger preparatory students) in a locality "exceedingly
healthful . . . peculiarly so to students from the South."[41] It was still a small
school with parochial reach, but its reach was slowly growing. Stamos Trikaliotes,
of Athens, Greece, graduated from ETU in 1841, the school's first recorded
international student.

The most immediate response to the new name and curricular range was a
public attack not against what had changed, but rather what had stayed suspi-

ciously the same. ETU remained a school with no church affiliation but, like most schools of its time, its faculty included a significant number of preachers—and, for one reason or another, they shared the same denomination as the school's long-dead founder.[42] As the size of the student body grew, so did its Protestant diversity (Knoxville's first Catholic parish was not established until 1855), and yet the Presbyterian domination of the faculty remained the same. Serving under the Princeton seminary dropout Estabrook, two out of five ETU minister-professors were also Presbyterian, and in 1841 the board of trustees considered firing them and replacing them each with a Baptist and a Methodist.[43] The motion failed, but for the next seven years faculty came and went, intimidated by the "great Presbyterian and Methodist war" developing around the university.[44] Tennessee's government did not grant Maryville College a charter till 1842 for fear of Presbyterian dominance among the educated electorate trespassing against the other growing denominations (the legislature's reluctance was probably also motivated by Maryville's openly abolitionist identity).[45] William Brownlow, a newspaperman and Methodist preacher who arrived in Knoxville in 1849, accused (probably baselessly) the ETU board of trustees of misusing state funds, thus arousing the suspicions of some state legislators. In 1850 the state government forced the trustees to add seats to their board and submit a regular report on the state of the school, marking the first time in any iteration of the school's history that it had been allowed anything but full institutional autonomy. Humiliated, Estabrook submitted his resignation, and the gun-shy trustees appointed Judge William Reese (Carrick's former student), the first president of any of the school incarnations with no formal clerical training. Reese was an able enough executive with deep local roots, but he did not have Estabrook's sense of aspiration, plus he was powerless in the face of the societal changes of the time. For the next ten years the school went through yet another period of instability, but this time due to conflict rather than indigence.[46]

Since John Gunn's complaint about ETC's "aristocratic" interests, other complaints against privilege had grown throughout Tennessee. The same year Estabrook took the reins at ETC, Tennessee held its first constitutional convention since the state's founding. The new document decreased property taxes on modest holdings (the 1796 constitution had axed rich and poor alike on a "uniform and equal basis"), and property requirements for voting and holding office were eliminated. But its more insidious legacy was an unprecedented formalizing of slavery and white supremacy. Conventioneers rebuffed calls for a program of gradual emancipation by including a clause making owner's consent an absolute necessity for freeing anyone from bondage. The vote was taken away from free men of color who had made up a small portion of the electorate since 1796. Tennessee would continue to have one of the smallest enslaved populations in the United States (in 1850 only 24 percent of the state's overall population was enslaved and only 22 percent of white households enslaved anyone), and arguably more open critics of slavery than any other Southern state (for instance, Maryville College had, by this time, established itself as an institution openly opposed to the institution). However, the events of the 1830s ensured that Tennessee was not only a "white man's country," but also firmly under the political control of the slaveowning minority of the white population. Perhaps not coincidentally, by virtue of its being the section of the state with the smallest minority of enslavers and the fewest enslaved people, East Tennessee's population and political capital continued to fall behind the middle and western sections of the state.[47] By the end of the 1840s, slavery was becoming a heated political topic, and those who defended it as well as those who abhorred it could at least agree that its existence was a major contingency in the future of the United States. Eight months after Estabrook's resignation from ETU, a group of white Southerners from six states met in Nashville to affirm the right of state secession in reaction to the federal government's limitations on slavery in western states.[48] In 1851 student-run "Southern Rights Association" at the University of South Carolina published a series of resolutions and asked that students from other Southern schools respond. ETU students complied, or at least responded, condemning the "spirit of treason, insurrection and civil war" evident in the South Carolina club's declaration. "Resolved," read the Tennessee reply in various newspapers, "That though the South has not obtained all that could have been desired, in the adjustment of the slavery question . . . we remain immoveable in our attachment to the Union, prompted, not by the rebellious principle which they advocate, '*Liberty first, and Union afterwards*,' but the noble and glorious sentiment, '*Liberty and Union, now and forever, one and inseparable*'" (original italics).[49]

Disunion was an unpopular idea in East Tennessee, and apparently abhorrent on its campus. But slavery, the impetus behind the ideas of secession and "Southern Rights," was fundamental to life in antebellum Knoxville. It is very likely that enslaved men built much of the ETC (and later ETU) campus buildings on Barbara Hill, particularly the brick Greek Revival flagship building Center College (eventually called Old College), and adjacent student life structures known as West College and East College, the school's first dormitories.[50] Substantial construction projects began under Estabrook's leadership including East College and West College, both attributed to "Tennessee's first contracting firm" headed by

Thomas Crutchfield (who also oversaw the construction of ETC's first building on Barbara Hill).[51] Crutchfield and his father-in-law, Samuel Cleage, (the latter the founder of the town of Athens, Tennessee) migrated from Virginia in 1823, bringing with them enslaved people "who were trained workmen . . . put to work making brick, cutting, curing, turning and polishing work, etc."[52] Operating in a cash-poor economy in the early years, Cleage was said to have occasionally taken slaves as payment for his and Crutchfield's constructions, and both men were slaveowners at the time of major campus expansion between 1828 and 1830.[53]

East Tennessee was a geographic crucible for the growing conflict over slavery, and its schools played a role, not by serving as a forum for public debate, but rather by attracting a diverse host of individuals to an area where slavery was less economically dynamic than elsewhere in Tennessee and the South. Going back to the days of William Blount, school trustees were invariably wealthy elites and many, perhaps most, profited from slavery. Longtime trustee and Knoxville booster and historian Dr. James Ramsey took the rare position of advocacy for reopening the international slave trade, but he was an extreme case (as early as the 1820s Ramsey had envisioned a railroad connecting Knoxville to Charleston and Savannah rather than closer port cities in North Carolina and Virginia).[54] Many antebellum Tennesseans expressed ambivalence about slavery, while others actively opposed it. A ways to the east of Knoxville, Jonesborough, Tennessee, was the home of the *Manumission Intelligencer* (later renamed *The Emancipator*), founded in 1819 as one of the first newspapers in the United States devoted entirely to ending slavery.[55] Under Isaac Anderson's leadership Maryville College became a hub of abolitionist ministry with (by Anderson's estimation) a student body made up of roughly half ardent abolitionists by 1838, and a small handful of African American students over the course of the nineteenth century.[56] Abolitionism was considered a radical position even among white Tennesseans who did not own slaves and those who resented the inordinate political power slavery carried with it in local and state government. ETU instructors perhaps did not criticize slavery as loudly as their Maryville neighbors, but antislavery sentiment was noted among its faculty during Estabrook's administration. After ETC chemistry instructor Reverend L.F. Clarke died in 1840, his friend Ezekiel Birdseye eulogized "one of the most ardent abolitionists," whose "labors among the colored population of Knoxville were successful and placed him so high in their affections that they yet speak of him with warm affections and lament his death."[57] ETU faculty who held less-than-sanguine feelings about slavery were probably best represented by Massachusetts native Horace Maynard, who came south to teach at ETU in 1838.[58] Aghast at the plight of enslaved people he saw around him in Knoxville, he excoriated slavery as "a curse to the country" the following year, but as his Tennessee sojourn continued, his feelings softened, and he began leasing slaves from his neighbors after he began practicing law (Maynard resigned from ETU in 1843) and contemplating a political career. Elected to Congress in 1856, Maynard was himself a slaveowner by the end of his first term.[59] Vocal public arguments over slavery were discouraged in the 1840s, and dangerous by the 1850s, but the growing tension was found in other facets of life. It is very likely that the interdenominational attacks on the Presbyterian-dominated faculty leading up to Estabrook's resignation were a sort of proxy war over ecclesiastical differences over slavery.[60]

Throughout the 1850s, ETU's board of trustees spent almost half of their meetings accepting resignations from faculty and attempting to hire replacements.[61] The board's extant records feature few indications of obvious rancor or dissent among teachers except for the faculty's collective protest against changes imposed to a standard pledge of good morals for the student body.[62] Reese resigned after fewer than three years, when the number of faculty was temporarily whittled down from six to one; his replacement, New Hampshire native George Cooke, was (according to contemporary Knoxville newspaperman Moses White) drummed out of his office in 1857 for being a Northerner (the trustees officially accepted Cooke's resignation three weeks before the Supreme Court announced its infamous *Dred Scott* decision).[63] Early in his term, the school was crippled by Knoxville's "Asiatic cholera" epidemic, and enrollments stayed low for years to come.[64] By the time of Cooke's resignation, Knoxville had been connected to Georgia via the East Tennessee & Georgia Railroad, replete with new commercial opportunities in and connections to the Deep South, for nearly two years.[65] With sectional feelings reaching a fever pitch and, locally, an unprecedented link to the land of King Cotton that had long hungered for East Tennessee corn, wheat, and livestock, New Englander Cooke was deemed suspect.[66] With Cooke's departure, ETU suspended classes for a year, a victim of prejudice brought about by commerce.[67]

Deadrick's advertisement for the 1859 summer session boasted of an "Institution . . . permanently reorganized and in successful operation," but lacking a specific mention of faculty size, and a tuition marked up 150 percent since 1850.[68] By this time most of the ETU student body were younger, preparatory-aged, and soon to lose their president yet again when Reverend William Carnes accepted another school presidency in Middle Tennessee.[69]

Before his departure, however, he oversaw ETU's official mandate of military education in 1860.[70] The nineteenth-century South had an affinity for formal military training for a combination of reasons, ranging from the institutionalized violence needed to maintain a slave society, to the recognition that "[h]abits of unrestrained indulgence . . . frequently laid the foundations of ruin of youths," who might otherwise "become useful and distinguished members of society."[71] The Virginia Military Institute began holding classes in 1839, and the South Carolina Military Academy (later renamed The Citadel) three years later, both with the stated intention of instilling dignity and masculine discipline in a young male population easily led astray. At least since the 1840s, the ETU administration had had to deal with disciplinary problems ranging from students leaving campus without permission to student drunkenness and "pistol packing" (guns on campus were strictly forbidden), and the school responded by introducing military education in 1844 under the guidance of engineering instructor Albert Miller Lea; it was discontinued after three years.[72] It is very likely that the nervousness of the 1850s compounded these problems (the board of trustees had discussed military discipline as early as 1855), and the new curriculum at ETU was just one manifestation of fixing a society that seemed to be fraying at its edges. It is difficult to determine how much military discipline had been taught on and around Barbara Hill before the Civil War began the following year when teachers and students were forced to make difficult decisions as to their respective loyalties to state and nation. The fact that a student named John M. Brooks was made "Instructor in Military Tactics" at the program's beginning suggests not only its popularity among the students, but also that the program may have begun as something approaching an extracurricular activity and a welcome diversion from the conventional classroom.[73]

Between 1794 and 1860, Blount College, East Tennessee College, and finally East Tennessee University each reflected the living conditions and political culture[s] of their respective timespans. The first iteration reflected the British sectarian tradition transplanted to the outskirts of a new republic at a time when *Tennessee* was still a transnational space, growing year by year at the expense of the Chickasaw and (more immediate to Knoxville) Cherokee Nations. The Commons of open land used by Native Americans and then settlers was taken away, but it took some time for the university to become itself a Commons. Although Reverend Samuel Carrick probably provided a thorough learning environment, a parson's guided readings of geometry and logic was a far cry from a truly formal education.

The second era resembled a society getting newly accustomed to calling itself a democracy—albeit a *herrenvolk* democracy representing only white men. Old hierarchies of wealth and privilege that had begun to deteriorate in the

Revolutionary era crumbled, and the nature of education at the school reflected that. The curriculum reflected the abandonment for the gentlemanly appreciation for classicism in favor of a more utilitarian education suitable for the sons of yeomen and budding common school teachers. It is telling that the college was attacked for sectarian reasons just as it was developing an educational identity attractive to a broader segment of society.

Finally, the third period replicated the balancing act of democracy and a slave society, culminating in the American Civil War. The war also set the stage for a permanent transformation of the school, one that reflected a heightened public responsibility for higher education and an unprecedented role for what Americans understood as a *university*. But the question of what role a university played within a democracy remained unanswered and, as decades passed, would only become more complex. The free flow of ideas at ETC and ETU had been hampered by power struggles, either over governmental philosophy, religion, or the prejudice and rancor generated by the debate over slavery, all *political* struggles in the purest sense of the word. The school's full potential for education would be inhibited by politics many times yet to come.

CHAPTER TWO
Means and Opportunities, 1860–1890

....

"Thorough training, large knowledge, and the best culture
possible are needed to invigorate, direct, purify, and broaden life;
needed for the wise administration of citizenship, the duties
of which are as sure to come as the sun is to shine, though today
or tomorrow may be cloudy; needed to overcome narrowness,
one-sidedness, and incompleteness."

—W. E. B. DU BOIS—
Black Reconstruction in America (1935)

Historian Stanley Horn once quipped that "Tennessee never seceded; [Tennessee governor] Isham G. Harris seceded and carried Tennessee along with him."[1] There is truth to the hyperbole, since no other eventual member of the Confederacy did so with a greater collective record of reluctance than Tennessee. White Tennesseans bristled at the election of Abraham Lincoln in 1860, but the overwhelming majority of the eastern population was reluctant to rashly follow their fire-eating West Tennessee governor out of the Union. Even after the federal attack on Fort Sumter in late April 1861, Harris maneuvered Tennessee toward secession, and alliance with the new Confederate government, but he felt obliged to do so in relative secrecy. When Tennessee's "Declaration of Independence" was presented to voters (white men over the age of twenty-one, a group making up well under 20 percent of the state's population), it passed with over 70 percent of the vote, although there remained heavy opposition in most of the eastern third of the state. Knoxville and a handful of other commercially vibrant valley towns in the Holston and Tennessee River Valleys were virtually the only spaces in East Tennessee where any inkling of pro-Confederate sentiment grew (at the time of secession, the town's white male majority probably did support the nascent Confederacy), and even there the nay-sayers were loud.[2]

Methodist preacher and newspaper editor William Brownlow had put aside his interdenominational antagonism to lambast any and all anti-Unionist activity, and to warn East Tennessee slaveowners that tempting the wrath of the federal government would ultimately bring about the end of their peculiar institution.[3] Brownlow was eventually imprisoned and later banished. It was not uncommon for Knoxville Confederates and Unionists to feel disillusionment or disgust with their own respective sides; for instance, most of the latter despised Abraham Lincoln and were aghast at the prospect of emancipation once that became a likelihood. In the words of the most thorough Civil War history of Knoxville, for most of 1861, "many of the townspeople chose sides begrudgingly and more or less privately, keeping their sympathies to themselves and hoping to pursue business as usual, 'without reference to politics,' for as long as possible."[4]

Life in wartime Knoxville was fraught with ambiguity, an ambiguity probably felt very keenly on the ETU campus during the 1860–1861 school year. It is very likely that paranoia over the election of Lincoln and enthusiasm for rebellion were felt more strongly on campus than in the parlors, stores, and newspaper offices of Knoxville proper. Moses White took note of the large number of "Students going to the Rebel army."[5] Students came from all over, including parts of Tennessee where secession was far more popular. Moreover, historian Amy M. Taylor has noted that, in the upper South, "young adults who had never known a time without sectional conflict," born less than a quarter century before the war began, seemed to have been typically more eager.[6] John Brooks, founder of ETU's student-led military education regimen, began drilling his classmates before the 1860 election, in apparent preparation for his own commission as a Confederate captain less than a year later.[7] Support for the Confederacy was not limited to students: Professor Alexander Blair helped recruit Confederate volunteers before himself becoming a Confederate chaplain.[8] The same month as the Battle of Gettysburg, Richard Kirkpatrick, who taught Latin, Greek, and mathematics, cofounded the *Southern Chronicle* to advocate the rebel cause until later that year when his newspaper office "fell into the hands of the Federals...."[9] In the early months of the war Unionists, and those suspected of being Unionists, were subject to persecutions even though sentiments in Knoxville were "nearly equally divided" in the spring of 1861, as pro-Union language professor Milford Butler wrote to his sister. Although he had already planted his garden, Butler reluctantly resigned his professorship and left Knoxville later that year.[10] Even native Southerners like Professor Robert Strong (a Knox County native) who feared coming to harm for "loving the Union" felt compelled to leave.[11] Education was, it seemed, subordinate to the necessities of warfare.

The Civil War was one of the greatest challenges to the very existence of East
Tennessee University, a school peopled by both rebels and Unionists.

Classes continued during the fall of 1861, even as they shrank in size. A rash
of bridge burnings convinced Confederate General Felix Zollicoffer to declare
martial law.[12] School ended in early 1862 after the Battle of Mill Springs (also
known as the Battle of Fishing Creek) in southeastern Kentucky brought the
large-scale war within 120 miles of Knoxville. Mill Springs was a major Union victory that ultimately resulted in federal control over Middle Tennessee by the end
of the year. However, Knoxville remained under Confederate control for another
nineteen months.[13] The ETU campus was requisitioned by Confederate forces
as a hospital, and it fell into disrepair.[14] The board of trustees met faithfully but
sporadically at least once a year throughout the war; they requested (apparently
without reply) assistance from the Confederate government to repair buildings
a year after Mill Springs.[15]

During the war, 1863 was the most destructive year for Knoxville, and the board did not meet again that year. That summer the city changed hands when Ambrose Burnside and the Army of the Ohio marched southward from the Cumberland Gap and repelled the dwindling Confederate forces (former ETU professor Robert Strong saw this as his opportunity to return home).[16] Knoxville was one of the last of Tennessee's major cities to come under federal control, and the Confederate attempt to retake the city a few months later became one of the largest engagements in all of East Tennessee. In November Confederate forces commanded by General James Longstreet laid siege to Knoxville with hopes of eventually gaining the city. After nearly two weeks he was commanded to make an offensive, and reluctantly chose a Union earthwork stronghold less than half a mile northwest of Barbara Hill recently dubbed Fort Sanders. After cannonade proved ineffective a CSA infantry charge was attempted, but their failure to contend with an unexpected ditch dug in front of the fort dealt Longstreet's men one of the worst proportional losses of the war. Longstreet claimed 813 casualties—129 fatal—in twenty minutes of early morning fighting, whereas only five Union soldiers were killed with eight wounded.[17] Knoxville remained under Union occupation during the following bloody sixteen-month slog toward eventual Union victory.[18] The campus continued to experience terrible wartime wear and tear as an ad hoc military hospital, the Battle of Fort Sanders by itself had little direct physical effect on ETU, other than to leave the war's imprint of memory on a piece of land that the university grew closer to in the following century. In March 1864, military photographer George Barnard stood atop Old College with his camera to record a visual seven-plate panorama of Knoxville for an official postbattle chronicle.[19]

Because Nashville and Memphis had been under federal control since 1862, Tennessee had officially been subject to political Reconstruction since shortly after the Civil War's beginning. Lincoln appointed Andrew Johnson as military governor, and the former tailor went to work quickly to punish any and all elements of rebellion in the state. When Johnson became Lincoln's running mate in 1864, he was replaced by William Brownlow, who replaced his old antagonism for Presbyterians with one for rebels. Both men required stringent loyalty oaths in exchange for political rights, so stringent that during their respective terms in office, the majority of Tennessee's white males of voting age were disenfranchised, and remained so for years after the war.[20] East Tennessee had a loyalist majority during the war, or at least far more so than Middle and West Tennessee, and its white male population largely either declared past allegiance or renounced rebellion after the war was over (Brownlow's successor, Dewitt Senter, was

The 1863 Battle of Fort Sanders took place near the East Tennessee University campus.
Although the battle itself did little damage to the campus, the school's usage
as a hospital for both Confederate and Union forces took its toll. By 1865
the buildings were heavily damaged and decrepit.

also an East Tennessean, albeit one more politically moderate). After 1865, the
Republican Party began finding favor all over the mountainous counties after
Brownlow himself, a former Whig (like Lincoln) became a Republican (white
Tennesseans who opposed them styled themselves intermittently as Democrats or
"Conservatives.") Tennessee was readmitted to the Union in 1866, shortly after its
legislature voted to ratify the Fourteenth Amendment, and left largely to its own
devices just as most other formerly rebellious states were about to come under
the jurisdiction of military Reconstruction. The next year Black men took part
in statewide elections, thereby growing the statewide Republican electorate.[21]
Quite suddenly, East Tennessee, and by extension Knoxville, found itself in a

more politically advantageous position than the two other grand divisions for the first time since before the Jackson era.

The effect of this new position was not felt immediately, especially not on the ETU campus. ETU's board reassembled in the spring of 1864 and this time resolved to request funds for rebuilding from the US government since the campus was being used for the same functions by federal troops as it had for the Confederates up until the previous year.[22] Conditions in Knoxville were still dire and uncertain, so another board meeting was not held until July of 1865, months after the war was over and calm relatively restored. The board elected one of its longtime members, Episcopalian sexton Thomas Humes, as ETU's new president so that classes could resume the following spring lodged in the relatively undamaged buildings housing Knoxville's School for the Deaf and Dumb (and yet another alliance with the Hampton-Sydney boys' school) with a four-man faculty.[23] Humes was the first president of the school native to Knoxville, an ETU graduate, and a board member since the age of twenty-three.[24] He was hardly the first ETU president with opinions, but there are no extant records indicating that his predecessors expressed them with his insistence. Like William Brownlow, he was an old Whig and staunch Unionist. Throughout Confederate occupation, Humes made no secret of his loyalist beliefs, and his role as minister to civilians and soldiers on both sides gave him an air of authority few Confederates were willing to challenge. East Tennessee had its share of rebels (including Humes's own namesake nephew), but many of them did not return to Knoxville and other localities after the war, and those that did tended to keep their own respective counsels.[25] Unionists like Humes were far from quiet after the war, especially if they were noted for bravely speaking their mind during Confederate occupation, and their publicity and prominence generated the general feeling in the North that East Tennessee was purely loyal. Humes did not mind propagating this sweeping oversimplification, and this, along with his dogged dedication to ETU, made him an ideal representative for a school whose only hope for survival (or so it seemed for a few years) was an appeal to the federal government.[26]

The war had laid waste to countless communities throughout the South, and even places that had remained loyal to the Union (or, at least, had only lukewarm tolerance for the Confederacy) were not guaranteed governmental assistance after the fighting was over. Sometime between 1865 and 1867 the US War Department gave ETU due diligence by examining wartime damage to its grounds and buildings, and assessed the damage at more than $15,000 before accusations emerged that former ETU trustees had supported secession. Considering the relatively high level of pro-Confederate feeling evident on the campus in 1861,

Rev.Thomas W.Humes, AM, S.T.D., Tenth President
East Tennessee University, 1865-79.
University of Tennessee, 1879-83.

Reverend Thomas Humes fought to keep
higher education, especially traditional
humanities classes, in Knoxville almost
as hard as he fought to suppress
pro-Confederate rebellion in Knoxville
during the Civil War.

this accusation was probably legitimate; if flight is a sign of disloyalty, at least
seven board members had fled town ahead of the Burnside's arrival in 1863.[27]
Nevertheless, ETU was still in a good position to receive relief since the signs
of the war were still visible on Barbara Hill. Even with rebels in its board of
trustees, faculty, and student body, after Tennessee's readmittance in 1866, it was
politically expedient to stress eastern Tennessee's loyalty. Furthermore, ETU had
stalwart allies in Congress: former professor Horace Maynard, who kept after
the War Department till the end of the decade from his seat in the House of
Representatives and, as of 1869, William Brownlow did the same in the Senate.[28]
In 1872, a Senate committee favored remitting $18,500 to the school by virtue
of its being "the only educational institution of known loyalty, in management
and influence, in any of the seceding States during the war," and surrounded by

a population known for their loyalty and sacrifices to the cause of the Union." Remarkably, Congress acknowledged that their own army had very likely caused more damage to ETU than the previous two years of rebel occupation, or the Confederate attempt to retake the city in late 1863.[29] In 1871 ETU graduated four students, its first graduating class since the war.[30]

The only barrier left was President Ulysses Grant, who vetoed the bill.[31] Grant had had to deal with more such appeals than any president before him, and although he knew all too well the physical damage caused by the Civil War, he believed that compensation for damages to private citizens was beyond the capabilities of the US Treasury. Furthermore, his own experience in Tennessee during the first half of the war probably jaded him to the idea that *any* section of any one state was wholly "loyal" and therefore deserving of recompense. Grant explained his position to Congress, expressing fear of opening a floodgate of later requests.

> If the precedent is once established that the Government is liable for the ravages of war, the end of demands upon the public Treasury cannot be forecast. The loyalty of the people of the section in which the university is located, under circumstances of personal danger and trials, thus entitling them to the most favorable construction of the obligation of the Government toward them, is admitted; and nothing but regard for my duty to the whole people, in opposing a principle which, if allowed, will entail greater burdens upon the whole than the relief which will be afforded to a part by allowing this bill to become a law, could induce me to return it with objections.

Grant suggested that, in light of "the claims of these citizens to sympathy and the most favorable consideration of their claims by the Government," Congress simply reconstrue the same amount as a "donation," which Hume and the board gladly accepted after a new bill was redrafted and passed by both House and Senate in 1873.[32] In the meantime, ETU had managed to build South College in 1872 and a new "Mess Hall" in 1873, the first new buildings on Barbara Hill since years before the war; the former was the only class building to outlast *East Tennessee University* as an institutional moniker.[33]

By this point it had been nearly a decade since ETU had made its first sally for federal relief, and in the meantime the school had already benefitted from a revolutionary source of governmental support that gave it permanent sustenance. In 1862, Congress passed the Morrill Act, an unprecedented allotment of federal funding for education that created and sustained what came to be known as "land-grant" schools. Echoing the land deal whereby East Tennessee College benefitted from Cherokee lands decades earlier, Morrill offered states certificates for federal land to sell in order to endow schools "to teach such branches of learning as are related to agriculture and mechanical arts, in such manner as the legislatures of the States may respectively prescribe," for "practical education of the industrial classes in the several pursuits and professions of life." The act cautioned that agricultural and mechanical pursuits need not crowd out "other scientific or classical studies" as well as "military tactics" already taught at schools that might receive grants (Morrill mandated military training at all schools benefitting).[34] Like the Homestead Act, which also used federal lands (mostly in the trans-Mississippian West) taken from Native Americans, Morrill's bill had been introduced before the Civil War but it was vetoed; critics feared that federal funding for education would wrest control of schools away from states and localities. But with most slave states no longer represented in Congress as of 1861, the "states' rights" dictum was no longer a dominating political bugbear, and the expansion of federal support for local concerns seemed a military necessity in the North.[35] As education historian Laurence R. Veysey has pointed out, federal funding for state education never translated into federal control over such, because revenues for land-grant schools, once distributed, were handled at the discretions of state legislatures who were not universally entranced with the prospect of publicly funded—let alone federally funded—education. Rather than increasing the power of Congress over education, the land-grant system actually funded a new empowerment of state governments.[36]

Perhaps more than many other comparable schools, ETU already had experienced the vicissitudes of politics since early in its history, and it was politics that allowed it to benefit uniquely from the Morrill Act, which was signed into law when Tennessee was seceded and therefore ineligible. Even before the war was over, an "old settler" in Minnesota brought the possibility of gaining a Morrill land grant to Andrew Johnson's attention when he offered to scout the "125,000 acres due Tennessee" a few months before Johnson was elected vice president.[37] Tennessee was the first state readmitted in 1866, too late to bid for a Morrill grant, but Congress extended the act essentially for Tennessee's sole benefit but with the provision that accommodations for African American applicants be made.[38] One Minnesota congressman unsuccessfully proposed an amendment denying anyone "who had ever held military or civil office under the so-called confederate government" a job in the school.[39] Governor William Brownlow cultivated a friendly relationship with congressional Republicans while also boosting his end of the state (including its educational institutions) against what was considered the recently disloyal middle and western thirds. ETU had once been caught up in Brownlow's "war" against East Tennessee Presbyterians, but the real war had changed things (for that matter, the postbellum president was an Episcopalian, a denomination that had never curdled Brownlow), and the governor took it upon himself to act as the school's booster. "Who shall say that this Institution has not done some good in the world, limited as have been its means and opportunities?" read *Brownlow's Knoxville Whig* in 1867. "But it is capable, under proper guidance, control and care, of doing even more in the future,—far more within the same period of time, than it has accomplished in the past. May it be prospered in all its educational labors, to the remotest generations!"[40] Later that same year the Tennessee legislature voted in favor of accepting a Morrill land grant with a view toward establishing a state agricultural college.[41] Considering the "denominational war" in his past, Brownlow's might well have felt sardonic assuring (as a member of a committee lobbying for ETU's appointment) the legislature that the school was strictly nonsectarian in order to meet the grant's parameters.[42]

Less than two years later East Tennessee University was given land-grant status, bringing sudden relief to the beleaguered school, but also sectional debate.[43] West Tennesseans said that an agricultural school in the eastern part of the state was impractical; agricultural practices suitable for other parts of Tennessee—namely the Mississippi River valley's cotton culture—could not be taught in Knoxville, and western farmers' children were less likely to afford a trip so far away from home. In 1870 a few railroads announced that ETU agricultural students would be given drastically reduced fares around the state, but this arrangement may have been temporary or, at least, did not have a universal effect. Potential students still struggled, notably the son of a "poor farmer" in northwestern Paris, Tennessee, who wrote to the school asking for train fare in 1884 or the young Alabaman who asked in 1883 if he could be enrolled and boarded, "and wait on me until I can make the money."[44] The demand for agricultural education was tied to agricultural development, and its need was felt in the South far more so than in any part of the nonrebellious states. The war lost Tennesseans nearly one third of their farm wealth (not counting the wealth represented by enslaved people which, if included, meant an even greater loss for former enslavers), and most of that loss had been in West Tennessee because of over-dependence on cotton cultivation. On the other hand, much of East Tennessee, especially the Cumberland Plateau just to the north and west of Knoxville, had never been agriculturally productive compared to the western Cotton Belt, the heavily commercial pastures and fields of Middle Tennessee (which was also the most heavily populated area), or even the nearby Holston and Tennessee River Valleys. The war had a dramatic levelling effect on the state's sections, one in which the relative equality of wealth in western planter country had become nearly like that of eastern yeoman farmland. Based solely on economic need, all three sections of Tennessee had legitimate claim to an agricultural school. The extraneous factor was the politics of Reconstruction that rewarded eastern mountaineers for being less rebellious than the rest of the state.[45] The Republican/Unionist character of the move was made plain by the act's inclusion of a section demanding that schools "foster, encourage, and inculcate loyalty to both the State and National Governments," as well as another forbidding the exclusion of any qualified male student "by reason of his race or color" and requiring "separate accommodation or instruction of any persons of color, who may be entitled to admission."[46]

The attempt to undo the ETU plan was immediate, but relatively short. Brownlow's departure to the US Senate, and a subsequent Conservative/Democratic victory in state legislative races, initiated in Tennessee what white Southerners would later call "Redemption": the end of Republican majorities and the return of all-white rule in 1869.[47] Almost immediately, the new majority attempted to divide the land scrip between two or more schools throughout the state.[48] "If the Legislature can thus tamper with vested rights, by taking this fund from the East Tennessee University," complained a correspondent to a Knoxville paper, "the fund itself is of no practical value as an educational one, for no College would desire it or accept it as an endowment in the view of the profitability that the next legislature *might* [correspondent's italics] remove it to some other place."[49]

Governor Dewitt Clinton Senter vetoed the legislative attempt to divide the fund, reasoning that one well-funded school was better than two or three poorer ones, regardless of location.[50] But, hailing from just east of Knoxville, Senter's veto (likely the first gubernatorial veto in Tennessee history) could also be interpreted as a sectionally partisan decision (in the words of one easterner praising Senter) "guarding the interests of East Tennessee."[51] It was a notably partisan move by a governor noted for being considerably less controversial than his predecessor (although Brownlow had had the luxury of never having dealt with an opposition-majority legislature). No eastern Republican would be elected again for four decades, but the first land-grant university in the former Confederacy was thereafter permanently in Knoxville, yet again a result of the city's attenuated Union loyalty. As a sign of ETU's new function, the board hired agriculture and geology professor Hunter Nicholson, a veteran of the Confederate army.[52]

Higher learning for white males in Tennessee was now far more democratic and accessible than it had been when John C. Gunn had called East Tennessee College a "temple of aristocracy," but it was also more subject to the whims, dogmas, and venalities of politicians. ETU had gained greater prosperity than it had ever had before, but only by trading away the autonomy it had in leaner days. As ETU president, Reverend Humes commended himself well to his board of trustees and the federal government, but, once the 1870s had commenced, the outspoken Unionist was bound to run afoul of a state government now under the control of former rebels and conservative "belated Confederates." Intrastate sectional tensions were generations old in Tennessee, but Redemption brought about an enduring effort to suppress the power of African Americans and white Unionists like himself. Humes's public persona was an unwelcome reminder to Southern partisans that the "Lost Cause" of Southern independence had its native naysayers. Within ten years after the war, white Southerners were spinning for themselves the myth that their rebellion had been a united front, so much that one disgruntled faculty member, a Virginia-born elocutionist named Edward Joynes, could conceive of Humes's presidency (without apparent irony) as "carpet bag rule" (it so happened that Joynes was an agricultural education advocate).[53] Tennessee Republicans also seemed to consider Humes and, by extension ETU, kindred; a Columbia, Tennessee, newspaper courted an ETU advertisement by boasting to Humes that it was one of only two extant Republican newspapers in Middle Tennessee.[54] At the end of 1882 the *Knoxville Chronicle* was trying to throw cold water on a controversy that had, by then, been growing for nearly a decade: "We only grieve that, at this late day, there live partisans so malicious as to strive to drown our schools in the venom of their spiteful tongues. It will be a sad day for our country when Democratic boys leave the schools where Republicans are in the majority, or when Republican boys leave a school because a majority of the students are Democrats."[55]

Students, especially resentful offspring of unreconstructed rebels, nicknamed Humes "limping Jesus" for his imperious moralism and an injury he supposedly incurred when he was shot in the leg while delivering a Unionist oration during the war.[56] Students and Knoxvillians protested when a Northern-born professor, John K. Payne, attempted to prevent a student from Blount County from delivering a eulogy to Robert E. Lee during an 1875 junior year exhibition on account of the mention being too laden with war feelings. It was generally believed that Humes sided with Payne since the former had previously allowed a similar eulogy for Union Navy Admiral David Farragut who happened to have passed away about two months before Lee's death in 1870 (the controversy surrounding Lee notwithstanding, Farragut's nativity in western Knox County, Tennessee, might have been a factor in allowing his remembrance). Students presented a petition warning that ETU depended "upon the patronage of the Southern States," and that "there is an opinion throughout the whole South that this College is run in the interest of the Republican Party," and further such censorship would "further augment this prejudice. . . ." The board of trustees was in agreement with Payne but decided against censoring the students, and the Lee eulogy was ultimately included.[57]

Redemption was felt in Knoxville as much as in parts of Tennessee, and perhaps more since the city was considered a loyalist mecca a decade earlier. As Reconstruction deteriorated further south, white Knoxvillians were more apt to express anti-Northern prejudice than they had been just after the war, especially with luminaries of Tennessee loyalism fading from prominence (Andrew Johnson and William Brownlow died in 1875 and 1877 respectively). The relatively cosmopolitan makeup of the ETU faculty was a common target of this sentiment. Owing to its role as state agricultural school, ETU was subject to opinion not only on campus and in Knoxville, but also in the state capitol. Multiple times after 1865 the Tennessee legislature added members to the board of trustees (it was considered imperative that every congressional district be represented on the board), and an increased number of voices from middle and western Tennessee cried out against Humes. As early as 1874 members of the board of trustees apparently agreed with the students' petition and informally discussed establishing an administration (and perhaps faculty) made up entirely of "Southern men" in order to attract more students from other Southern states (the intimation was that "Southern Men" did not include Humes even though he was a Tennessee native). Class enrollments had fallen during the 1870s, but there was no proof that it was due to Humes's reputation (it was just as likely that enrollment had been artificially high early in the decade because other Southern states lacked land-grant schools). *Knoxville Tribune* editor Charles Charlton reported that an increasing number of trustees and citizens felt that Humes was "not acceptable to the South on account of his intense, and perhaps, bitter Republican proclivities" and that former Confederate general Joseph E. Johnston might make a suitable replacement as president as a "business matter" (at the time Johnston was involved in a Gulf Coast canal project and would soon mount a successful congressional run in Virginia).[58]

In March 1877 the Tennessee General Assembly appointed fifteen new trustees, among them five Confederate veterans.[59] That summer, the board reorganized the faculty, voting to keep Humes in office (by a sheer nineteen to seventeen) but dismissing Payne and another Northern-born professor. One Knoxville newspaper remarked that Professor Payne and his colleague B. S. Burton's "only fault" was having been "born north of the famous so-called Mason and Dixon's line."[60] "The actions of these southern trustees is an outcropping of

Students of the University of Tennessee in the late nineteenth century wore different uniforms; the military fatigues that befitted the school's paramilitary role, and the athletic garb suitable for a new sport that was sweeping college campuses: football.

the same narrow spirit which existed in the old slavery days, a spirit which is not seen in the north, and which hardly existed here during the warmest days of the war," said a Connecticut newspaper which erroneously counted Humes as one of the Northern-born faculty. "No college which hopes to be successful can afford to turn away good instructors on account of their political beliefs."[61] A partisan Nashville editor shot back at Northern censures, calling Burton a "profound snob," and defended the board's decision in an anti-intellectual sectional tirade: "A class of insolent puppies come South and expect to be inefficient in position, and yet hold place by their New England-born right to rule the world. It would be just as well for these eye-glassed snobs from the center of the universe to understand that we will move on our own course in our own way regardless of their clamors or opinions."[62] A more sober assessment from the same newspaper later noted that although the board of trustees had a Democratic majority, the reorganization of the faculty was also motivated by ETU's failure to serve its function as an agricultural school.[63] The school's curricular purpose and postbellum politics had become entangled.

One of the most notable new hires was new professor of agriculture John McBryde (Hunter Nicholson was moved to natural history and later became university librarian).[64] McBryde revolutionized his program, building the university's first greenhouse and initiating unprecedented crop experiments. Decades before soybeans became a major cash crop in Tennessee, he had joined a small number of agriculture professors (most, if not all, of them outside the South) in growing the legume on American soil for the first time.[65] His brief time at the school (he left in 1882) marked the practical beginning of ETU's existence as a research institute.[66] He was also a veteran of the Confederate cavalry and the Confederate treasury, facts probably cheered by the more conservative trustees and instructors as much as the academic acclaim he brought to ETU; during the search for a new agriculture professor, Joynes admitted to a friend that he was less concerned with whether the new hire knew "much about agriculture" than with installing "some good Southern man."[67] The reorganization came just months after the end of the Grant administration and the inauguration of Rutherford B. Hayes, the "compromise" decision that marked what many historians consider the official end of Reconstruction (following a contested, violent election, Hayes had promised to pull federal troops out of the last three Southern states still subject to military occupation). Tennessee had not been subject to Reconstruction for more than a decade, but the reorganization, even if strictly a business matter as Charlton contended, was a notable coincidence with what many white Southerners called "self-rule."

As the first state to reenter the Union, Tennessee had been left to its own devices, and as a result neither the legislature nor ETU had taken measures to fulfill one of the Morrill Act's key requirements: education for the state's Black population. By the 1870s, Tennessee had only one Black legislator (elected in 1873) and most white Republicans were scarcely more concerned with the education of freedpeople and their children than were conservatives and former rebels.[68] Even as they created a new constitution mandating that "no school established or aided" by the state could "allow white and negro children to be received as scholars together," state legislators simultaneously tried to ruin ETU's claim on the Morrill fund by chiding the school for not accommodating Black students; Humes blithely replied that there had been no Black applicants.[69] In 1871 and 1872 Virginia, South Carolina, and Mississippi all used federal money to establish agricultural and mechanical education for African Americans.[70] In

One of President Humes's best hires
was John McBryde, who revitalized the
Agriculture Department. An early advocate
for soybean cultivation, McBryde's brief
tenure marks the university's turn toward
becoming a research institution.

South Carolina, the political apogee of radical Reconstruction, Black politicians served on the state university's board of trustees, and Black student enrollment rose from zero to ninety percent between 1873 and 1876.[71] But Tennessee (with a much smaller Black population than those three states) lagged behind. In accordance with Morrill, ETU made military training a large part of the curriculum, forcing students into uniform and, as of 1875, mandating a military regulation code designed by a West Point graduate.[72] This made the stakes of racial politics higher since the sight of Black "cadets" sharing the same uniform as their white peers would have been too much for many white Southerners, especially serving under Samuel Lockett, a commandant of cadets who told a friend upon arriving in Knoxville that he and his family were "very happy at being back again among white-folks."[73] Even white Republicans who had once made Tennessee a political vanguard for the rights of freedpeople in the 1860s were not willing to risk their livelihoods for African Americans, and it was left to the latter to stand up for themselves. In 1880 four Black men were elected to the state legislature, and they immediately set to work calling attention to the agricultural school's gross inequity, selecting a dozen young Black men for admission, and demanding "arrangements for persons of color who may be entitled to admission."[74] They challenged the school by nominating students to attend even though state segregation laws would have required not only separate buildings, libraries, and equipment, but also a separate faculty.[75] Historian Samuel Shannon observed that Black Tennesseans did not go so far as to challenge the state's mandate of segregated education, but rather they "used the specter of integration as psychological leverage," intimating that the school had an obligation to any "'colored [male] youths'" not accepted to schools designated for Black education.[76] A meeting of Black Knoxvillians in the summer of 1881 protested the board of trustees' failure to establish a specific policy of biracial education.

> Yet, we have exercised that patience, endurance, discretion under wrong, for which the negro is fast gaining an enviable reputation. In the meantime, the board of trustees of said University have not informed the negro of his rights to attend, nor made provisions for his accommodation, nor has any representative been just, progressive, and bold enough to appoint a single negro student, and, with a single exception, none has applied for admittance. During all these years we have yielded to the deprevation [sic] of these educational advantages and have silently acquiesced in the enjoyment of them by our more favored fellow-citizens.[77]

The board of trustees was faced with the task of upholding a modicum of what would later be called "separate but equal" in order to fulfill their Morrill obligations without incurring the wrath of Tennessee's white supremacist majority, who believed "an intermingling of races would completely destroy the college."[78] The trustees arranged temporarily for Black students to attend Fisk University, a private freedman's school founded in 1866 (indirectly answering the ongoing complaints of distance from middle and western Tennessee), and then established a more permanent relationship with a newer institution, Knoxville College, beginning in 1884.[79]

Knoxville College was founded by the United (Northern) Presbyterian Church in 1875 short miles north of ETU.[80] Neither the board nor the legislature objected to the school's denominational association (even though it violated state law) because its inclusion solved an issue that had developed on campus. Despite its being the state agricultural school, faculty members objected to the idea of white students actually engaging in "compulsory and unremunerated" physical farm labor (a fact that perplexed a visiting legislator in 1877).[81] Through its inclusion, Knoxville College's students would serve as the university farm's labor in

A view of campus around the time East Tennessee University became
the University of Tennessee, ca. 1879.

exchange for pay (the contract arranged by the board of trustees covered Knoxville
College students' tuition but not their room and board). The unequal arrangement
lasted into the twentieth century as the reach of "Jim Crow" legislation broadened
in Tennessee and the rest of the South's public spaces.[82] As a result, many students
lacked the advantages of residential learning that whites took for granted. For
instance, one Knoxville College student, in 1898, noted the inconvenience of
having no library near his east Knoxville home when he left campus for the day.
"A hidden intellectual hunger gripped me," he wrote years later, "with no chance
to satisfy it."[83]

By this point, East Tennessee University had undergone its final name
change, becoming the University of Tennessee (UT). The change in title came
in 1879, establishing, once and for all, the school's statewide constituency and
its broadened purview and perhaps to deaccentuate how far east its campus
was (or, from the state legislature majority's perspective, to claim the school for
the whole state *despite* its geographical placement). "It is now become in name,
as it has been in its usefulness and welfare, with the whole State of Tennessee,"

Founded in 1875, Knoxville College was East Tennessee's premiere historically
Black university. Knoxville College served as the executor of the Second Morrill
Act's provision that land-grant schools provide biracial education even though
the University of Tennessee was unwilling to desegregate. Decades later, the
latter school was forced to desegregate thanks to activism from Knoxville College
students and other members of the city's Black community.

Humes intoned at the June commencement. "It is henceforth, by virtue of recent
wise and efficient State legislation, an integral part, and also a leading factor
in the public school system of the State."[84] It was a statement that could be
taken as an expression of either magnanimity or irony. Tensions between the
school and the state government were at an all-time high, mainly because of
lack of funding during an especially trying decade (the Panic of 1873 had set off
a national recession that lasted for at least four years). "We do not know that
the Legislature which meets to-morrow at the State Capitol, will have any new
scheme for obstructing our State University," a Knoxville editor complained a
few weeks before the name change. "The treatment heretofore given it by the
State, as compared with the treatment given many of the agricultural colleges,
is simply shameful."[85] The legislators reserved the right to appoint tuition-free

cadets from their respective districts without making up the loss to the cash-strapped school. The state was not ready to radically change its funding policy (conservatives assumed Morrill money was enough to train farmers), but the changes that came with the new institutional title were dramatic. UT became a doctorate-granting institution, thus joining the ranks of new research institutions popping up in the United States—Johns Hopkins University was founded in Maryland three years earlier—although UT's doctorate of philosophy would not be a commonly awarded degree for some time. They also created a Board of Visitors, an extra oversight body that would periodically inspect the school and report its upkeep to the governor. The main thrust of the changes was an effort to make good on UT's (by this time) decade-old role as agricultural school amid what a past history of UT called "A full-scale attack on the time-honored study of the 'classics'" entangled with the growing neo-Confederate attitudes in and around the school.[86]

Thomas Humes had arguably guided the school into land-grant status as little more than a life-support system for an educational program that had remained virtually unchanged since the days of Joseph Estabrook: a practical education in letters and sciences fortified with a gentleman's focus on philosophy and ancient languages (the latter subject Humes taught himself), scholarship that one newspaper lampooned as "too much 'befo' the 'wah' aristocracy."[87] In 1873 Humes told his eight-man faculty that a curriculum for training normal school teachers should be brought back and somehow fit into what had become a fully military institute. Training for normal school teachers had ended at the end of the 1840s after being initiated by Joseph Estabrook who bucked against the sort of classical traditionalism that Humes usually espoused. With that in mind, Humes's suggestion may have been an attempt at compromise with faculty and trustees who wanted a greater focus on science. Humes's "normal" school idea apparently faded within two years of its introduction, very likely from lack of interest, although it did reappear in 1879 and lasted almost halfway through the 1880s thanks to funding from philanthropist George Peabody.[88] And it did seem that even the science faction appreciated the need for common schools in the state to act reciprocally with its university. In 1878 Hunter Nicholson delivered a paper calling for teacher training for the sake of scientific development, which had become "the entire framework and running-gear of modern civilized life."[89] It was an apparent public rebuke of Humes. A contingent of faculty led by elocutionist Edward Joynes and trustees led by longtime board member Oliver P. Temple believed that Humes was holding the school back with his pedagogical conservatism, and soon after UT took its new moniker factions had formed along these lines.[90] Humes's public reputation as a "radical" Republican exacerbated this conflict, although, since Temple (who dedicated decades to service as an active trustee) had been a fellow Unionist during the war, it is likely that he had compartmentalized the two controversies. Temple was a judge and Knoxville's postmaster and a New South booster who considered practical education in farming (the business of most Tennesseans) and industry to be of vital civic importance; students who wanted to read Horace and other classics read at the school since the days of Samuel Carrick could enroll in one of Tennessee's private institutions (by the end of the 1880s, Tennessee had more than forty degree-granting institutions, many of them founded or reorganized since the war).[91] Tennessee suffered from the same postbellum lack of development as the rest of the South, with the requisite problem of poverty, and Temple most likely considered a full concentration on vocational training to be the more democratic option. In short, UT came into being amid a struggle between the advocates of the humanities and the advocates of physical science and technology, a struggle familiar to American educators long after the days of Humes and Temple.

It was perhaps ruefully appropriate that, after years of persecution from those around him, defender of the humanist tradition Thomas Humes finally resigned over freedom of expression— but also nepotism—in 1883. His nephew Charles Humes ran afoul of members of the faculty for his involvement with UT's literary magazines, the *Chi-Delta Crescent* and an underground satire screed innocuously titled *The Weekly Bulletin*, in which he criticized chemistry professor Thomas Brown. Charles Humes let loose in a *Crescent* article, casting rhetorical stones at the city of Chattanooga, the state government ("It is the only Legislature in the United States that has not voted its State University an appropriation"), the board of trustees ("They might suggest to them to pay a little bigger salaries, and then they would not have *any* [Humes's italics] lazy instructors"), and at Brown, suggesting he was among the aforementioned lazy instructors.[92] Brown had him expelled, but the young man extra-legally appealed to the board of trustees university laws that kept trustees and students at a mutual distance (probably for just such an occasion). The board overrode the dismissal at his uncle's prompting, infuriating the faculty and prompting seven resignations.[93] The board may have noted that Brown was overly sensitive (having not been named specifically in the last piece), and that Charles Humes's latest piece was a defense of UT against its many critics. Still, enough members of the board already wanted rid of Humes (especially Temple), and his nephew's strange malfeasance was a useful final straw. The trustees asked for Humes's resignation in late August 1883, after which the board managed to retrieve all but two members of the faculty (Brown was one of the two permanently departed).[94] Memphis's *Public Ledger* noted that the resignations came about out of a longstanding divide between teachers and trustees, "difficulties that have been noticed more or less freely by the Tennessee press," with both parties losing more and more patience with Reverend Humes. "The trouble originated in conflicts of authority, not in any objection, as far as any surface indications point, to any member of the faculty." The *Ledger* complimented Humes's record with the school, but also let slip that his "connection with the institution date[d] back of the war. . . ."[95] After sewing up his postresignation duties for Fisk University (which he reported to the board of trustees on UT stationery), Humes never took a professional role on the campus again.[96] He became Knoxville's first city librarian, remaining in the post until his death in 1892. His nearly two decades as president loomed large in the minds of Tennesseans who were concerned with their state university. Mail addressed to Humes, particularly from prospective students and teachers, continued to arrive at the university until at least as late as 1884.[97]

The next four years were among the strangest in UT's history. UT's board of trustees ran the school without a president, as they collectively worked to fully transform UT into their vision of a school fully dedicated to farming and mechanics. The historical record suggests Oliver Temple was the most active at attempting to secure a new president but, in the meantime, the board maintained the school as best they could, most likely giving the faculty as much free rein as possible after the Charles Humes affair. Throughout this period enrollment in UT's agricultural school remained low, a trend that one observer noted, soon thereafter, was because "Farmer's sons especially were disposed to take other courses of study and escape the farm life to which they had been brought up." Perhaps still fearful of losing land-grant status, in 1886 the board fixed it so that all courses excluding engineering included some amount of instruction in agriculture. The measure did little to improve agricultural education among students who would potentially use it, but it did magnify UT's identity as a school of agriculture.[98]

Temple led a campaign to hire his friend John McBryde as president, and a series of negotiations began to get him to return from his position at South Carolina College (which had expelled its Black students shortly before McBryde had taken up residence there). As perhaps the South's greatest academic authority on experimental agriculture, the prospect of a President McBryde offered the clearest path to Temple's vision for UT, and the two had kept up a de facto partnership toward that end for years before Humes stepped down.[99] The board of trustees was amenable to McBryde's return, and made him complimentary offers of pay and housing, but McBryde begged off multiple times, claiming that, although he was under attack already in South Carolina, he feared he would be facing unforeseen challenges back there. He changed his mind when he heard Congress's passage of the Hatch Act (which fortified the Morrill Act after a quarter century with further federal money for agricultural experiment stations connected to land-grant schools) would likely pass.[100] In summer 1887, McBryde accepted the UT board's offer, but then suddenly withdrew his acceptance after a health scare followed by a counteroffer from South Carolina.[101]

The board turned instead to Charles Dabney, a figure who measured closely to McBryde as a Southern agricultural "progressivist," and one of the most transformative presidencies in UT's entire history.[102] Dabney was a great believer in the revolutionary potential of agricultural education in the South, one who ultimately surpassed even the most ambitious hopes of Oliver Temple and the other land-grant visionaries (for his part, Temple's greatest contribution to agricultural education at UT was made after his death, when his daughter presented the university with $25,000 earmarked for agricultural education in 1919).[103] While Humes's advocacy for classical education was viewed as obstinacy and stasis, Dabney's vision for UT involved completely changing the school's form and complexion, creating for all intents and purposes a school completely different from the one that had existed beforehand. Perhaps just as important, Dabney was the embodiment of the "good Southern man" hoped for during the waning days of Reconstruction. During the war his childhood home in Virginia had been an ad hoc Confederate hospital. His father had served with distinction as Stonewall Jackson's chief of staff and hagiographer before becoming one of the postbellum South's most influential Presbyterian theologians (and, as it happened, an apologist for slavery and a severe critic of public education!).[104] In his memoir, Dabney himself promoted the memory of Jackson's commander, Robert E. Lee, but extolled his postwar role as a college president, not as a general. After the war when he was made president of Virginia's Washington College, Lee had believed that "the hope for the future [of the South] lay not in political agitation but in economic and industrial development, and that the College must lead in this work" by creating for itself schools for agricultural demonstration, chemistry, commerce, and (owing to Lee's distant past in the US Army) engineering.[105] "I shall devote myself now to training young men to do their duty in life," Charles Dabney quoted the general in a 1892 article.[106] Dabney also applied post-Redemption white supremacy to his philosophy of teaching, believing that the "arts" of farming and engineering were for whites only, while Black Southerners need only learn "how to work and labor."[107] He did not apparently extend the same patronizing attitude toward other non-white races;

Few presidents left such a lasting imprint on the
University of Tennessee as Charles Dabney. Under
his leadership the school focused more on science and
agriculture, established a summer program for training
school teachers, formed a law school, and accepted
women as students for the first time in a century.

late in his presidency Dabney requested that eight students from the war-ravaged
Philippines be brought to Knoxville and enrolled at UT, the only Southern
university to do so ("Southern agricultural education" held purported benefits
for tropical inhabitants).[108] The exchange program was deemed a failure after he
left office since white UT students themselves ostracized the visiting students
"owing to their brown skins."[109] Under Dabney, federal funding for agricultural
education provided by the Hatch Act was not equally divided between UT and
Knoxville College as the act stipulated. Instead, it was allocated to UT and the
state government allowed the larger "white" school to dole a smaller portion

to Knoxville College as the former saw fit.[110] Dabney's racism, though hardly unusual among white Southerners of his generation, held Knoxville College back—and higher education for Black Tennesseans in general—for his entire term as presidency.[111]

The beginning of Dabney's administration was UT's final escape from the complicated legacy of the Civil War and its replacement with an uncomplicated one. As an outspoken Southern-born Unionist, a Republican and perhaps a "Radical," Thomas Humes was a constant reminder to the detractors among his faculty, students, and trustees that they lived under a cloud of what they considered societal downfall in the form of Confederate defeat. In a more complicated manner, Humes was a reminder that not every white Southerner had been of one mind between Fort Sumter and Appomattox, an annoying fly in the buttermilk at a time when former Confederates were coming together with conservative Unionists like Oliver Temple to construct a united Lost Cause mythology. The fact that Humes stood (allegedly) in the way of agricultural education at UT was not entirely unrelated; Lost Cause mythology and agricultural and industrial education were not a strange pairing in the hands of men like Temple and Dabney. The idea of gathering a faculty made up only of Southerners was long past, a silly artifact of the Reconstruction era, and Dabney's faculty was eventually full to bursting with Northerners (having a Southern president, however, was still an unwritten rule for the time being).[112] Since then, forward-looking white Southerners had accepted that their home rule had to be bolstered with Northern support, while most Northerners involved were happy to lend good will and capital to the South without gainsaying the perpetuation of its antidemocratic practices. Like most New South men, Dabney was happy to fly the Lost Cause banner while simultaneously accepting Northern or federal money, be it provided by the Hatch Act, the largesse of Northeastern investors and philanthropists, or the second Morrill Act that passed Congress at an opportune time during his presidency in 1890.[113] To men like Dabney this behavior was not hypocritical nor even paradoxical. It was practical for the sake of a prosperous future for white Southern farmers and businessmen.[114] Dabney was probably present when, also in 1890, Knoxvillians gathered with veterans of the blue and the gray at the site of Fort Sanders to see an aged General Longstreet, and to hear attorney and ETU alum (and future trustee) Joshua W. Caldwell proclaim that "we [white Unionists and Confederates] were never enemies. We were of one race. We were one in history and hope."[115] It was a selective memory that would prove profitable for white Southerners, white Northerners, and whites-only schools such as the University of Tennessee.

Reverend Thomas Humes's memory of the war was also selective. Shortly after he was deposed as president, Humes wrote *The Loyal Mountaineers of Tennessee* (1888), part memoir, part historical homage to the pro-Union sentiment of East Tennessee that Humes believed was an innate characteristic of the Southern mountaineer dating back to the days of the Revolutionary War (Humes said relatively little of the large number of ETU students who had openly supported rebellion). Like many, if not most, Gilded Age descriptions of Appalachia, Humes emphasized the physical and social remoteness, and resultant unpretentious primitivity, of a region "shut in by rock-ribbed mountains." East Tennessee Unionists must have been virtuous and sincere, Humes claimed, because "in a region of country so isolated from the great world . . . its actors could have no stimulus to their constancy in the heard applause of admiring spectators." "To whatever causes their conduct may be attributed," Humes asserted, "it at least conveys the impression of their strong individuality as a people and invites the closer observation and study of the political philosopher."[116]

It is likely that Humes was attempting to shame those who had accused him of supporting "aristocracy" by advocating a traditional liberal arts education. He was also probably scolding those around him who had taken up the Lost Cause banner *after* the war regardless of what they had done *during* it. After all, East Tennessee University had become the state's only land-grant school because state and federal Republicans wished to reward eastern Tennessee for its relative loyalty, *and* because Humes and other Unionists like him had worked hard after the war to make sure their school won the spoils of war. Many Tennessee schools had not survived the war or the lean years that followed, especially in parts of Tennessee that were more associated with rebellion.[117] It is very likely that the school once known as East Tennessee University would have ceased to exist without Yankee dollars, and Humes knew this even if most of his contemporaries preferred not to think about it.

Humes's description of his native territory as shut off from the "outside world" was, like many other contemporary descriptions of Appalachia, either duplicitous or unintentionally ironic. The East Tennessee of his lifetime was certainly more connected to the "outside world" than it had been when a Pennsylvania-born Presbyterian preacher named Samuel Carrick ventured down the Great Valley to a place soon to be named Knoxville a decade after the Revolutionary War. Humes should have known better than anyone that East Tennessee was exposed to forces outside of its immediate environs, especially on the campus to which he had dedicated much of his professional career. Blount College, ETC, ETU, and finally UT had attracted educators and students from faroff places (most notably the North) for nearly a century at the time of his writing, even though many of them had had to endure regional prejudice during his presidency. By most accounts, East Tennesseans had been quick to choose sides once it became clear that there would be rebellion against the United States—perhaps they had done so unpretentiously, but more likely they were influenced by political or economic concerns that connected them to places, North or South, far beyond the banks of the Holston River. Most likely they were influenced by the politics of slavery, even though Humes disingenuously insisted that Tennessee mountaineers "felt no concern about the institution" (interestingly, in his own history of Tennessee Unionism, Oliver Temple similarly contended that "The question of slavery did not enter largely into their [East Tennesseans'] minds," Temple reasoned because "seven-tenths of the Union men were non-slaveholders").[118]

After the war, Humes and the ETU board of trustees had hedged their "strong individuality" enough to accept federal support to permanently transform their scrappy school into a permanent public service for their state and nation. Humes's own work directly belied his own words, which were intended to praise his neighbors (and perhaps himself—Humes had been a bold Unionist even during Confederate occupation of Knoxville) and even though he had left UT against his own wishes, he had left it a school comparable to other land-grant institutions outside of the impoverished South. Moreover, he had asserted his own vestigial belief in classical learning at a school that grew into a rarity in the United States: an institution that doubled as a land-grant school and a state's primary public university. It was a dual identity that insured that UT was to have a very interesting future.

CHAPTER THREE

The University of Tennessee in the New South, 1890–1930

· ·

"Ultimately and philosophically, science is the organ
of general social progress."

—JOHN DEWEY—
Democracy & Education (1916)

"I firmly believe that before many centuries more,
science will be the master of men."

—HENRY ADAMS TO CHARLES
FRANCIS ADAMS JR.—
(1862)

Since 1794, there had been a judge and plenty of clergymen in the president's chair, but Charles Dabney was the first president of the University of Tennessee (UT) to hold a doctorate. It was a sign of the times, a signal that the school was in tune with national trends in higher education. Doctoral degrees were earned through research, and during the early Gilded Age research played a miniscule role in most colleges and universities. That changed rapidly beginning in the late 1870s after private institutions like Johns Hopkins University (founded in 1876) came into being, and older state schools like the University of Wisconsin expanded their respective purviews to become centers for public service rather than just degree-conferring academies.[1] UT's conflict between the sciences and humanities had its own Southern flavor since it took place during and after the sectional rancor of Reconstruction, but it reflected a broader national tendency stretching from Harvard in Massachusetts to Stanford in California through which the American university was becoming something new.[2] Dabney's administration represented the culmination of a process that had begun during that of Joseph Estabrook, and accelerated after East Tennessee University achieved land-grant status: a drift toward the teaching of "practical" arts and science, and away from the classical learning valued in the days of Samuel Carrick but considered vestigial in an era of steam power and dynamos. As education historian Dan R. Frost described him, Dabney was among "the Progressive educators who freed Southern higher education from academic conservatives . . . helping to create a 'great educational awakening' in the South after 1900."[3] Under Dabney's leadership, UT was part of a region-wide vanguard of reform, an acknowledgement by Southerners that the postbellum South was in dire need of repair and "renationalization" within the United States.[4]

Like many American PhDs of his time, Dabney received his highest degree in Germany, following his University of Virginia mentor to the University of Göttingen in the 1870s to study chemistry after teaching a year at Virginia's Emory & Henry College.[5] While teaching at the University of North Carolina he became involved with the Watauga Club, a group of young, highly educated white Southerners that has been credited with bringing Progressivism to the South. The Wataugans espoused reforms ranging from state funding of scientific agriculture to publicly funded higher education for white women.[6] The memory of the Lost Cause may have been sacrosanct to many white Southerners, but Watauga visionaries revolted against the "fossils" and "mummies" of the aging political leaders of the Confederate generation who placed no value on education for the masses. Dabney and his fellows were chagrined to see so many farmers' sons leaving the soil behind for jobs in mill villages and railroad hub towns and casting votes for politicians who had little interest in spending money on improving the drudgery of farming they had left behind.[7] He was convinced that, despite the intended effects of the Morrill Acts, there was no "true polytechnic institute in the South," since the intended funding had "in nearly all instances fallen into the hands of the old-foggy, leterary [sic] institutions."[8] They also resented the contention that the South need import its engineers and scientists from the North. In the mid-1880s, Dabney and company fought for the creation of an agricultural school in North Carolina before the effort was taken up by the state's Grange movement, organized farmers who would soon thereafter coalesce into the Populist, or People's, Party.[9] Dabney accepted UT's invitation soon thereafter, perhaps to escape the stultifying irony of agricultural reformers running afoul of farmers. Even after his experiences in North Carolina, Dabney brought with him a firm belief that he could form a mutually beneficial relationship between farmers (even ones skittish about change in a turbulent national economy) and experts like himself.

Dabney arrived at UT with fresher eyes than any new president since before the Civil War, and his initial impression of a "horribly mismanaged" campus that aroused shame among the "educated people" of Tennessee inspired a thorough house-cleaning.[10] The controversy over Thomas Humes and his nephew had resulted in a demoralized faculty, and the school was in one of its frequent moments of class roll decline and financial crisis. Dabney decided his only recourse in Tennessee would be to consolidate as much personal control over his new school as possible. In 1888 he rearranged eight of the ten-man faculty, reinstating some in new positions and dismissing others, particularly the humanities positions.[11] He filled the positions he was most concerned with, namely anything related to agriculture, with a select group of men, including a few Northerners. He created and organized departments, combining mechanical engineering with physics, and dividing his own field, chemistry, between Organic and Applied, the better to make the former more of a tool for agricultural research and education.[12] Dabney had made clear to the board of trustees in his acceptance that he would require an unprecedented executive authority over faculty, and former understandings based on kinship (many relatives of board members had taught at the school over the years) would no longer be recognized. Hiring and dismissal had previously been the board's sole domain, but the mutual desire for reform, along with the probable hurt feelings following Humes's presidency, jettisoned the previous relationship between the faculty and the board in the interest of progress. Dabney, it was recalled a few years after his presidency, "showed great sagacity and rare judgment in the selection of his professors, [gathering] about him a group of men of singular fitness and approved skill, young in years and full of zeal."[13]

To further create a stable learning environment, Dabney appointed UT's first dean to oversee the professors and curriculum.[14] In imitation of the University of Wisconsin and other Midwestern schools, he gradually did away with UT's preparatory school, classes for younger, less-prepared "subfreshman" students that had been made available since before the Civil War.[15] Dabney believed that the inclusion of what amounted to secondary education had no place in a modern university, even though high schools providing proper preparatory education were few and far between in postbellum Tennessee (even if they were becoming common in the states Dabney wanted to model his school after). The hope was that, even as UT accepted fewer students proportional to Tennessee's population, the raising of academic standards by the state university would motivate the state government to move toward standardization and improvement of its public schools. Elimination of the preparatory program earned UT its first-ever accreditation membership, a place in the Association of Southern Colleges and

At the end of the nineteenth century, a majority of Tennesseans were farming for a living, and agricultural education was crucial. The University of Tennessee's College of Agriculture remains one of the school's greatest contributions to the state's welfare.

Preparatory (or Secondary) Schools soon after it was founded by a Vanderbilt University professor in 1895. This gave UT a distinct advantage, at least in terms of bragging rights, over the Universities of South Carolina and Georgia, both under the leadership of visionaries Dabney considered his fellows who were far slower to shed their need for preparatory education.[16] "No southern institution has a higher standard or examines candidates more thoroughly," the *Atlanta Constitution* announced a week before UT sent its cadets to the famed 1895 Atlanta Exposition. "Students and professors alike are most enthusiastic over the situation and prospects of the institution."[17]

Throughout, Dabney's chief passion was agricultural research conducted in the school's experimental stations. Tennessee was undergoing its own agrarian political movement, albeit one that did not have the lifespan of the North Carolina Populists. In 1886 Democrat Robert L. Taylor beat his Republican brother in a colorful gubernatorial race known as the "War of the Roses." Taylor was no expert on agriculture, but he and newspaper editor John McDowell were adept at the anti-elite politics that had reverberated in Tennessee public life since the days of Andrew Jackson. Just as East Tennessee College before it, UT became a target. In his opening message to the legislature briefly before Dabney took office, Taylor recommended what he called "practical training" at UT, rather than "an ideal institution for a constituency that does not exist."[18] Taylor later criticized Dabney for hiring professors from outside of Tennessee and from outside of the South (some of Dabney's more notable hires came from Massachusetts, New York, and Maine).[19] West Tennessean McDowell kept up the old Reconstruction-era sectional battle in 1889, deriding UT's entreaty for building funds on campus, protesting that a large number of future farmers had never benefitted from the school's resources. Leonidas Polk, national leader of the Farmer's Alliance and usually a proponent of scientific agriculture, stepped in as well, arguing that "'practical' farmers" understood that "the purely technical methods of improving our methods of farming" was "not a force or remedy" for Tennessee farmers.[20] Within the agrarian movement of the 1880s and 1890s there coexisted impulses favoring strengthened public support for agricultural education as well as a generally egalitarian (except on matters of race) reliance on the wisdom of the crowd, the latter of which did not jibe well with Dabney's vision. The purpose of land-grant education, Dabney told the Tennessee legislature, was not "to train farm laborers, miners, mechanics, and mere artisans," but instead what he called "trained experts," engineers, agriculturalists (i.e., farmers, but farmers who had time and money enough to experiment on new techniques for the market and the greater good), and metallurgists.[21] In any case, despite all of his differences with Dabney, Taylor was swift in approving for UT the funds provided by the second Morrill Act in 1890. Suddenly, the school's revenue was increased by nearly 40 percent.[22] Nearly three decades after the Civil War, the promise of federal support was finally fulfilled in a meaningful way.

Charles Dabney reciprocated by accepting an appointment as assistant secretary of agriculture during Grover Cleveland's second presidential term, a move that confirmed to many of Dabney's detractors that he did not share the interests of Tennessee farmers.[23] The faculty, however, agreed that a dual appointment as university president and federal employee would increase UT's national profile, and the board of trustees approved Dabney retaining the presidency during an extended leave of absence in the District of Columbia, provided he take a cut in yearly university pay from $5,000 to $2,000 and visit campus at least four times a year.[24] This dual appointment earned him some of his harshest criticism, and not only from Tennessee's other two sections. "'Tis strange that professional, rather than practical farmers get all the pie from this great department, created especially for the farmers," groused one East Tennessee newspaper. "But so it is."[25] Chattanooga Republican Henry Clay Evans was more forthright, calling Dabney's $2,000 yearly state income "robbing the children of the state."[26] Dabney's move inspired yet another legislative attack on UT, in which lawmakers proposed a bill replacing the board of trustees with a state-appointed board of regents in order to put a final end to the measure of state-guided autonomy the school had operated with since 1807.[27] The bill failed, leaving behind uncertainty as to the university's constitutional status. But Dabney's federal position probably benefited more than harmed UT, especially its experimental stations. Dabney handled most of his Department of Agriculture business from Knoxville, and his exposure to federally funded scientific research helped him formulate a vision of science and education "entirely removed from political interference."[28] Dabney's federal position ended with the Cleveland administration in 1897, but it left him with a new understanding of what would become the chief problem of public higher education in the next century.

Historian Robert Wiebe described Dabney's era as a national "search for order," a time when experts like Dabney were influential, and secluded "island communities" became more integrated with national and international statuses quo.[29] Dabney's goals for UT and education in Tennessee fit this characterization well. Universities were a rare enough thing in the United States at the end of the nineteenth century—let alone in the impoverished South—that Dabney was very loosely bound by what a university needed to be. For one thing, while higher education may have traditionally prepared young people for public service, Dabney believed that the university itself could be a source of public service. As he told an assemblage at the Virginia Polytechnic Institute in 1896, his vision of education marked a dramatic break with the past.

> In 1865 the South awoke suddenly out of mediaeval night and found itself in the midst of a scientific age and a day of tremendous material development. She [c]ommenced to appreciate for the first time her birthright of almost boundless material resources, and set bravely to work to build up her waste places and

win back the wealth she had lost. She commenced asking herself, What good are coals, iron ores, zinc ores, hard wood, water powers, marbles, and such things, unless utilized? Why not train our own young men to manufacture these things into commercial products? Is not the fact that these things still lie in the mountains unused chiefly owing to that other fact that we have no men who know how to use them? Hence it was determined that Southern boys, at least, should have an opportunity to secure a scientific and technical education and thus be qualified to assist in the development of the material resources of the country.[30]

Even though it was the official state university at the time of his arrival, UT was still a relatively provincial, impoverished institution with most of its high regard coming from Knoxville and the East Tennessee countryside (resentment from Middle and West Tennessee was still palpable). Tennessee itself was as beleaguered by poverty and lack of internal opportunities as was the rest of the South, and Dabney believed that the key to uplift was consistency: if all parts of the state could be brought to the same (hopefully elevated) standard of educa-tion, it could achieve a larger portion of what his contemporaries were touting as the "New South." Dabney had as great, or greater, an ambition for UT as Joseph Estabrook had for East Tennessee University before the Civil War. Fittingly, one of the many new buildings constructed at UT during Dabney's presidency was an engineering building named posthumously for Estabrook that stood till nearly two decades into the twenty-first century.[31] Unlike his predecessor, Dabney would not be brought down by anything so antiquated as denomina-tional prejudice.

In many ways, Charles Dabney did not so much transform UT as change what was already there: agricultural and mechanical education, military discipline, and athletics. Dabney did not eliminate the cadet program, but he did create a "civilian" student government and disciplinary system overseen by a dean rather than a commandant.[32] Athletics took on special consideration at the end of the nineteenth century because of new fears that industrialization was having an enervating effect on Anglo-American masculine vigor. A doctor's son in Win-chester, Tennessee, asked to transfer to UT in 1889 "in order to get the benefit of [UT's] military drill" on account of "not having a sufficient amount of exercise" at Vanderbilt.[33] The Young Men's Christian Association capped off a decade of proliferation on American campuses by building a gymnasium on Barbara Hill, as well as school sites as far away as Dartmouth and the University of Iowa, in 1890. Thereby UT became one of the South's first colleges to join in on the Victorian era's international trend of civic organizing (and Christian evangelicalism) while also augmenting its athletics.[34] Students had engaged in sports since antebellum days, but Dabney, whose presidency coincided with the first modern era Games of the Olympiad held in Greece in 1896, saw to it that track and field events, baseball, and football took on the organized form they had in the Ivy League and at new Midwestern schools that were coalescing into the precursor to the "Big Ten" conference; in turn, UT was invited into the Southern Intercollegiate Athletic Association (founded by a Vanderbilt professor) in 1895.[35]

Along with sports, under Dabney's leadership UT took on the accoutrements of a college or university that would become familiar, or even obligatory, to American higher learning in the twentieth century. Greek letter organizations were founded and legitimized by the school. Students began publishing a yearbook, *The Volunteer*, in 1897, thus giving a nickname to sports teams that would later receive mention in the local press (the *Knoxville Journal and Tribune* was calling UT's teams "the Volunteers" as early as 1902, reportedly in imitation of an Atlanta paper that had already called them that).[36] By 1897 the school recognized thirteen other student-led organizations including a monthly magazine, three literary societies, five social fraternities, and an engineering club.[37] In 1898 UT held memorial services for two graduates killed at the Battle of El Caney in the US war against Spain, the first UT graduates killed in a foreign war; the next year UT students raised funds to educate a Cuban student to be chosen by officers of the occupying forces.[38] In 1899 Dabney pushed through the founding of a Phi Kappa Phi chapter, an honors fraternity that, unlike the more famous Phi Beta Kappa, recognized students in all educational fields rather than just the liberal arts.[39] In 1902 UT brought its brass band (founded as one of the first cadet measures in 1869) to the Sewanee game, beginning a game day tradition that had become de rigueur by the 1920s. Mortarboard caps and gowns were worn for graduation ceremonies for the first time in 1903, the year before Dabney's departure.[40] Three years later, students founded the *Orange & White*, a publication that would go on to become the school's most long-lasting student newspaper. UT students, working together with their administration, laid the groundwork for the twentieth century in a few short years.

One change, the admission of women in 1892 was quite revolutionary, especially within the realm of Southern higher education. Dabney's presidency included the centennial of Blount College, and also the hundredth anniversary of the school's education of five women. Since the early republic era, a public role for women in the United States had been discouraged, even as female education became more acceptable and popular. Women—at least white, middle-class women—were, by the early nineteenth century, expected to pass to their children the virtues necessary for a strong republic, and for that some measure of education was deemed necessary, although men still considered woman suffrage too radical. Tennessee quietly led the way in providing women with the then-standard "classical" education; in 1855 Mary Sharp College in south-central Tennessee was the first school in the United States to award women bachelor's degrees considered equal to those given to men. Before it fell to economic hardship in the 1890s it had few imitators other than East Tennessee's Tusculum College, which began admitting women in 1872.[41] The sudden population loss after the Civil War popularized women common schoolteachers, necessitating the growth of women's academies. But even after the war, education for women, even white women, was slowed by the demands of Southern white supremacy.[42] By the 1890s, the South was dotted with private women's colleges that served the upper crust of white society, but public universities allowed women sporadically. Flagship universities in the South were relatively quick to accept women into the classroom, but reluctant to build female dormitories until the 1920s. Many land-grant schools, in contrast, did not accept women until after World War II; of land-grant schools in the former Confederacy, only Alabama joined UT in including women in the early 1890s.[43]

The "propriety" of accepting women as students was discussed by the UT trustees as early as 1880 when demand for coeducation began to make itself known.[44] The board revisited the topic eleven years later and decided to open the teachers' department to women. Four attended during the 1892–93 school year, after which it was quickly decided to open up the rest of the university to women.[45] Forty-eight women attended the following year. Reflecting his rearrangement of the school's governing structure, Dabney made coeducation a referendum for the faculty. "The University has never stood as high in the educational world as it does to-day," a press release boasted in June 1893, "and it is doubtful whether similar advantages on such favorable terms are offered women anywhere else in the South."[46] Not everyone agreed, including a male student who expressed his displeasure in rhyme in 1895:

Not long ago, upon 'The Hill'
The Board n' consultation
Decided, after much delay,
To have co-education
Next day 'twas published far and wide
In every town and city,
And every man who heard it said:
'Alas, and what a pity.'

When women joined the student body in the 1890s the University of
Tennessee took a giant step forward toward the model of higher education
that defined the twentieth century. Not the first Southern state university
to "go co-ed," it was also far from being the last.

So now the men all stay at home,
And nurse and sweep the floor:
No longer are there 'lady' cooks,
As in the days of yore
Thus all these honors, all these crimes,
All this male degradation,
Are due in part—in fact, they're all—
To this co-education.

The one literary plaintiff was probably not alone in his chauvinism (in early years male students were said to have called their classmates of the fairer sex "floozies"), but his voice was quickly made irrelevant by women thriving at UT, although, by 1900, they still numbered less than 15 percent of the student body.[47] But their numbers grew and, within a few short years, young women and men at UT were interacting in ways that would later seem familiar on campuses all over the United States: one Halloween, male students attacked the women with flour but were turned back when members of the fairer sex counter-attacked with a water hose.[48] In 1913, University Dean James D. Hoskins saw fit to ban popular dance steps, like the "turkey trot" and the "grizzly bear," he deemed unbecoming.[49] The "co-eds" of UT had ushered their school into the twentieth century.

The addition of white women as students might be termed UT's entrance into, or first contribution to, the Progressive era, a time of change directed by an idealistic middle class determined to push the boundaries of democracy while also creating a more orderly, educated American society. President Dabney was a great admirer of Midwestern universities, particularly what was known as the "Wisconsin Idea," the concept that universities like the University of Wisconsin could be (building upon the ideals of the Morrill Act a generation earlier) a center of social re-design, and a school for all citizens, not just official students.[50] "Not Yale or Harvard or Princeton is the typically American university," he told an assemblage, "but Cornell, Michigan, Wisconsin, and Stanford."[51] Perhaps not surprisingly, Midwestern state schools led the way nationally in opening up coeducation; Wisconsin's university normal school first enrolled women in 1860, while Michigan's did same ten years later. Most of the old sectarian schools of the Northeast remained all male until well into the twentieth century (Princeton University, the school that had an indirect formative influence over the school that would become UT did not accept women until 1969).[52] By the 1890s female education was growing in national—and Southern—popularity, but not without trepidation as to *what* women were to be educated to know and do. Months before UT began accepting applications from women, Tennessee newspapers

re-printed a *Harper's Magazine* column by philosopher Anna C. Brackett omi-
nously warning that "some schools" replaced "frivolity [and] lack of consistent
purpose and thoroughness" for "real reverence for the truth of her own woman-
hood."[53] "Our girls are well instructed in grammar, history, music and art, but
very few are taught to cook," wrote another columnist.[54] Ten years after women
began attending, Dabney answered that charge by establishing a home economics
program run by UT's first female instructor, Anna Monroe Gilchrist, a former
instructor at Columbia University's Teachers' College, and later by Jessie Harris,
UT's first academic dean.[55] Beforehand Dabney had noted that only the most
serious female students came to UT since the school had no training in music or
fine arts, the "so-called accomplishments" of "young women who merely want to be
polished or 'finished' from entering the institution." Instead, UT offered women
what Dabney called a "thorough, liberal education for some profession," except
for classes where they might be "physically disqualified or especially exempted
by the Faculty. . . ."[56] Home economics went on to become a popular part of the
school's extension service and public demonstrations for rural women and "all
women desiring to take the courses."[57]

UT had to deal, for the first time, with Victorian mores regarding the sexes
and their respective separate roles, this at a time when the American middle class
was roiling with tension over changing gender roles. But the female student body
organized almost immediately in a concerted effort to resist coddling. In the first
years, women were not allowed residency on campus, and were obliged to live
with families approved by the faculty (one of the stipulations was that they could
not reside in homes already housing male students).[58] In 1894, UT's Woman's
League protested plans to assign them a "matron" without also providing them
a dormitory. The league asserted that all UT students were old enough to be
"capable of conducting themselves properly." "We consider self reliance in matters
of conduct as well as in study one of the chief advantages gained by a University
education," their executive committee wrote at the end of the 1893–94 school
year, "and we believe that this benefit is best secured by the Woman's League and
would be seriously impaired by the profound form of government."[59] The school
did, however, appoint an unpaid (initially) Dean of Women, Angie Perkins, the
wife of a physics professor who was succeeded by English professor Florence
"Lady Skeff" Skeffington.[60] The first women's dormitory, Barbara Blount Hall,
was finished in 1901.[61]

From the perspective of the all-male board and faculty, women's presence
on campus meant that the male student body had to adhere to unprecedented
decorum for the sake of "the fairer sex." In 1900 Dabney attempted a crusade

Blount Hall, the university's first women's dormitory, stood
from 1925 to 2014, was a fine example of UT's early-twentieth-
century dedication to Collegiate Gothic architecture.

against cigarettes on campus, announcing during a student assembly that he had
noticed a correlation between smoking and poor grade performance. The anti-
cigarette campaign was apparently unsuccessful; within a quarter century, once
the sexual revolution associated with the "Roaring '20s" had set in, women had
openly joined their male classmates in openly puffing away at Tennessee's chief
cash crop despite the efforts of dean of women Harriet Greve.[62]

The historical record of UT during Dabney's term suggests that attempts
to regulate student behavior were rare, and crusades to improve the structure of

public education *en masse* were his true passion. Dabney hearkened to Jefferson's emphasis on common education, and criticized the "educated men" of the South "who hold to the theory that general education of the masses is not desirable. They prefer rather the education of the masses, whom they would educate only in a very limited degree."[63] His later years on Barbara Hill were his most active in this respect, most notably his founding of the "Summer School of the South" in 1902 (in imitation of a program initiated by the University of North Carolina in the 1880s), and UT's Department of Education at the beginning of 1903 (education gained full status as a discipline with its own college within the university twenty-three years later).[64] Both were motivated by Dabney's goal of training a large quantity of public school teachers for the state and region; and the postbellum Southern nationalism that had pervaded the school during the Humes administration played a role as well. In 1903, one of the Summer School's more "eminent lecturers," Georgia-born historian Ulrich B. Phillips, spoke of the "unique civilization" created by the antebellum "plantation regime," and praised the "aristocratic ideals" that the descendants of old Cavalier Virginia had brought west with them that ultimately "proved a leaven among the backwoods people."[65] Phillips's presence, and his message, provided white Tennesseans with not only a rosy view of the Old South, but also the New South's "intellectual justification" for the continued subordination of Black Southerners.[66] It was a racist sermon tailor-made for UT in the Dabney era. But, in the mind of the white South at the time, it came amid a great democratic expansion of educational opportunity sought on Barbara Hill since the days of Joseph Estabrook.

Philander Claxton, a native North Carolinian and East Tennessee University alum who would go on to become a US commissioner of education, served as superintendent of the Summer School. Known as the "Horace Mann of the South," Claxton kept the Summer School going for years after Dabney's presidency. Claxton had attended ETU/UT during the rancorous years under Humes, and he shared Dabney's passion for breaking with the Southern past via "practical" education.[67] Dabney and Claxton participated in what might be considered the quintessential Southern Progressive organization, the Southern Education Board, founded in 1901.[68] The Southern Education Board was a conglomeration of northern philanthropists and white Southern educators; Booker T. Washington, the most famous and respected Black educator of the day, was not invited to join even though he was friendly with most of the founders. The organization was described as "an investigating and 'preaching' board for carrying on a propaganda of education" which happened to include advocacy for "free public schools for all the people, blacks and whites alike, and compulsory attendance laws."[69] Near the end of his presidency Dabney enlisted Claxton in a series of campaigns to establish a relatively uniform, state-funded public school system in Tennessee, the better to solve the problems he had witnessed when he first came to the state. Dabney and Claxton convinced the state to establish county school boards in 1907 (rural schools had previously been left to very local district control) and to set aside an entire quarter of gross state revenues for schools (later increased to a third) fortified with county-collected taxes two years later.[70] By this point, Dabney had been gone from UT for a half-decade.

With women on campus as students, and an organizational dedication to broadening public education established, UT took one step closer to the democratic education for which many of its leaders had strived almost since its beginnings, but during the Dabney era its all-white student body remained an obstinate symbol of the South's—and indeed, the nation's—antidemocratic color line. The second Morrill Act (1890) included language advocating (perhaps too gently) equal access to public higher education, at least among schools receiving federal support.[71] By the end of the decade, West Virginia, Maryland, Louisiana, Oklahoma, Kentucky, Georgia, Florida, and Delaware had established African American colleges with land-grant status.[72] Dabney continued UT's "industrial department" at Knoxville College teaching farming and mechanical arts to fewer than twenty students per year, crowing that the smaller school provided "the 'brother in black' the kind of education which he needs most," leaving out the fact that said education was funded by only 15 percent of Morrill allocations to Tennessee.[73] The Supreme Court's decision in *Plessy v. Ferguson* (1896) established the "separate but equal" doctrine, but Dabney (who openly called Black Southerners "a child race, at least two thousand years behind the Anglo-Saxon in its development" and "a millstone about [the South's] neck") and most other Southern white elites saw this more as license to continue state-maintained inequality while increasing separateness.[74] In 1900 Knoxville College was forced to end one of its most ambitious projects, a five-year-old medical department, one of the only medical programs available to African American students in the South.[75] In 1901 the state went so far as force Maryville College, the old private bastion of Tennessee abolitionism, to remove their small number of African American students.[76] From the end of Reconstruction to the turn of the century, the white-dominated state government's policy toward its Black citizens had transformed from neglect into hostility.

Black Tennesseans recognized that their access to education was being continuously smothered during the era dubiously dedicated to "separate but equal," and protested the "failure to do anything for the established Negro institutions" and the "neglect and discrimination in its worse form by the state."[77] After Dabney's departure, Claxton joined forces with African American newspaper publisher Henry Allen Boyd to lobby for Tennessee's first actual land-grant source of education as part of the General Education Act of 1909.[78] Boyd and most of the other black lobbyists lived in Nashville and understandably wanted the school in or near their city, so the Tennessee Agricultural and Industrial Normal School (TA&I), later renamed Tennessee State University (TSU), opened there three years later, finally fulfilling a key provision of the Morrill Acts of 1862 and 1890.[79] The lobbyists had at least one ally left in the federal government, J. C. Napier, a white Tennessee native working in the Treasury Department who used the UT/ Knoxville College arrangement as a demonstration to Congress and President William Howard Taft that there was "not a state in the Union where the black man [was] getting his due," mandated by the Morrill and Hatch Acts.[80] The UT trustees voted to end its claims and responsibilities regarding Knoxville College, and the official relationship between the two schools was permanently severed.[81] Knoxville College was once again a fully private institution. UT would remain all white for decades to come. The result was that while UT was relatively well-funded, it suffered intellectually from the prejudices of its leaders, while Knoxville College lost a significant source of funding but, free from Dabney's racism, was able to broaden its education beyond his narrow "industrial arts" vision to become a liberal arts institution in 1931. Both Knoxville College and Tennessee Agricultural & Industrial (which became an accredited state university in 1946) defied the bigotry of lowered expectations by becoming training grounds for both schoolteachers and professionals in the twentieth century.[82] Meanwhile, "separate but equal" persisted unequally. As a demonstration of white academic attitudes of the time, Dean James Hoskins represented UT at the University Commission on Southern Race Questions, a series of meetings of all-white Southern universities in the 1910s called "in an effort to bring about a better understanding of the negro problem."[83]

By this time, Charles Dabney had been gone for nearly a decade, having accepted the presidency of Cincinnati University at a salary nearly double what UT could manage. Although Dabney admitted to a friend that he had left UT "too fast and too independently," his presidency and his efforts through the Southern Education Board had been met with what he considered "insurmountable prejudice, narrowness, sectarianism, sectionalism, demagoguism, and profound stupidity of the leaders of these people and of the masses of the people themselves. . . ."[84] As historian Natalie Ring observes about Dabney and other Southern Progressives, the "New South Creed" that inspired the children of the Civil War generation in the 1880s was subsumed by the national image of the "Problem South" by the first decade of the twentieth century.[85] Dabney's lament was a common one among Progressives in the South or elsewhere, a recognition that politics was often a bitter adversary of education. Still, Dabney was more successful than any previous president in navigating political (or, in Joseph Estabrook's case, denominational) adversity in his school's history.

His successor, engineering and physics professor Brown Ayres, continued Dabney's expansion of UT's size after he arrived in 1904. But, unlike Dabney, he did not see his school as a means to a lofty Progressive end during his fifteen years in office.[86] Ayres was known as a brilliant physicist so passionate about education he turned down a lucrative job offer from Alexander Graham Bell.[87] But he knew that his was not the only discipline. Ayres was aware that an English professor from North Carolina had declined the presidency before it was offered to him, quite possibly because he saw little hope for his own field at a school that was obviously centered around the physical sciences (although Dabney apparently favored Ayres in the first place). UT was a land-grant school with the responsibilities that entailed, but it was also the state university, and the changes Ayres initiated during his fifteen years in office suggest that he felt a need to expand the school's scope. Agricultural education did not decline, but it did not have the same absolute centrality under Ayres as it had under Dabney. In 1905, UT established the College of Liberal Arts (renamed the College of Arts & Sciences in 1994), a callback to the past of Samuel Carrick and Thomas Humes.

Since the 1870s, the school had gone through a series of changes leading toward its status as a school that would represent the entire state of Tennessee. The Dabney presidency had done much to make this a reality, and students came from all over the state to get their educations. These efforts were fully realized under Ayres. Between 1905 and 1909 Philander Claxton secured a permanent allocation from the state, a longtime goal for presidents and trustees going back decades (years later Dabney said Claxton "made the greatest contribution to the cause of public education . . . of any man since Jefferson.")[88] In recognition of the new relationship with the state government, the board of trustees agreed to a drastic reform within their own numbers. In the previous century the board had grown to thirty members, mostly from East Tennessee. In 1908 the board was reduced to an even dozen with representation throughout the state, including a required third made up of UT alumni, as well as a required third "members of the principal opposition political party to that now in control of the State government," changes suitable for the school's first West Tennessee–native presidency (having studied and taught in New Jersey, Virginia, and Louisiana, Ayres was originally from Memphis).[89] UT ran an active extension service in cooperation with the USDA, and western, middle, and eastern Tennessee hosted at least two experiment stations by 1920.[90] Ayres was a frequent speaker at farmers' gatherings, and the old distrust between experimental and "practical" agriculture felt during Governor Taylor's administration seemed to have faded. For instance, after UT agronomists advocated the eccentric idea of adopting soybeans as a crop for feeding hogs, the legume eventually became one of Tennessee's top cash crops.[91] The Summer School of the South, Dabney and Claxton's most influential legacy, continued on the campus through the last summer of Ayres's presidency, making UT a center-point of Southern Progressivism—although Ayres himself griped that attendees damaged campus property and diminished the university's function with too much emphasis on primary education.[92]

Dabney had envisioned UT as a resource for the country gentry of a largely rural state, but by the early twentieth century a lot of farmers' sons were moving to the towns and cities and becoming workmen or professionals. Somewhat younger than Dabney and an urbanite himself, Ayres saw UT as a place to train the latter group. Ayres was, as one Chattanooga newspaper pointed out, "never at any pains to conceal" he was "to the manner [sic] born," and did not share Dabney's egalitarian educational vision.[93] Attorneys and physicians had been trained in a master-journeyman fashion until just after the Civil War when a nationwide demand for standardization of professional work grew. UT had answered the call soon after Dabney became president by organizing a legal curriculum in 1890, although the training of young lawyers at UT was carried out by no more than two senior jurists at one time for nearly twenty years and was little different from the old American tradition of reading Blackstone under the direction of an amenable judge. Under Ayres, UT Law became its own college in 1911, and the college was given its own building thirteen years later.[94] To provide UT-trained lawyers with flush clients, Ayres founded UT's school of commerce in 1914, a school that would later become a college of business. It is hard to determine how much the new school improved the various Tennessee bars since, as late as 1936, the state still did not require lawyers to have more than a high school education preceding their two years in a law school or law office.[95]

Nineteen-Eleven also marked the establishment of UT's medical college, an undertaking that had been envisioned ever since the Estabrook administration. Medical education in Tennessee had long reflected Knoxville's developmental lag behind the other two major cities. A private medical school was established in Memphis in 1846, and one was established in Nashville in 1850, followed by a dental school two years later.[96] UT adopted Nashville Medical College as the state medical college in 1879, but the lack of trained doctors in East Tennessee remained noticeable, and the Nashville school had practically no relationship to UT anyway (the medical school deposited its own fees and tuition and simply had the latter's name on its diplomas). In 1889, just as the state government was assembling a medical examiners board, another branch of Tennessee Medical College was founded on the corner of Gay Street and Main, the first formal higher education in downtown Knoxville since the days of Blount College.[97] But Knoxville's subordination to larger cities was still a problem. Dabney started a pharmacy school in 1898 but low enrollment necessitated the school be transferred to Memphis after twelve years. Between 1911 and 1913, all medical education associated with UT was reconsolidated in the Bluff City, and medical training did not return to the Knoxville campus until shortly after World War II.[98]

Back in Knoxville, the Ayres years were a period of tempered expectations in comparison to the Progressive zeal of Charles Dabney. Ayres led UT during the first world war, an ordeal that did not challenge the school's existence as past trials had done (indeed, it is very likely that the US war effort strengthened UT), but instead displayed the unprecedented home-front role that universities could play during wartime. The "Great War" began in Europe in 1914, and its effects were felt on campus at least three years later. Just under a thousand students matriculated in the fall of 1916, but the number fell to 826 the next fall after the US declared war, and 751 in 1918 (this after enrollment had increased 417 percent between 1887 and 1916), while instructors from UT's vaunted military training program were called away for service.[99] Men returning to campus in 1919 and 1920 were placed in Student Army Training Corps, which introduced military drills to students who were not otherwise part of the cadet program.[100] After commanding a brigade in northern France, UT military science professor Lawrence Tyson was awarded the Distinguished Service Cross. His son McGhee was lost in action thirty-one days before the Armistice while serving as a naval pilot in the North Sea, and posthumously became the namesake for Knoxville's first airport in 1930. A much larger, more permanent, airport named for him was built in neighboring Blount County five years later.[101]

A month after the Armistice, Ayres announced an immense building program on the Hill, including a large class building to stand in the place of Old, East, and West Colleges, the old East Tennessee College buildings from the 1820s.[102] The following month he attended a conference of land-grant college presidents in Baltimore where the body resolved to form a multicampus reserve officer training corps.[103] Early the next week the president died unexpectedly "as a result of acute indigestion."[104] Dean Hoskins served as acting president until Dean of

UT played a special role during the "Great War," owing partly to its decades-old
position as a center of military science education.

Agriculture Harcourt Morgan was unanimously selected as Ayres's replacement
the following summer.[105] Blanch Bingham, a "pretty cheer leader for Co-Eds" from
Middle Tennessee, was honored with laying the first brick of the new building
Ayres had announced eleven months earlier.[106] Three years later, a UT alum living in West Tennessee told his local newspaper that, during a recent visit to his
alma mater after forty-two years, he had recognized only one building.[107]

The Morgan administration was not the first tumultuous era in the school's
history, but it was the first time hard times were defined more by embarrassment
than by existential danger. Since Dabney's term, UT had grown not only in size
but also in prestige, and Knoxville had grown around it; between the 1880s and
the war, the city annexed dozens of surrounding square miles, including the
campus-adjacent residential neighborhood that grew up around the ruins of Fort
Sanders. Its population increased more than threefold between 1890 and 1920, to
just under eighty thousand, and reached more than 100,000 by the beginning of
the Great Depression. In the 1920s alone, more than six thousand houses were
built.[108] In 1921, there were reportedly 116 churches (forty Methodist congregations, thirty-six Baptist, a dozen Presbyterian, plus other smaller denomina-

Canada-born UT president Harcourt Morgan
probably enjoyed talking to Tennessee farmers
more than he did faculty members. He left
the president's office in 1933 to serve on the
inaugural board of directors for the
Tennessee Valley Authority.

tions) with more than 34,000 souls in attendance.[109] African Americans made up slightly over 18 percent of churchgoers, and over a quarter of the city's general population. Since the 1880s, Knoxville had made itself a manufacturing town, and its Black population increased by four times between 1870 and 1920, with a late surge during the Great War as part of the nationwide Great Migration. As in many other cities in the South and Midwest, in the "Red Summer" of 1919 a white mob attacked the city's Black population en masse (this just short months after the founding of Knoxville's chapter of the National Association for the Advancement of Colored People).[110] Most of the violence took place on Vine Street, more than a mile east of the UT campus, but one newspaper account mentioned one segment of the mob "in the bottoms near the university" (probably the area around Second Creek on the east side of The Hill).[111] Members of the

The Hill, ca. 1919. For more than a century, the school that became the
University of Tennessee was centered around Barbara Hill, named for Barbara
Blount, daughter of William Blount and one of Carrick's students.

Fourth Tennessee National Guard attempted to restore order, and made it clear
by practically all accounts that they held Black Knoxvillians more responsible,
even though the latter were never on the offensive.[112] Rather than condemning
the rise in racial violence, local newspapers lamented the curse of mass society
making its way into East Tennessee. "While the riot in Knoxville Saturday night
is to be deplored," opined a Greeneville editor, "it only goes to prove how close to
home the mob spirit is reaching."[113] A few months later the city's streetcar drivers
went on strike, seemingly confirming (at least to those not directly involved) that
the urban "mob spirit" had indeed arrived.[114]

    Urban growth and an expanding number of students and professors exposed
the city and the university to other national trends and uproars, beginning with
the Prohibition movement. Southern universities like UT led the way in popu-
larizing Prohibition, even if students were known to tipple from time to time.

In 1907 UT students even rode a water wagon in a parade through Knoxville supporting a law that banned liquor sales in large-sized towns. Not all students were convinced, however; Joseph Krutch, a recent Phi Kappa Phi inductee, was nearly expelled in 1915 for writing an essay for the literary magazine attacking the authoritarianism of Prohibition and "blue laws" that regulated commerce on Sundays.[115] The war made alcohol consumption more visible, and grosser in the eyes of temperance advocates, and Tennessee passed its "Bone-Dry" law a few months after the war declaration. By the time the Eighteenth Amendment was ratified (with overwhelming support from Tennessee's congressional delegation and state legislature) alcohol sales in Knoxville had been strictly illicit for two years.[116] As demand for banning hard drink increased, national observers like *The Literary Digest* noticed that "college heads" in the South were seeing to it that "the mint julep and eggnog [would] soon be no more," and related it to the new educational emphasis on science over the old Southern love for language and veneration of the past.

> The bowl which once flowed with rhetoric, fond recollection and faint regret is now filled with nuts and fruits, which contain no conversation. Thus, we are led to believe, have their own and the National Prohibition Laws changed the old order and set a new one on the ways. The South has changed in many respects, not more, perhaps, than in departing from the method with which it welcomed and sped the parting guest and in which it regaled itself as occasion and season required. A new state has crept upon us. Cotton is still king, the Colonel still smokes, and chews a little; but, we are led to believe, he and his sons have given up their Bourbon.[117]

It is likely that many of UT's "college heads" missed their legal tippling, but complaints about federal overreach were few. Prohibition was widely popular in the South and the old white Southern demand for "states' rights" was somewhat muted in the 1920s. Illicit liquor and beer were famously available in Knoxville for those who wanted them. Finally, UT was still the domain of Tennessee's relatively well-to-do young people and temperance, if nothing else, was a sign of middle-class respectability even in the "Jazz Age." Nevertheless, as the 1920s progressed, Prohibition, and the will to prosecute for it, wore thin on the UT campus as it did everywhere else. A local "prohibition administrator" reported that "about seventy-five" liquor bottles were confiscated in the bleachers during the 1929 Alabama–Tennessee football game (which Tennessee won 6–0), but no arrests were made.[118]

Like elsewhere, Tennessee's middle class was divided between the older

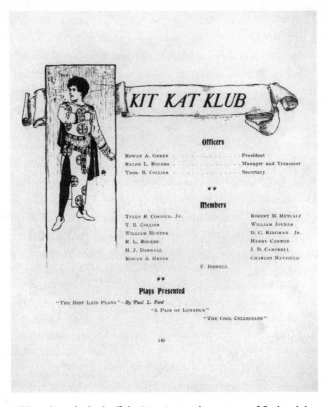

UT students kicked off the Jazz Age with a variety of flashy clubs,
including the theatre-centered Kit Kat Klub.

Victorian zeal for Protestant piety, and the newer forces and trends collectively
(and imprecisely) referred to as "modernism." One battleground for the burgeon-
ing battle between the traditional and the modern emerged from the seemingly
sudden arrival of mass consumption entertainment and a sexual revolution that
followed World War I.[119] UT students and faculty probably discussed the relative merits of the evangelist Billy Sunday, the sardonic nihilism of Baltimore
journalist H. L. Mencken, the promises or threats presented by the Bolshevik
Revolution, and the sudden national popularity of an African American art form
called jazz. They probably watched with interest as former UT student William
Gibbs McAdoo attempted to win the Democratic presidential nomination in
1920 and 1924, the second time with an endorsement from a new iteration of

the Ku Klux Klan.[120] This new version of the white nationalist organization, last heard from in Tennessee a half century earlier, set up its largest urban "klavern" in Knoxville, attracting the white working and middle classes with the promise of a country restored to "100% Americanism."[121] In an apparent braying response, UT men formed their own KKK, the "Kit Kat Klub," a drama club that occasionally featured Vaudeville-inspired gender-bending casting. Women students joined in the fun with their own troupe named the "Rouge & Powder Club."[122] Historian William Bruce Wheeler notes that the university "appears to have taken no part in addressing Knoxville's confounding problems" in the years immediately after the Great War.[123] Perhaps UT was aloof from its immediate surroundings, but in the early days of cinema, radio, and mass market publishing, higher education in Knoxville was obliged to reflect the national mood. And, curfews notwithstanding, students had some exposure to city life during Knoxville's most boisterous decade.

In some ways, UT president Harcourt Morgan was Dabney redux. Although he was not a Tennessean or a native Southerner, the Canadian scientist enjoyed mingling with Tennessee farmers and appearing at various county extension service events all over the state. He expanded the Dabney-era experiment stations in Middle and West Tennessee to assuage old sectional spites and advertise "the practical message of commercial value to the people of the state," according to one contemporary Knoxville booster.[124] Science at a land-grant school and its satellites was synonymous with profit in the 1920s, unless it involved one of the hottest controversies of the day, Darwinian evolution. Charles Darwin's *Origin of the Species* (1859) was published almost exactly sixty years before Harcourt Morgan assumed UT's presidency. Nineteenth-century readers debated the book, for not only its religious implications, but also its merits in contrast to other contemporary evolutionary theorists like Jean Baptiste Lamarck and Thomas Huxley. Some of the debates came close to home in Tennessee relatively early. In 1878 professor of geology and zoology Alexander Winchell was dismissed from Vanderbilt University, then a school associated with Methodism, for teaching polygenetic evolution (a theory that different races of humanity had different origins).[125] Shortly thereafter, Robert Dabney, Charles Dabney's father, had stirred up a controversy over evolution among Southern Presbyterians, disputing its truth but more for its alleged damage to Christian doctrine than its empirical possibility.[126] The controversy was later in coming to UT, possibly because so much of the late nineteenth century had been more a struggle for institutional survival than an opportunity for rancorous debate. UT professors of the era did not seem to see much problem with evolution. The younger Dabney did not see the same inconsistency between Scripture and laboratory, speaking of Huxley (whom he called "the greatest teacher of natural science our century has produced") in the same breath as Paul of Tarsus and the Sermon on the Mount in an address to another Southern university.[127] During the Humes presidency, UT commandant and mathematics professor Samuel Lockett told medical students that the study of evolutionary science like Darwin, Huxley, and John Tyndall, would lead to an end to disease in the near future.[128] By the first decade of the twentieth century, the teaching of evolution did not seem to conflict with the larger aims of a school that promised in its yearly register to "promote the religious spirit and life" of its students while also promising "to promote no creed nor exclude any."[129]

Scientific advancement moved at a rapid pace, but not as rapid as the Progressive "search for order," notably Charles Dabney's dream of scholastic consistency throughout Tennessee. By 1910 students throughout the state had unprecedented access to public education, and textbooks were no longer catch-as-catch-can in local school districts, thanks to the Uniform Text-book Law passed in 1899.[130] Simultaneous to this development (what historian Charles Israel has called "the formalization of public education and politicization of moral questions that had previously been settled on familial and local community levels"), was a quantitative revolution in the educational publishing industry, with many of the newest available textbooks displaying the influence of Charles Darwin or other provocative (but less popular) evolutionary theorists like Tyndall and Huxley.[131]

In 1922 UT education professor Jesse Sprowls adopted one of these, James Harvey Robinson's *The Mind in the Making: The Relation of Intelligence to Social Reform* (1921), a best-selling, civilization-spanning history that actually mentioned Darwin by name only once, but nevertheless suggested a pattern of human societal development guided by forces other than the Hand of the Judeo-Christian Deity. Robinson's book also protested the limitations on freedom of expression and assembly placed on the United States by the administration of President Woodrow Wilson during the war.[132] Altogether, Sprowls's adoption was not so much an endorsement of evolution as it was an attempt to expose his students to a lengthy text that embodied practically everything conjured by the term *modernism*. It happened to coincide with former presidential candidate (and Wilson's first secretary of state) William Jennings Bryan's national campaign against the teaching of Darwinian evolution that eventually led to bills introduced in six states seeking to stymie or outlaw its teaching in publicly funded schools. Reacting to the heated atmosphere developing in Tennessee, Dean of Liberal Arts James Hoskins tried to quietly circumvent Sprowls by cancelling the professor's book

order after the School of Education dean had tried to dissuade the young professor. Sprowls appealed to President Morgan, but he was rebuffed. Morgan presided
over a university with unprecedented support from the Tennessee General Assembly and the governor's mansion, and as a scientist he was genuinely scared
of the prospect of anti-evolution legislation, so he feared what might happen if
he made too much of a stink over academic freedom. Morgan initially refused
Sprowls's resignation but supported the Education dean's decision to dismiss
Sprowls for purportedly unrelated reasons. Morgan asserted that he and other
UT professors had addressed evolution in their classes, although perhaps not
with as direct an application to human existence as Robinson's text (Morgan was
trained as an entomologist, a specialist in insect life, with personal expertise on
boll weevil eradication).[133]

Over the next year, professors offered Morgan their own resignations in protest of Sprowls's treatment. In the summer of 1923, UT dismissed five professors,
including the president of the local chapter of the American Association of University Professors (AAUP), an organization founded by John Dewey and Arthur
Lovejoy in 1915 to protect academic freedom and professorial employment.[134]
Hoskins, whom Morgan assigned to lead an internal investigation of unhappy
faculty, believed that many professors were using the dismissal of Sprowls to
express their own grievances and embarrass UT for spite. Indeed, many of the
"insurgent movement" within the faculty made claims unrelated to Darwin or
Sprowls: UT's alleged violation of the rule that placed a certain number of alums
on the board of trustees, the illegal hiring of a foreign citizen (Morgan had never
become a US citizen), and excessive purchase of heating coal.[135] During the summer of 1923 Sprowls made sure that newspapers in Knoxville and other Tennessee
towns were kept abreast of the disarray under Morgan and Hoskins, ignoring
advice from a friend that he "should seek a new position" rather than "seek[ing]
now revenge."[136] By the end of the year, UT had lost thirteen instructors, nearly
one fifth of its faculty, leaving Morgan, Hoskins, and the board of trustees with
the biggest rebuilding chore in decades.[137]

UT students protested the Sprowls firing within days by publishing three
editions of *The Independent Truth*, an anonymously composed and edited underground journal. One history professor declared the screed "dignified and re-
strained," and a better forum for "airing student grievances" than the *Orange &
White*, which had thus far ignored Sprowls's predicament.[138] *The World*, a popular
national magazine, compared Hoskins and Morgan's UT to the Soviet Union's
Sverdloff University.[139] But the worst indictment of UT's handling of its faculty

came from the AAUP. The AAUP slammed UT for its treatment of its faculty, particularly its lack of a tenure system (Sprowls and all of the other departing instructors were on one-year contracts).[140] A rumor spread that an administrator had admitted that the mass dismissal was a purposeful purge of atheism, and Morgan found himself in a position where he was pilloried by both fundamentalists and modernists, in Tennessee and beyond, each assuming he agreed with the other side.[141] It was not the first time the school had sacrificed education for politics, but it was the first time a school president had been responsible for doing so.

Amid the high dudgeon on campus, in the spring of 1925 the Tennessee legislature passed the Butler Act, a law banning the "Evolution Theory" in all universities and public schools receiving state funds (a similar bill had failed to pass in 1923). Butler's was not the first bill to make this attempt, and many Tennesseans in government and private life considered the law too far-reaching regardless of their personal feelings on evolution. Governor Austin Peay signed the bill into law with no apparent hesitation. Many Tennessee scholars at private institutions protested the Butler Act, including the president of Fisk University, Vanderbilt's English Department chairman, and Arlo Brown, president of the University of Chattanooga, who fought within his Southern Methodist denomination by refusing to ban Darwin from his classrooms, emerging as Tennessee's bravest voice of defiance to intellectual censorship during the 1920s.[142] But Harcourt Morgan was afraid to complicate his school's relationship with a friendly governor (who had plans to expand UT), and he not only kept silent about his misgivings but also urged UT's faculty to do so as well.[143] Morgan pleaded to Peay that the bill be amended so that it referred only to "man's ascent from a monkey," so as not to impede "civilized man's [development] by breeding and selection to improve as many forms of plants and animals as are economically worth while."[144] He assured the governor that UT would nevertheless bow out of the controversy since "Evolution so intricately involves religious belief," an element of life that the nonsectarian school "has no disposition to dictate." Peay assured himself and the public that "nothing of consequence" in any of the books being taught by Tennessee schools at the time would interfere with the new law. "Nobody," he predicted, "believes that it is going to be an active statute." Meanwhile, UT students protested the Butler Act just as they had the firing of Sprowls, sarcastically suggesting that lawmakers in Nashville consider regulating gravity and the speed of light after they got done with biology.[145]

Peay's prediction about the Butler Act proved mostly true for most of its forty-two-year existence, but the immediate reaction created a national sensation and became one of the most misapprehended events of American history. After the American Civil Liberties Union (ACLU) announced that it would finance a test case challenging the Butler Act's constitutionality, a group of booster-minded businessmen in Dayton, Tennessee (less than a hundred miles south of Knoxville), colluded to have a local substitute teacher named John Scopes put on trial. The "Scopes Monkey Trial" brought national attention to East Tennessee where it was widely believed the recent war between modernism and fundamentalism would be settled once and for all. It began as an attempt to assert freedom of speech that had been threatened continuously since the war, but it ended as a referendum between science and religion, with the two star attorneys—Bryan and celebrity trial lawyer Clarence Darrow—taking absolutist positions against each other. John R. Neal, an eccentric former legislator and law professor who had been one of the firing victims of 1923 (and an early advocate for Sprowls), served as one of Scopes's defense attorneys, and he attempted to have Harcourt Morgan called as an expert witness on the subject of biological evolution, but the presiding judge barred the move.[146] Scopes was found guilty, the law was upheld, and Dayton did not secure the new wealth its businessmen sought. Historian Paul Conkin observed that the trial of Scopes (who ended up going to graduate school after having his fine paid for him by his allies) had a broad stultifying effect on science education since most publishers could not directly address the Darwinian theory until well into the 1950s if they wanted to sell textbooks.[147] It had a stultifying effect on Tennessee too. In the American mind, Tennessee and the South had lagged behind the rest of the United States in education and even general intelligence, just as they had lagged behind in material wealth since the Civil War. The Scopes trial seemed to confirm their intentional benightedness, and UT, entangled in state politics and administrative timidity, did nothing to suggest otherwise. It also stood as an odd rebuke not only to UT itself, but also to the vision of education that men like Charles Dabney had once held for education in Tennessee. Bryan's mootable victory in the trial, and his overwhelming support from white Tennesseans, was a strong indication that both the politicians and the general public rejected empirical knowledge as a matter of course. UT was bound to receive collateral damage; before the trial had even ended, the dean of Columbia University's pharmacy school declared that Tennessee had "reverted to slavery[,] this time intellectual," and recommended that his school "refuse to recognize any scholastic training from that state as basis for entering college here. . . ."[148] Four decades later, UT zoology professor Arthur Jones convinced the board of trustees and school vice president Edward Boling to lobby for the Butler Act's repeal, which finally happened in 1967, shortly before similar laws in Arkansas and Mississippi were struck down in court.[149]

Harcourt Morgan's last act of obsequiousness to the politicians came in 1927 when popular Midwestern writer Homer Croy published an article exposing the existence of an American Association for the Advancement of Atheism (AAAA) chapter at UT and seventeen other universities.[150] Paranoia over organized atheism had been riding high since one of the most high-profile nonbelievers in the United States, Clarence Darrow, had deconstructed William Jennings Bryan's literal belief in the Bible during the Scopes trial, as well as the growth of the ACLU which Croy claimed was behind the AAAA. As before, letters poured into Morgan's office, most expressing confidence that the UT president would uphold Christian values. Unlike the kerfuffles over Darwinism, the atheism scare was short-lived. There was circumstantial evidence that at least one student had corresponded with the AAAA, probably in the wake of the publicity following the Scopes trial and may have attempted to form a cell with no university sponsorship.[151] The rights, or lack thereof, of students to form clubs or assemblages on their own was never discussed. Hoskins and Morgan were personally and publicly concerned that their school had a reputation for "Godlessness" in any way, shape, or form. In 1928, they helped found the Tennessee School of Religion, a partnership of several local Protestant congregations that used UT facilities and offered Bible classes that counted for UT credit but was technically chartered as a completely separate organization. The following year UT initiated an annual midwinter convocation with open promotion of Protestant Christian theology. The School of Religion continued for three decades before faculty members raised the question as to whether or not the arrangement skirted the boundaries of separation of church and state too much. In 1965 UT established the Department of Religious Studies and severed its official relationship with the Tennessee School of Religion (although faculty and administrators continued to serve on the latter's board of directors). The last convocation was held in 1968. From then on, religious life on the UT campus remained active via many churches and organizations, but fully voluntary and left to students' individual discretion.[152]

Harcourt Morgan was no ideologue, but his desire for stability caused him to unintentionally help ideologues. In 1930 East Tennessee's Lincoln Memorial University dismissed faculty and students it considered radical rabble-rousers in a move far more arbitrary and draconian than UT's firings of 1923. The smaller school's new president publicly insulted students he believed wanted to have

Campus as it looked in the Roaring Twenties.

Lincoln Memorial "Leninized," and claimed that UT had offered to lend faculty members to replace the professors who had been forced out.[153] Like many former teachers who became administrators, Morgan's ultimate destiny was politics rather than education. In the summer of 1933, Harcourt Morgan was selected to serve on the triumvirate committee of the Tennessee Valley Authority (TVA), a federal organization that would go on to irrevocably change Knoxville, East Tennessee, and a fair chunk of the rest of the South. He was chosen by another member of the committee, Arthur Morgan (no relation), because of his expertise in Southern agriculture.[154] Harcourt Morgan was approved by the US Senate (despite the better of politically influential John R. Neal who still despised Morgan's cowardice and coveted the TVA position for himself) and became the committee's dark horse as Arthur Morgan and its third member David Lilienthal feuded over the TVA's ultimate purpose. Arthur Morgan was drummed out in 1938 and Harcourt Morgan became chair. For the next decade, the former UT president became a conscientious defender of Tennessee farming (for instance, opposing putting some of the state's richest farmland underwater).[155] He wrote with broad flourish of the importance of understanding humans as part of a precipitously balanced ecosystem and preventing natural disasters.[156] In a 1936 letter he wrote to James Hoskins (his successor as UT president) about the "new frontier" promised by the school's partnership with the TVA, his happiness, and perhaps relief, is palpable.[157]

But Morgan's departure did not mark the end of controversy. In 1939 the AAUP accused the Hoskins administration of arbitrarily firing education professor A. D. Mueller in 1937.[158] The Mueller case placed UT on the AAUP's list of censures, where it stayed until after World War II when the school (by then a much larger institution) began adhering to AAUP tenure policy.[159] Hoskins was probably unbothered by the loss since the AAUP usually advocated for professors who did not match his utilitarian vision for education in Tennessee. "After all," Hoskins intoned in 1940, "a state university has but one reason for existence, and that is to create for the state. Gone are the days when a university was merely an institution for classical learning where knowledge was regarded as its own reward. It is not enough to train a person to be intelligent. He must be intelligent for some useful purpose."[160]

UT's experiences in the 1920s proved that education was valuable only if people chose to value it. The Progressive era that Charles Dabney helped initiate in state and nation came to a grinding, horrible halt. Brown Ayres had been a source of stalwart, if not ambitious, leadership during a decade of constant change and growth. Harcourt Morgan was more representative of the sentiment articulated in newspaperman William Allen White's eulogy for Progressivism: Americans were "tired of issues, sick at heart of ideals, and weary of being noble." Morgan's belief in the superiority of knowledge to politics (assuming he had such a belief) was tested multiple times during his presidency, and he failed to uphold it each time. Morgan apparently believed that discretion was the better part of valor even when the science he had once dedicated his life to teaching was under attack, and free speech itself was in danger. The Scopes trial put a definitive end to the Southern Progressivism Charles Dabney had helped initiate. It confirmed to many the "prejudice, narrowness, sectarianism, sectionalism, demagoguism, and profound stupidity" that had driven Charles Dabney to the North twenty-one years earlier. Northern observers declared the South hopeless, while Southern idealists wrung their hands and tempered their idealism. And yet the controversy had only emerged because of the uniformity of statewide education (particularly legislative oversight over textbooks) that Dabney believed would be a cure for all Southern ills. Although Tennessee became the battleground for a fight between religion and science, the question of creationism versus evolution did not ruin UT. It did, however, reveal what former presidents like Joseph Estabrook and Thomas Humes had discovered the hard way: in public education, the search for truth was too easily subordinated to the dictates of politics.

CHAPTER FOUR

A University Finds a New Purpose, 1930–1955

. . . .

"The delicate thing about the university is that it has a mixed
character, that it is suspended between its position in the
eternal world, with all its corruption and evils and cruelties,
and the splendid world of our imagination."

—RICHARD HOFSTADTER—
Columbia University Commencement Address, 1968

The 1920s was, in the words of historian Calvin Lee, "The golden age of Joe
College," a decade when college education became more visible in American
culture than ever before (even though it remained economically inaccessible for
the majority of Americans). F. Scott Fitzgerald's *This Side of Paradise* (1920)
used Princeton University as a setting for the literary initiation of the Jazz
Age, establishing "the stereotype that was to cling to an entire generation of
college youth."[1] College students came home for summer break talking about
T. S. Eliot, James Joyce, and an Austrian scientist named Sigmund Freud, and
before long products of the avant-garde ended up as dinner table discussion and
subject matter in middlebrow family publications like *Saturday Evening Post*. The
same students came back in the fall and filled the bleachers on the sidelines of
newly graded football fields and, more and more, they were joined by fans with
no direct connections to the college or university (in illustrations of the time
these enthusiasts were often pictured wearing raccoon fur coats and equipped
with a team pennant and secreted pocket liquor flask). University of Illinois
halfback Red Grange became a celebrity in a decade of celebrities by playing
ball for free before he went on to a nine-year professional career. The "Four
Horsemen," Notre Dame University's relentless backfield, achieved nationwide
fame thanks to creative sportswriting and the coaching genius of Knute Rockne.

By the end of the 1920s football had expanded Americans' interest in colleges and universities, but not necessarily as sources of learning. In the Marx Brothers' *Horse Feathers* (1932), the first of many college film comedies, the prevailing joke is the subordination of education to success on the gridiron. Others, most of them light romantic comedies, such as *College Humor* (1934), *College Rhythm* (1934), *College Holiday* (1936), and *College Swing* (1938), were considerably less acerbic in their portrayal of higher education. Their proliferation demonstrated a public appetite for, and curiosity about, the lighter moments of college life during a time of economic uncertainty.[2] Colleges and universities were, perhaps quite suddenly, a part of popular culture even though the overwhelming majority of Americans did not attend them. And yet, even as higher learning earned higher visibility, organizations like the AAUP were becoming increasingly concerned that colleges' dedication to sports would be their undoing by subverting their true mission.[3]

By the end of the 1920s UT had been fielding an intercollegiate football squad for most of four decades. During his last years as president Thomas Humes lamented how UT students seem[ed] to have abandoned athletic games and [instead] to idolize 'shows.'"[4] Students took up the implied challenge soon after Humes's departure, casually playing baseball (by far the more popular sport in the nineteenth century) and organizing a football club as early as 1884.[5] UT students began playing other schools in 1891 under the tutelage of UT instructor Henry Denlinger, a veteran of Princeton University's team (a year after what was probably the state of Tennessee's first intercollegiate football game between Vanderbilt and Nashville College and twenty-two years after Princeton played Rutgers in the first recorded intercollegiate football game).[6] The rise of football reflected contemporaneous events in Knoxville. Extractive and manufacturing industries grew in Knoxville and its surroundings during the economically unstable 1890s, and a new generation of northerners were arriving in Tennessee—many of them carrying with them a sport formerly associated with Philadelphia's Main Line, Boston's Back Bay, and other elite Gilded Age enclaves. The loosely defined UT squad took on a variety of challengers, including local athletic clubs (all the rage among the 1890s male middle class, who strived for what Theodore Roosevelt called the "strenuous life") and prep schools, but its first intercollegiate game was a loss to Middle Tennessee's Sewanee (also known as the University of the South). After an 1892 win against Maryville College the following year, UT football entered into a brief period of irregular play and indeterminant statistics; after all, there was little official about the game, and other sports, especially baseball, took precedence on campus. The administration lost interest in officially fielding a team, but a handful of students, led by William Stokely, kept practicing and inviting competition until 1896 when UT joined the Southern Intercollegiate Athletic Association (SIAA) along with Vanderbilt, Sewanee, and schools from nine other Southern states.[7] A series of journeyman head coaches were hired between the interruptions in sport caused by the Spanish-American War and the Great War, most producing more wins than losses in seasons lasting seven to nine games and staying at UT three seasons or less. Somewhere along the way, probably just after 1896's 4–0 season, the team began wearing athletic sweaters in varying shades of orange.[8]

College football almost perished in the first decade of the twentieth century because of its physical dangers and numerous fatalities around the nation, as well as concerns that unscrupulous coaches and school presidents would use graft to hire "ringers" for their teams. Manifold concerns among administrators led to a series of meetings that culminated in the creation of the regulatory National Collegiate Athletic Association (NCAA) in 1906, a body that gradually expanded its reach over the next two decades.[9] UT could not avoid the epidemic of serious accidents on the field even after such reforms as the forward pass and ten-yard first downs (lengthened from five) theoretically made maiming injuries less common after 1909. In a game against Vanderbilt in October 1915, UT left halfback Bennett Jared suffered a spinal injury, causing paralysis and his untimely death twenty-one months later.[10]

The SIAA avoided the controversy suffered by higher profile schools in the Northeast and Midwest (Vanderbilt and the University of North Carolina were the only SIAA schools to take an initial interest in any national regulatory organization), but internal disputes over freshman play led to a multischool revolt and the creation of the Southern Conference in 1921, the same year UT finished grading off Shields-Watkins Field, the school's first permanent playing space for football, with bleacher seating for about 3,200, on land purchased not long after the construction of Ayres Hall.[11] Women were given a new role on football game days in 1925 when bandleader Ernest Hall added a female drill team to the marching band performances. The team's early Southern Conference successes were sporadic; in 1923 the Volunteers made a rare trip outside of the South just to lose a season opener to Army 41–0. The next season they began the season 3–0 against smaller neighboring schools but lost every single game for the rest of the season. UT's foray into heavily commercial, nationally recognized football did not come with instant success.

Meanwhile, women's basketball premiered in 1920, an outcome of the wartime easing of gender norms and, perhaps, in celebration of the ratification of the Nineteenth Amendment. Mary Ayres, the daughter of recently deceased UT

Engineer Brown Ayres had a different vision for UT than past
presidents, one that involved massive expansion, notably the striking
Gothic Revival building atop Barbara Hill that bears his name.

president Brown Ayres, briefly coached the Pioneer Girls' Basket Ball Team of
the University of Tennessee, later nicknamed the "Volettes," long enough for UT
women to ask for "equal rights and privileges" with male athletes including team
travel, increased funding for the women's program, and representation on the
UT Athletic Council.[12] Women's assertions of their rights and privileges came
across as a threat to men's sports at a time when college sports, especially football,
were becoming commercially crucial to many schools including UT. In 1923 the
Women's Division of the National Amateur Athletic Federation (WDNAAF)
was founded to blatantly counter the growth of competitive women's sports,
theoretically to avoid the type of corruption already growing within men's
sport. The organization's effects were felt on the UT campus. A 1926 editorial

in the student newspaper *Orange & White* protested the forced end of women's intercollegiate sports at UT:

> Boys on any campus gain recognition more quickly through athletics than through any other means. However, at present, it appears that the U.T. co-eds will be deprived of what recognition, honor, and glory which they have received through basketball. Next, some authorities will say that basketball is injurious to the health of girls. Only girls in the best of health are allowed to go out for basketball. The season for basketball is short. It is constantly being said that co-eds do not get a sufficient amount of exercise, and then when they do play basketball it is said that they are getting too much exercise.[13]

Ayres moved to Pennsylvania in 1926. Other than sorority-based intramural competition (which also included volleyball, softball, and swimming), women's basketball would not return to UT for a half century.[14] By 1932 UT offered women no intercollegiate sports opportunities whatsoever.

Volunteer football's fortunes changed for the better shortly after a young army officer and ROTC instructor named Robert Neyland was hired as assistant coach in 1925 at the behest of engineering professor Nathan Dougherty (a star guard for the Volunteers in 1908 and 1909 and one of the Southern Conference's chief architects) and promoted to become the team's eleventh head coach the following year.[15] The Texas native's employment at UT coincided with a relatively sudden unprecedented exhibition of Southern clout in college football. He came to UT the same year the Southern Conference joined other major conferences in voting to ban "professionals" like Grange from coaching their teams, the better to keep coaching the domain of faculty members like Neyland and maintain distance from the private sector football leagues that employed paid players that were starting to pop up in various cities.[16] The Southern Conference gained national attention when an undefeated University of Alabama earned a trip to the 1926 Rose Bowl, beating the University of Washington 20–19.[17] In October of 1927 Georgia delivered an astonishing 14–10 upset to Yale in New Haven. It would be decades before Southern universities could claim regional mastery over football. But the region's first major forays in that direction came about short years after the formation of the Southern Conference, and almost immediately after Tennessee and other Southern states had attracted the negative attention that came with the 1925 Scopes Trial (John Scopes's occupation as a high school football coach remained a notable coincidence). As a sign of the times, the trial and an increasing number of ballgames in every region were broadcast on radio.

With the exposure of the airwaves, more and more fans wanted to see the games firsthand, and those with the spare time and disposable income traveled by car and train for an autumn weekend getaway in an otherwise strange town. Nearby hotels and restaurants reaped the bounty. By 1930, Shields-Watkins had seats for an audience of nearly eighteen thousand.[18]

UT's own invasion of the North and West would come later, after Neyland initiated what can only be termed the golden age of Vols football. In his eighteen nonconsecutive years as head coach (interrupted by stints of military service in Panama and mainland Asia) the Volunteers eventually had six undefeated seasons and four national championships (although only one, Neyland's last one in 1951, is undisputed), including a 1939 season without a single point scored by opponents.[19] In his first six seasons of coaching, Neyland led the UT Volunteers to fifty-three wins, one loss, and five ties (in an era when ties in football were common and accepted).[20] The 1931 season was particularly remarkable, an 8–0–1 regular season record coached by Neyland and fellow officers Paul Parker and W.H. Britton, which likely would have earned a bowl game had the late-season tie with the University of Kentucky not spoiled it.[21] The Vols' success was largely attributed to the return of agile senior 185 lb. halfback Gene McEver, who had skipped the 1930 season with a knee injury sustained while playing baseball in Virginia (McEver went on to be UT's first All-American and a longtime coach at Davidson College).[22] Instead of a bowl, UT celebrated the postseason by beating New York University 13–0 in the newly built Yankee Stadium in an exhibition organized to raise money for families left destitute by the Great Depression.[23] It was a relief for a program that had recently been charged—but eventually cleared—of violating the same freshman practice rules that had inspired the Southern Conference formation in the first place.[24] It was not the last time UT football would be accused of, or implicated in, malfeasance but end up walking between the raindrops.

At a December 1932 meeting at Knoxville's Farragut Hotel, UT and other Southern Conference schools formed the Southeastern Conference (SEC), a collection of thirteen football powerhouses (ten state schools and three private institutions) in seven states south of the Ohio River. Tennessee was the only state with three members—Sewanee (departing the conference in 1940), Vanderbilt, and UT—and the creation of the new conference ultimately bolstered UT football's national success and prestige.[25] Each school paid $50 to join, a paltry sum even by the standards of the day, and a wise investment, considering the revenue windfall that resulted for practically every school involved.[26] The SEC invented the accolade of conference championship and, in 1935, became the first conference to authorize athletic scholarships covering tuition, room, and board, a practice that was not imitated by other programs until after World War II. The new reform demonstrated sympathy to young American men recently done under by the Great Depression who could still earn an education through athletic prowess—a special boon in the American South, which President Franklin Roosevelt proclaimed the country's "economic problem number one." But it was also an acquiescence to the "black market" in athlete enrollment burnished with an official patina; the SEC legitimized the enrollment of students for the sake of competitive performance and, although scholastic requirements were mandated, the temptation to find loopholes became permanent. Southern schools competed

This page from the 1935 yearbook conveys aspects of campus life during the middle of the Great Depression.

for star players in a manner deemed unbecoming among many northern schools, and essentially illegal according to several NCAA resolutions passed in reaction to the SEC's actions. However, the latter was a small matter since the national governing body had no regulatory arm at the time.[27] Quite suddenly, the athletic departments of a handful of Southern universities rose to prominence within their respective administrations.

UT and Neyland may or may not have made more frequent or more skillful usage of football scholarships than other SEC schools, but the Volunteers did enter into its best years just a few seasons after the big change. In 1938 three teams (Sewanee, Clemson, and Louisiana State University) managed a total of sixteen points against the Volunteers, generating enough excitement for UT to add twenty-five new seats to the Shields-Watkins press box and a press release desk to the athletic department. The season was also notable for the relatively sudden national prevalence of Southern football, providing sports journalism with a North/South sectional drama to accompany the cinematic release of *Gone with the Wind*. "The 1939 football season to date," wrote a Philadelphia sportswriter in mid-October, "has been spent proving to the country that the football powers are those teams hailing from Dixie." UT and other SEC teams (as well as those that had remained in the Southern Conference) were "as good [as] if not better than the best from other sections, [and] we can watch these pigskin juggernauts go to work on each other." That same week (short days before UT defeated Alabama 21–0 in a game broadcast on two radio networks), a Rodgers & Hart musical entitled *Too Many Girls* opened on Broadway (featuring a young Cuban actor and musician named Desi Arnaz) using the University of Tennessee squad as the unseen "heavies" set to play the scrappy fictional underdog team.[28] Less than two weeks later crooner Bing Crosby discussed the Volunteers on his National Broadcasting Company radio show, predicted (based on the "dope" from sports columns all over the country) their eventual trip to the Rose Bowl, and talked up star running back Johnny Butler before singing the UT alma mater "The Spirit of the Hill." Reflecting his team's exposure on Broadway and national radio, Butler earned a rare privilege for a college student while in California: a photograph with movie star Lana Turner arranged by Hollywood director and UT alum Clarence Brown.[29] The relatively provincial state university had gained unprecedented national attention.

UT arguably contributed to the Southern football mystique more than any other program, save perhaps Alabama, and even the latter school owed much of its national reputation to its storied interstate rivalry with the Volunteers played out every third Saturday in October since 1928 (the two teams first met in 1901

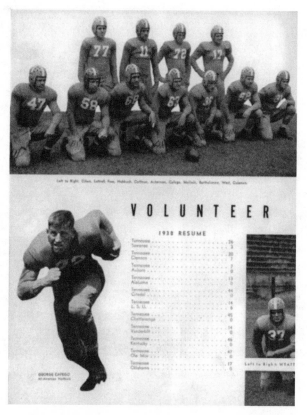

The late 1930s were salad days for Volunteer football.
UT achieved national attention before World War II
necessitated a season without football in 1943.

in a Birmingham-hosted game that ended prematurely at 6–6 after thousands of heedless Alabama fans rushed the field).[30] In the first third of the twentieth century both schools, and most of their SEC fellows, used football to become "booster colleges," institutions that justified their existence to politicians and taxpayers through their capacity for spectacle and entertainment rather than for education.[31] During his time at Texas A&M, future Alabama coach Paul "Bear" Bryant famously justified his being paid more than an English professor because "fifty to sixty thousand" people watched him coach weekly, while fewer than fifty watched the latter give exams.[32] By the same token, a rousing radio broadcast, an embellished story in the newspaper sports section, or even what

Shields-Watkins field during the golden age of Vols football.

was then a relatively affordable ticket (two tickets on the fifty-yard line cost $2 in 1927, and had doubled by 1948), were all more economically accessible than college attendance, especially in an impoverished state like Tennessee.[33] College football had been around for more than a generation before the 1930s, but the Great Depression made college sports a practical necessity for maintaining a relationship between the institution and the public.

By Neyland's last year as athletic director, the teams of the SEC had collectively established a uniquely Southern football culture that belied the game's origins in Atlantic Seaboard Yankeedom. What followed was decades of paradoxical intermingling of innovation and tradition through which UT maintained a national reputation even in its seasons of modest performance. Honoring the latter tradition, as well as the success found by turning UT assistant coaches into coaches, the UT athletic department demonstrated an ability to compete on a national scale while keeping up the appearance of a "traditional" institution defined by lineage and fictive kinship.

The spectacle and entertainment, just like the education, fell far short of being truly democratic. The all-shutout 1939 season was followed with the University of Southern California (USC) shutting UT out on New Year's Day 1940, a loss that nevertheless earned UT $130,000.[34] USC's short trip to the championship was less of a surety than UT's, given the dominance of their chief conference rival, the University of California–Los Angeles (UCLA), a team with four African American players, including future major league baseball icon Jackie Robinson. UCLA was not the first major university to integrate its sports, but it was the first football program with Black players in starting positions. Many reporters and fans anticipated a matchup with the heavily favored UCLA despite the probability that UT would have to demur from playing against opponents identified as colored. Their prior invitations to the Sugar and Cotton Bowls (games guaranteed to be against fellow lily-white teams) insured UT would have other options, albeit less prestigious and less profitable ones, and Neyland refused to comment on UCLA when asked (according to sports historian Lane Demas, most commentators watching the situation felt assured that Neyland would have the final say on the subject rather than the president or trustees). Sportswriters spared UT from having to make the decision by selecting USC after a raucous 0–0 conference championship, after which Neyland immediately announced UT's openness to a Rose Bowl invitation. A year later, Boston College allowed UT a similar dubious consideration by leaving their lone African American player, running back Lou Montgomery, at home when they came south to play the Volunteers in the 1941 Sugar Bowl (Montgomery had similarly been exempt from the Cotton Bowl in 1940).[35] UT's antidemocratic enforcement of organizational racism, like that of other Southern universities in the twentieth century, was not only a product of their own will but also the non-Southern coaches, journalists, and administrators who were just as willing to play ball with Jim Crow.

James Hoskins assumed the UT president's office in 1934, and in his twelve-year tenure oversaw changes on campus just as dramatic as the school's sudden national sports profile, not least of which included surviving the Great Depression and participating in a global war. Despite the embarrassments of the 1920s, it was a revenue-heavy decade, and Governor Austin Peay went to greater executive lengths for the school than any governor had since the state capital had removed from Knoxville a century earlier.[36] A second university campus was created in 1927 when the state purchased a West Tennessee Baptist school to establish the University of Tennessee Junior College in rural northwestern Tennessee (it became the University of Tennessee's Martin branch twenty-four years later). In 1929, two years after Peay's death, Harcourt Morgan had accepted an unprecedented

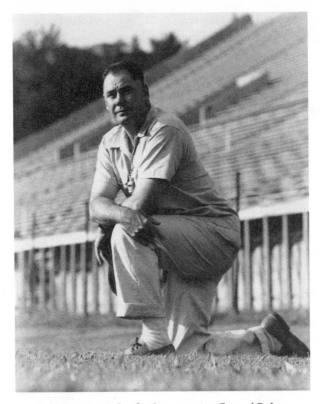

In between periods of military service, General Robert
Neyland coached UT football for the better part of a
quarter century, and established an expectation of success
among Vols fans that lasted long past his tenure.

$1,000,000 appropriation from the state but, by the time he departed for the TVA
committee, the state was broke and had disastrously attempted a tax reform that
the state supreme court declared unconstitutional.[37] During the worst years of the
depression, UT's faculty shrank considerably in number, and those who remained
underwent 20 percent pay cuts. Older professors took the opportunity to retire.
The university library went years without buying new books.[38] Most banks in
Knoxville failed, as did many locally owned businesses, and even though tuition
remained low for state schools, even the relatively affluent students who could
aspire to a college education (a thin minority in impoverished Tennessee) were
more hard-pressed than their forbears in the "Roaring Twenties." Nevertheless, the
largesse of the Peay years allowed for significant construction: several science and

Junior College campus and buildings with the Junior College farm in the background.

THE JUNIOR COLLEGE
MARTIN, TENNESSEE

Since its founding in 1927, more than 3,000 have been enrolled at the Junior College. Of this number, more than 1,500 have continued their studies here on the "Hill" at Knoxville.

This yearbook photograph from 1945 shows the Junior
College in Martin, Tennessee, that would one day become
the University of Tennessee at Martin.

administration buildings on the Hill (including Peay's namesake), a new library
that was eventually named for Hoskins and, between the foot of the Hill and
the football field, the visually iconic neo-gothic Alumni Memorial Gymnasium.
Alumni Memorial served as a basketball court, but it also became a cultural
mecca for East Tennessee. In the 1930s, such swing luminaries as Glenn Miller,
Jimmy Dorsey, and Benny Goodman played there, and it was still Knoxville's
prime location for live music decades later when Nina Simone, Janis Joplin, and
the Clash played on the same stage. Beyond football season, the new performance

ORGANIZATIONS

New and Old Gymnasium

Alumni Memorial Hall, named in honor of the school's
World War I war dead, served as a gymnasium and
concert hall for some of the most famous musical acts
to ever visit East Tennessee.

space gave Knoxvillians with no affiliation with the school a reason to come to
campus.[39]

UT's greatest asset in the 1930s (perhaps second to football), and the cause
for its becoming a true research institution, was the nearness of the Tennessee
Valley Authority (TVA), one of the New Deal's most ambitious and long-lasting
emergency stimulus measures. Even after Charles Dabney's scientific revolution,
UT had by 1933 a faculty that was (in the words of a past institutional historian)
"primarily a collection of schoolmasters," with relatively little to show for research
(and what there was of it was mainly published in regional agricultural journals).[40]

That was soon to change, as UT and state universities in neighboring states gathered to form their own state planning agendas in cooperation with the federal government's.[41] The "new frontier" Harcourt Morgan promised Hoskins in 1936 involved a significant expansion despite the relative austerity brought about by the depression.[42] UT's agriculture college expanded into forestry and wildlife management at Morgan's behest. TVA's personnel were trained on campus and, by the end of the 1930s, its presence had coalesced into a new set of courses in public administration and, in 1941, a political science department. UT's graduate program also got a boost. Master's degrees had been awarded in some disciplines since 1919, but some faculty members (notably Elisha Kane, a professor of European languages) began suggesting the enrollment of doctoral candidates around 1930 (one common reaction to the decreased job market for many relatively privileged Americans was to simply return to school). In keeping with the school's recent history, the first department to offer a doctoral program was chemistry, but not until 1943. Within three years physics and botany were included, as well as one humanity: English. Math and psychology joined the group by the end of the 1940s, as did History in 1954.[43] UT hired its first archeologists in 1934 to survey and excavate Native American sites encroached on by TVA construction (as well as that of the Civilian Conservation Corpsnd the Works Progress Administration, both of which hired from UT's school of engineering), although they were housed in the history department for years before the school founded an anthropology department.[44] Under Hoskins the additions of doctoral programs were decided by secret ballot, an immense power incomparable to any enjoyed by faculties under past presidents.[45] The need to attract doctoral students meant faculty should publish more themselves, and the board of trustees authorized the creation of a university press just before the war, although the University of Tennessee Press did not come into being functionally until 1957.[46]

UT had become far more diversified in its variety of educational offerings than it had been under Charles Dabney, but Dabney's vision of agricultural education and service, with federal cooperation, could scarcely have been larger than what was accomplished with the TVA partnership. Ironically, while the organization improved the efficiency and cunning of local farming, it created new jobs in Knoxville (including the TVA's own headquarters which was originally in Muscle Shoals, Alabama) and other nearby towns while its dams flooded former farms, thus leading to urban— and ultimately suburban— development in East Tennessee. "Technically, the T. V. A. was clear of responsibility for the valley inhabitants after they were paid for their lands," the *Washington Star* reported in 1941, "but the Authority, in co-operation with the University of Tennessee helped the people re-locate in their new homes and to become adjusted to strange environments. Most of the families moved to nearby counties."[47] East Tennessee and its university would never again be the same.

The TVA, and the new relationship with the federal government that came with it, were good preparation for the next great change. When the Volunteers made their Rose Bowl appearance Europe had been at war for nearly four months, with the Soviet Union embroiled in an invasion of Finland, and Britain struggling to devise an effective air strategy against the German Luftwaffe. More than 5,700 students were enrolled on the Knoxville campus in 1939, but the following school year coincided with passage of a federal Selective Service act passed in September, a factor that would keep enrollment down for many years to come. The draft, initiated for the possibility of war, applied only to male students, but UT was then still a male-majority school. At least one UT graduate, thirty-five-year-old Walter Kent, had already been killed when he was shot down by Japanese warplanes while piloting a Chinese civilian airliner in 1940.[48] Even though it was late in 1941 before many Americans considered warfare likely (and only a certainty after the Japanese bombing of Pearl Harbor on December 7), former and current students volunteered or were drafted, leaving the Knoxville campus almost devoid of activity by the summer of 1942 (regular enrollment reached a low of nineteen hundred the following year).[49]

By one estimate, about 6,500 UT students and alums were in military service by 1943, enough to necessitate cancellation of the football season for lack of players (within the SEC, only Georgia, Georgia Tech, LSU, Tulane, and Vanderbilt fielded football teams that fall), and women out-numbered men on campus two-to-one, with an overall enrollment of 1,325 at the time of UT's 1944 sesquicentennial (the student body had numbered over 5,700 in 1939).[50] By the war's end, at least 250 alumni would be killed in combat or listed as missing in action.[51]

Military science students (who were now part of what was called the Reserve Officer Training Corps) of the class of 1943 were allowed to finish their degrees and disembark just as the campus erupted in a new phase of activity. With the US war effort fully underway, droves of Army Air Corps cadets fresh from basic training began arriving to receive five months of military training along with relatively standard college instruction in English, geography, history, and other subjects deemed helpful to an officer or skilled enlisted man. The women who remained as regular students were shunted off campus to private homes so that dormitories could be occupied by men in uniform.[52] Later in 1943 UT hosted a segment of the Army Student Training Program and an Army Specialized

Training Program for engineering and chemistry (the latter of which had future novelist Kurt Vonnegut as a student).[53] Air Corps cadets readying for risking their lives were not willing to adhere to the same strict traditions and rules as regular UT students, and one physical education professor was scandalized to find several playing tennis on Sundays (this in a city with some of the last enforced blue laws in the US).[54]

Suddenly, Knoxville was a destination for people from faraway places, both soldiers and civilians, many of whom found Southern conservatism and racism stultifying.[55] By March 1942, Knoxville factories had accumulated nearly $8 million in government contracts, a plurality involving textiles. Women took up nondomestic labor in droves and, according to a survey conducted by the *Knoxville News Sentinel*, wanted to keep their wartime jobs even after hostilities were over in 1945.[56] In nearby counties, rural settlements that barely constituted villages were turning into towns of considerable stature. To the southwest, Alcoa, Tennessee, came into being at the behest of the Aluminum Company of America, while a few miles further north a discreetly constructed "city behind a fence" that would later become known as Oak Ridge was on its way to becoming Tennessee's fifth-largest city and the birthplace of nuclear power.[57] Symbolic of its new brush with cosmopolitanism, UT's Alumni Gymnasium hosted a recital by Sergei Rachmaninoff in the winter of 1943 weeks after the famous Russian composer became a US citizen (his performance of a funeral march from Chopin's *Piano Sonata No. 2* proved prophetic since it was his last performance before he succumbed to cancer weeks later).[58]

In June 1944, President Franklin Roosevelt signed into law the Servicemen's Readjustment Act, commonly known as the GI Bill of Rights or the GI Bill. The act basically insured servicemen's access to affordable or cost-free higher education or vocational training and took a major step toward making college accessible to the middle class (or, assuming the optimal effects, the expansion of the middle class). Overall, the GI Bill increased American college attendance to 15 percent of the US population (a white male segment; various administrative failings made the GI Bill scarcely available to Black veterans) by 1948 from the prewar rate of 10 percent, thus planting the seed for nearly one third of the next generation to attend later in the twentieth century.[59] Between the GI Bill, the nearness of Oak Ridge and TVA, UT's student body tripled between 1940 and 1950, while its faculty, in the same amount of time, increased fivefold. In 1946, well on its way to being one of the largest universities in the South, UT closed enrollment for the first time in its history after the student body exceeded eight thousand.[60]

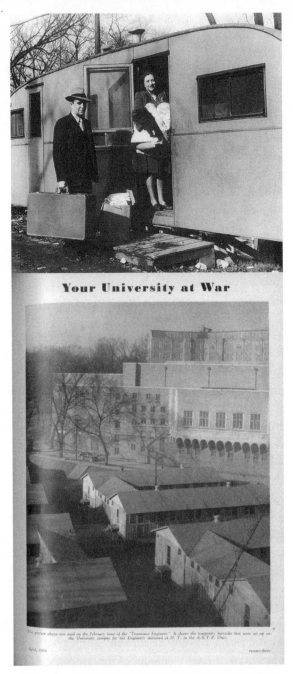

Your University at War

The picture above was used on the February issue of the "Tennessee Engineer." It shows the temporary barracks that were set up on the University campus for the Engineers stationed at U. T. in the A.S.T.P. Unit.

April, 1944   twenty-three

World War II changed the face of higher education, and
it changed the look of the UT campus for a number of
years as veterans took advantage of the GI Bill of Rights.

For the second half of the decade the UT campus was in a state of perpetual construction. In 1942, the agricultural education building built in 1880 was destroyed by fire, as was the Young Men's Christian Association building from the same era the following year.[61] Older class buildings needed refurbishing or replacement but the primary concern was student housing. Quickly summoned mobile homes made housing available for a population that had been practically nonexistent before the war: married students, many of them well over the age of twenty-five.[62] Except for some employees, the campus remained an all-white space. But, unlike any time beforehand, UT was peopled with a relatively diverse group of students, many of whom had "seen the world" via military service and many of whom were first generation college students.[63] And the trailers, though deemed unsightly by some, symbolized (in the words of one UT professor of education) "the democratization of American higher education."[64] Further, although most students still got around on foot, there were far more automobiles on and around campus than ever before, slowly introducing UT's permanent struggle for parking. Even students who lived on campus now kept traffic going, working jobs in Knoxville businesses and the various outdoor amusements showing up on nearby TVA lakes and adjacent to the Great Smoky Mountains National Park.[65] The new park was also a boon to scientific research. Botany professor Harry Jennison collected thousands of plant samples from the Smoky Mountains' unique biosphere and published *Flora of the Great Smoky Mountains National Park* (1939) at a time when few UT faculty members got a chance to publish their research on any topic—let alone regarding what was soon to become the US's most-visited national park.[66] The park was, and remains, yet another massive federal expenditure that has enhanced UT's existence almost by happenstance.

Seventy-five-year-old James Hoskins agreed to retire in 1945 to be replaced as president by dean of agriculture Cloide Everett Brehm.[67] Hoskins had ended his long period of leadership on a high note in contrast to the high-handedness and hostility to professors he had shown during the 1920s. In a missive notifying Tennessee Governor James McCord of his impending retirement, Hoskins wrote (apparently with no irony intended), "I do not believe that any institution in the Country has come through the trying period consisting of the last twelve years with less friction than the University of Tennessee."[68]

The search for a new president was conducted, as usual, by the board of trustees, but for the first time in cooperation with an advisory committee made up of faculty. The state of Tennessee had slashed funding for the school while it was practically under federal possession in 1944 and 1945, but Hoskins initiated a personal crusade to restore it. Brehm, who was meant to be an interim but stayed

James Hoskins served as university president for years with
a conservative temperament and an eye toward keeping up
with other comparable American universities.

in office after an exhausting two-year search, began his tenure by hiring fifty-seven new professors.[69] They arrived in the middle of a construction frenzy, including the Frank McClung Museum, the first of a handful of twentieth-century buildings recalling a surname associated with the school since Charles McClung sat on the inaugural Blount College board of trustees in 1794.[70] In 1950 a new library was completed, a dignified neo-Gothic building between the Hill and the Fort Sanders neighborhood named in honor of the retired Hoskins.[71] Brehm established UT night classes to be taught in Nashville, presided over the absorption of UT–Martin in 1951, and fought hard to expand a UT presence into Memphis by absorbing Memphis State College, but Tennessee's old east/middle/west sectional rivalry reared its head in the legislature, and the Pennsylvania native's plans were quashed (Memphis State, later renamed the University of Memphis, was given full university status in 1957).

Hoskins's departure seemed to be the signal to the AAUP to end its blacklist of the school, and it reinstated the school in 1947 after the trustees agreed to abide by its "Academic Freedoms and Tenure" parameters devised early during the second world war.[72] But within a few short years, the school was yet again embroiled in controversy that threatened the rights of free speech and association. The Brehm presidency came in time for the fading of wartime idealism and the onset of a national paranoia over the alleged dangers of communism initiated by President Harry Truman's 1947 executive order requiring loyalty oaths for federal employees. It was an echo of the Red Scare that had come after the first world war when middle America feared bolshevism was creeping in among the foreign-born working class. But this second Red Scare targeted the upper and middle classes, professionals and intellectuals in business, education, and entertainment. In the South, the Red Scare was leavened with the authoritarianism of Jim Crow and region-wide resistance to the federal government's incremental approach toward enforcing equal constitutional protection for people of all races. In the words of Southern historian John Egerton, the Southern anti-communism "pathology bordered on the absurd, and would have been laughable had they not been so dangerous," as "emboldened [white] witch-hunters, sensing how utterly safe they were, imagined themselves slaying red dragons at every turn."[73]

The zeal for hunting down "radicals" in and around Knoxville often took on farcical form even when it was at its cruelest. UT was not a campus known for radical creativity. In the 1930s some UT students supposedly formed their own chapter of the leftist Student League for Industrial Democracy, but local "campus pinks" were hardly disruptive to campus life before the war.[74] What happened after the war was probably more a product of the off-campus paranoid imagination than it was the politics of students and faculty. In 1948 a Knoxville Methodist minister accused a briefly-ly employed UT English instructor and folklorist named Mary Barnicle of distributing Henry Wallace campaign pamphlets to her students, and spread a rumor that she was being investigated by the FBI (her New England origins were probably an exacerbating factor given 1948's "Dixiecrat" political revolt). Barnicle did not have the protection of tenure and therefore, nor did she have AAUP protection, and she left the university before the fall semester in 1950.[75] That same year philosophy professor Howard Parsons (reportedly also a Progressive Party supporter) was attacked by Knoxville's American Legion for comparing the South Korean government to Francisco

Franco's dictatorial Spanish regime in an exam question.[76] Years later Parsons was denied promotion, but by this time the more direct cause was his involvement with the National Association for the Advancement of Colored People and the Southern Conference Educational Fund, notably partisan organizations in the years after *Brown Vs. Board of Education.* Parsons submitted his resignation in August 1957, almost exactly a year after Clinton (a small town just north of Knoxville) became the first desegregated school in the South.[77] It was clear that a large segment of fear of communism in and around the UT campus in the 1950s was motivated and fortified by racism.

Samuel Baron, a history instructor from New York, bore an even larger burden from the local Red Scare.[78] In 1952, a few weeks after silent film star Charlie Chaplin was denied reentry into the United States, UT students decided to show four Chaplin films on campus, plus *Alexander Nevsky* (1938), a film by Russian director Sergei Eisenstein. The latter film was produced in the Soviet Union, while Chaplin had gained a reputation for leftist leanings since he directed and starred in a satirical portrayal of Hitler, *The Great Dictator* (1940), so the scheduling had the appearance of a provocation of prevailing norms (although the film group's faculty advisers, Baron and a music instructor, said they did not see it as such). The local keepers of prevailing norms took the bait; John Duncan Sr., Knox County attorney and local American Legion commander, demanded the Chaplin movies be canceled, and the Republican *Knoxville Journal* echoed him, adding that *Alexander Nevsky* was bound to contain Soviet propaganda. After the Legion officially demanded the films be banned and that all future films be reviewed for content, Brehm folded and even apologized to another Legion commander.[79] Students protested, but to no avail.[80] The next semester Baron was questioned, to little immediate effect, in front of a state senate committee about the content of his Russian history textbook. State representative Judd Acuff called the committee a coverup, and accused Baron (who was Jewish) of being Russian born and anti-Christian [81] Acuff accused Baron's department head of making disparaging remarks about the US Army and democracy itself, and also said that unnamed members of the faculty were communists or members of the socialist League for Industrial Democracy. Baron denied all of Acuff's charges and some of the latter's fellow legislators called his attacks pointless, but the UT administration gave him no protection. At some point historian Ruth Stephens, UT's first woman to become full professor, allegedly broke into Baron's office to find evidence of his communist leanings.[82] Baron's contract was not renewed, and he left UT in summer 1953, the victim of a cruel and pointless attack. Shortly before Baron left, a student newspaper editorial lamented the fears felt by both students and faculty at the attacks on free speech.[83]

Brehm did not want a repeat of the problems seen during the Hoskins years, especially since the AAUP (a much more nationally authoritative organization in 1953 than it had been in the 1920s) had apparently elected to recognize his school because of his becoming president. The next year he submitted a draft of a statement written by UT's AAUP members outlining freedoms of teaching and research to the board of trustees. Members of the board griped about the statement's emphasis on liberties over responsibilities even though the document did include a gray area cautioning faculty against teaching or commenting on subjects beyond their field. With news of the Supreme Court's *Brown v. Board* . . . decision current, one trustee expressed concern that the new "Statement of Principles Governing Freedom, Responsibility, and Tenure" would encourage biracial socializing between faculty members at UT and Knoxville College. Still, the final draft assuaged concerns all around. Even though the statement protected tenured faculty, it did nothing to assuage combat the right-wing paranoia and opportunism emerging from the latter stages of McCarthyism (Joseph McCarthy himself had lost practically any semblance of national following by the time the Statement of Principles was finalized) or the new spirit of "massive resistance" against desegregation that pervaded the South. At the beginning of the 1950s the espousal of radical economic ideas attracted red-baiting. But, by the end of the decade, accusations of communism were more often aimed at anyone who challenged white supremacy.[84]

Conservative complaints against campus activities did not always amount to much. In winter 1958 the *Knoxville Journal* attacked a speaker on campus, Pacifist Methodist minister Henry Hitt Crane, for his leftist tendencies, although Crane apparently did his talk without incident (it was not his first visit to the UT campus). The *Journal* also attacked arrival of economist and journalist George Soule for a one-year visiting position at UT, citing his association with the unabashedly left-leaning Highlander Research and Education Center, and an odd accusation that Soule was a follower of Keynesian economics, a demand-sided system very much in place in the 1960s US to fight the Cold War 1960s and the basis for a local economy that united Oak Ridge, TVA, and UT.[85] The *Journal's* editors had apparently confused Keynesianism with socialism. Unlike past victims of red-baiting, Soule was a giant in his field and relatively impervious to parochial attacks, although he did bring suit against the *Journal* for libel. Also, by this point, Brehm had been succeeded by president Andy Holt who was not afraid of controversy and wryly told the board that the UT economics department was probably in need of a socialist even if Soule was not one.[86] Soule finished out his year.

Perhaps the only individual on the UT campus safe from accusations of disloyalty or excessive free thinking was Robert Neyland. After Coach Neyland's return from service in World War II, he was reinstated as the Volunteers' head coach, and took little time to renew the level of success seen in the early years of the war. Neyland coached the Volunteers to a career 173–31–12 record, four bowl appearances, and UT's first nationally recognized national championship in 1951. He coached one more season after that (a successful, but relatively modest, 8–2–1 season that ended with a 16–0 loss to the University of Texas in the Cotton Bowl) before stepping aside to become UT's first athletic director. The next three coaches won a collective sixty-four games out of 113, a moderate decline that included a 14–6 home upset by the University of Chattanooga in 1958 that resulted in a campus riot that had to be suppressed by fire hoses and tear gas.[87] Neyland held the AD position until his death in 1962, but only after turning down an illustrious offer from one of his old West Point classmates. A few months after Samuel Baron's dismissal, President Dwight Eisenhower offered Neyland the TVA board chairmanship (decades before, the two generals had been West Point classmates and football teammates). Neyland turned down the offer, reportedly saying, "You do me a great honor Ike, but I'd do you irreparable harm because I believe half those sons-of-bitches over there are communists."[88] Neyland was also safe from accusations of infractions that were all too real. In late 1954 or early 1955, Brehm revealed to his vice presidents that the coach had maintained an unauthorized "slush fund" for most of the time he had led Volunteer football, a glaring violation of NCAA policy. Everyone at the meeting agreed that any attempt to discipline the coach would result in trouble with the trustees (treasurer J. J. Walker recalled a 1938 board meeting in Memphis when the only subject discussed was football) and the less said, the better, especially with new coach Bowden Wyatt coming aboard to serve under Neyland's athletic department. Not a word was said. As university business manager James Hess noted, "There are some things it is better not to know."[89]

By the mid-1950s football had become a definitive element of life at UT, just as it had on countless other campuses, and on occasion it gave the school's educators something new to be cowed by when trustees and politicians were otherwise leaving them alone. Before he handed the president's office over to Andy Holt, Cloide Brehm proved that Harcourt Morgan and James Hoskins were not the only twentieth-century UT presidents who were either passively scared of politicians or actively willing to let politics intimidate educators and education. He, his vice presidents, and his contemporaneous trustees were apparently the same way when it came to the importance of football to his school's "booster" status established before his presidency. Football had likely saved many schools during the lean years of the 1930s and, in the years after World War II, the sport was an apt accompaniment to the new complexity of university life; it had only been a half century since the state had even allocated UT its own funding appropriation, but by the 1950s there was enough cash flow for account books to get hidden or cooked. The circumstances of college sports in the mid-twentieth century had caused leadership to compromise their school's integrity, although perhaps in a way that barely affected academia. It was a permanent compromise, and one that administrators, students, and (perhaps reluctantly) faculty learned to live with. Perhaps no one was more pleased than the public, who demanded more and more every year that UT be as successful on the gridiron as it was in teaching the young or helping to launch the United States into the Space Age. The ten years leading up to World War II, the war itself, and the ten years that followed it amounted to more change in a quarter century than UT had ever experienced. But the most dramatic changes were yet to come.

CHAPTER FIVE

Race, Riot, and Rocky Top,

1955–1970

. . . .

"The paradox of education is precisely this—
that as one begins to become conscious one begins to
examine the society in which he is being educated."

—JAMES A. BALDWIN—
"A Talk to Teachers" (1963)

No one was using the phrase "baby boomer" yet in 1960, but in January of that year, newly installed UT president Andy Holt predicted to the Knoxville chamber of commerce that his school would be welcoming an unprecedented "tidal wave of young people" within the next two school years.[1] Judging by post–World War II birthrates, Holt expected the student body to double by the following decade. In fact, UT's population explosion reflected Tennessee's modest statewide population boom; in 1970 it was the seventeenth-largest institution of higher learning in the US, serving as state university for the state with the seventeenth largest population.[2]

Holt did preside over an immense expansion of UT to accommodate a 60 percent increase in the student body in his last five years in office, a far greater increase than the population explosion precipitated by the GI Bill of Rights in the 1940s.[3] In 1961 the student body passed the ten thousand mark, but by the early 1970s, UT had a student body enrollment of more than thirty thousand, close to six times its size when Holt took office.[4] UT's first preparation was its inaugural self-study for reaccreditation by the Southern Association of Colleges and Schools led by UT vice president Herman Spivey. The self-study's final report included a handful of suggestions for efficiency and improvement, including a streamlined registration system and the creation of a faculty handbook.[5] But most of the changes to come were physical. By 1967, UT had spent $73 million on construction in less than ten years, adding an estimated yearly $70 million back to the Knoxville economy (up from an estimated $10 million in 1959) under the oversight of Holt's hand-picked campus development czar, Tennessee's finance commissioner (and UT graduate) Edward Boling.[6] The size and appearance of campus changed drastically during this time period, operating under the authority of an urban renewal amendment added to the 1949 Federal Housing Act. Starting in 1963, 341 buildings on the west side of the main campus were razed, necessitating the relocation of four hundred families. In the days of Ayres and Morgan, the campus had taken on an architectural consistency described as "Collegiate Gothic," replete with bastioned roofs and sculpted archways. But under Holt, seventeen modernist buildings built over the course of two years made exposed concrete and a wealth of glass the standard in this newer section of campus.[7] And these were larger buildings made for a much larger student population. The daily student-run *Daily Beacon* replaced the semiweekly *Orange & White* in 1967 to befit an expanded university.

When a new state regional University of Tennessee campus was established in Chattanooga in 1968, Andy Holt became the inaugural president of what became known as the UT System.[8] Holt was an able administrator who knew how to couch serious work in populist, unpretentious language whenever he had difficulty proving the value of expanding public education to even the most obstinate old Tennessee politicians. The West Tennessee native had begun a career as a public school teacher before earning a doctorate at Columbia University, and he was rare among school presidents for being able to combine able administrative skills with a folksy, approachable public image attractive to students, faculty, and politicians.[9]

Holt was a good fit for a university that was growing at an astonishing rate while maintaining a mostly provincial identity. UT had been a school in the American South for a long time, but the post–World War II years came with a new self-consciousness of being *Southern*. Citizen soldiers brought new accents and ethnicities to the campus during the war. But, as of 1945, they were gone. The next year UT and thirteen other universities founded the Oak Ridge Institute of Nuclear Studies (renamed the Oak Ridge Associated Universities during the Holt administration) to give science faculty and students access to the facility. In 1961 the university purchased a transistor-based twenty-kilobyte IBM 1620 computer "the size of a large office desk" and installed it in the Glocker Business Administration building, to be used by faculty and students from engineering, math, and various science departments around the clock.[10] In 1964 the UT Space Institute was built out of a wartime aeronautics facility in Tullahoma

THE STATE IS THE CAMPUS OF

THE UNIVERSITY OF TENNESSEE

President Andy Holt, appointed in 1959, presided over an unprecedented
period of growth in the university's history.

(a town 160 miles southwest of Knoxville).[11] As of 2019, nine Space Institute
alumni had become NASA astronauts.[12] East Tennessee's cutting-edge scientific
organizations linked to UT continued to attract newcomers from all over the
country (and, eventually, the world) throughout the 1960s but, while many of
them lived in Knoxville, they worked and played far from downtown. In the
decade following the war's end, Knoxville probably seemed more like the sleepy,
unattractive factory town it had been before the 1940s despite being close to the
cutting edge of the Space Age and a major contributor to what Eisenhower called
the military-industrial complex.[13] In his description of downtown Knoxville in
the 1950s, novelist and two-time UT student Cormac McCarthy recalled the
"Countrymen com[ing] for miles with the earth clinging to their shoes," who
would "sit all day like mutes" in Market Square just as they had before the war
as the city grew around them without aesthetic logic. "The city constructed on
no known paradigm, a mongrel architecture reaching back through the works of
man in a brief delineation of the aberrant disordered and mad."[14] As *Knoxville*

News Sentinel columnist (and future UT English instructor) Wilma Dykeman observed in the following decade, "Provincialism is not always confined to rural areas."[15] In 1948, journalist John Gunther described Knoxville as "the ugliest city I ever saw in America, with the possible exception of some mill towns in New England," and criticized its "puritanical" lack of proper night life.[28]

In the age of jets and atoms, vestiges of the past seemed all the more noticeable and, to many Tennesseans, attractive. In 1948, a Chattanooga lawyer named Estes Kefauver (UT class of 1924) sported a coonskin cap while running (successfully) for US Senate, thus invoking East Tennessee's early republic "frontier" past. Kefauver adopted the gimmick as a show of defiance to Tennessee's Democratic nabob, Boss Crump, but it also reflected a popular interest in the American past that would impact Knoxville and its surroundings in a unique way. The post-World War II years brought with them a consumerist renaissance and an unprecedented level of mass consumption for practically every product Americans used. In response there grew a societal demand, in the words of anthropologist Allen Batteau, for "an escape from the commodity system," that fueled interest in preindustrial "folk" crafts, particularly from southern Appalachia (as the growth of the tourist economy in Sevier County just to the immediate Southsouth of Knox County shows, the "commodity system" eventually caught up with the alleged demand to escape it).[16] UT's sudden zeal for embracing the image of its early republic origins came perhaps less from its dedication to agricultural education than to the country's desire to reembrace frontier myths to be used as cultural bulwarks for fighting the Cold War; three years after the first Smokey prowled the sidelines during a UT game, the US military began development of a small surface-to-surface nuclear projectile weapon nicknamed the "Davy Crockett."[17] It might also have reflected a need to re-negotiate the university's self-identity as *Southern* at a time when the South was undergoing massive change. Regional identity and veneration of the past had a currency probably unseen since before the 1925 John Scopes trial. The new nostalgia fit well with UT's Volunteer mascot, who wore a coonskin cap and fringed buckskins and carried a facsimile of a flintlock rifle. In 1953 he was joined by Smokey, a "Houn' Dawg" who represented the faithful canine companion to the "sturdy, hardy, courageous [Euro-American] pioneers" who had settled Tennessee.[18] The new canine presence was selected via halftime contest during the September 26 season opener against Mississippi State (26–0 Mississippi State), and the winner was Blue Smokey, an alert, howling male bluetick coonhound owned by local pastor Bill Brooks.[19] At this writing there have been eleven dogs to fill the role (not counting the bipedal "human" Smokey that began joining the actual dog at games in 1982), most of them related to Blue.

UT's renewal of Southern identity was probably not entirely happenstantial given the new tension over civil rights and the "Second Reconstruction" going on in US federal courts. The war mobilized thousands of Black Southerners both as soldiers and as citizens, and the old color line that maintained the power dynamic of Jim Crow was growing finer and hotter. In late February 1946, a violent confrontation between a recently discharged Black navy veteran and a white store clerk in Columbia (a Tennessee county seat town forty miles south of Nashville) led to the formation of a white mob and an ad hoc self-defense formation by the Black population before the arrival of the Tennessee national guard. The following August, a white deputy shot an elderly Black man in the back after the latter cast a vote in a hotly contested election in Athens, another county seat just south of Knoxville.[20] The same November of Kefauver's victory, one of Tennessee's twelve electoral votes went to the "Dixiecrat" ticket formed to protest the national Democratic Party's new civil rights plank. During the 1949 football season UT's marching band "brought back the colorful black-face," a feature the student yearbook bragged "has not been done by any other band to date." The spectacle was adopted to enhance the band's performance of "timely dance steps" to songs from "old minstrel days" ("Sewanee," "Carolina in the Morning") but, consciously or unconsciously, the show reflected the recent reassertion of white Southern belligerence against desegregation.[21] That same year *Knoxville Journal* sports editor Ed Harris dubbed the ensemble the "Pride of the Southland Band."[22] A few years later the Pride of the Southland marched in President Eisenhower's first inauguration parade, the first of more than a dozen such appearances in the nation's capital.[23]

Most white Southerners, Democrats or otherwise, were not ready for the idea of racial equality, and a significant number, like the Dixiecrats, fought it actively, though perhaps not quite as hard as African Americans fought *for* it. Although Black Tennesseans were essentially (in the words of one white student attending at the time) "invisible" on the UT campus in the late 1940s, the time was quickly coming when the age-old segregation of students in Tennessee would wither away. But Andy Holt and other white leaders would see to it that the change would be, or at least appear, gradual, anticlimactic, and subject to their elite say-so.

The doctrine of "separate but equal" had been challenged beforehand, notably in 1936 by an aspiring pharmacist named William Redmond. Recognizing that Tennessee did not offer pharmaceutical training for colored students, Redmond sued for entry into the School of Pharmacy in Nashville.[24] Redmond's suit was denied on the basis that Meharry, the state's Negro medical school, had a Black president who made the decision whether or not to have pharmaceutical education, so the state government was not at fault.[25] Although he lost the case, members of the state legislature were scared he or someone like him would try again, and so they cobbled together legislation to provide small scholarships making up the difference between "the expense at the nearest college admitting Negroes" for higher degrees in pharmacy, architecture, law, engineering, and liberal arts.[26] Attempts to test segregation at UT were put on hold for most of the 1940s, but during that time the US Supreme Court passed down a handful of telling decisions. In *Smith v. Allwright* (1944) the court put an end to the "white primary," a means of keeping Black voters out of internal political party votes (a technique never used in Tennessee on a statewide level at least). *Shelley v. Kraemer* (1948) made race-based housing "covenants" unrecognizable in courts of law, thereby chipping away at residential segregation.

But these sort of gains did little to solve Black Southerners' most grinding problems, poverty and unemployment, especially in cities like Knoxville where the wartime boom ended quickly. Between 1940 and 1950, Knoxville's Black population increased by more than 19 percent. But, by decade's end, race-based layoffs led to their being less than 6 percent of the city's industrial workforce, and their average income was nearly $1,000 less than the city average. Less than ten years after the war's beginning, Knoxville was showing signs of urban blight. [27]

Restaurants, hotels, and practically every other public space in Knoxville was segregated, and UT was no exception. Leaders like Hoskins and Brehm had no interest in desegregating the student body, but the attendant inequality was beginning to embarrass them, especially since more and more faculty members could be counted among the number now being called integrationists. In 1952 UT hosted the annual meeting of the Southern Historical Association (SHA), an organization that had eliminated *de jure* segregation internally but whose Black members still faced discrimination at meetings held around the South. UT history professor Leroy Graf was determined to make the SHA's five Black attendees (including John Hope Franklin a leading authority on Southern and African American history) feel welcome, but was stymied at the last minute when he was told that the Farragut Hotel on Gay Street had backed out of its earlier promise to allow an integrated conference banquet. A local country club agreed at the last minute to host the affair in integrated fashion. To make matters worse UT's own Sophronia Strong Hall's cafeteria, the setting for a conference luncheon, refused to seat Black attendees with the white majority.[29] It was becoming clear that the Southern edict of segregation could not be reconciled with the ideals represented by Southern universities—at least not by those who wanted to keep up with the times.

The white order saw tensions growing, and action was taken to make separate equal in fact rather than in name only. In 1951, with demand for higher education at an all-time high, Tennessee elevated TA&I to university status. It was a small step toward the state's promise made in 1943 to "make [TA&I] for Negroes equivalent to UT for white students."[30] Bethel College, a Cumberland Presbyterian school in West Tennessee opened itself to Black enrollment in 1953, while Vanderbilt enrolled a Black divinity student in 1953. The next year Maryville College, the institution that had once been on the forefront of biracial education before the Tennessee legislature forced it to segregate, reintegrated for the first time in more than a half century.[31] But most private colleges were expensive (despite its announcement, Bethel had no Black students during its first year of integration), and the university in Nashville was hardly accessible to every Black Tennessean with college aspirations. Shortly after the Supreme Court's *Brown v. Board of Education* (1954) five Black applicants to all-white Memphis State University were denied, leading to five years of federal court cases. The next year a Memphis NAACP head enrolled in a UT night course being taught in Memphis and managed to shame the dean of admissions into allowing him to remain after it was revealed he was not white.[32] In September of 1955, *Time* Magazine gave grades to the states undergoing the process of desegregation. The five states of the Deep South were given Fs, while Missouri was the only state awarded an A. Befitting its history of lukewarm politics, Tennessee (along with Delaware) received a C.[33]

Like Memphis State and many other Southern state universities, UT dragged its feet on desegregation. In 1950 Gene Gray and Jack Alexander (applicants for UT Graduate School) and Lincoln Blakeney and Joseph Patterson (prospective law students) hired a Knoxville law firm to challenge the state's arrangement for Black graduate education at Tennessee A&I (the school lacked graduate training in the sciences and law). Gray and his co-plaintiffs won and, by 1955, sixty-eight Black graduate students were enrolled at the Knoxville campus. Lillian D. Jenkins of Bristol, Tennessee, became UT's first Black recipient of a graduate degree, having earned an MS in Special Education in 1954 before continuing her graduate education at Ohio State University.[34] Two years later, R. B. J. Campbelle became the first Black recipient of a UT law degree; in 1959 Harry Blanton was the first African American to earn a UT doctorate. Interviewed years later, Blanton remembered no active scorn from his classmates, but instead the feeling of being "the invisible man on the campus."[35]

By the time of Jenkins's graduation, *Brown v. Board* (which had direct bearing only on primary and secondary public education) had given educational integration a national profile, but it had also hardened the resolve of white Southern politicians. Even moderates and liberals otherwise open to gradualism lamented that the Southern states would lose another fight with the federal government (as they had nine decades earlier).[36] Tennessee Governor Frank Clement favored school desegregation in principle (hoping quixotically that it would not "become a political issue"), and unlike some contemporary white Southerners, "recognized [the Supreme Court] as supreme," but he was unwilling to flout the wishes of a more conservative legislature and board of trustees.[37] Having earlier favored a gradual desegregation for undergrads, one newspaper complained after *Brown v. Board* that a "middle course" for Tennessee politicians had become untenable, and Clement et al. decided in 1955 to postpone the desegregation plan indefinitely.[38] The high school in Clinton, Tennessee, a small town one county north of Knoxville, became the first to successfully integrate a white public school system in the former Confederacy to allow black students in 1956 while the leaders of most of the state's state colleges. Two years later Clinton High School was dynamited by anti-integration terrorists.[39] Violence against school de-segregation occurred in other parts of the South, and it would be years into the next decade before the glacial edict of *Brown v. Board* had a comprehensive effect on Southern education.

Under the moderate leadership of Governor Clement and President Holt, UT was promised to be fully integrated on some undetermined day of jubilee, but it took grassroots activists—namely students from neighboring Knoxville College—to actually make it happen. In the spring of 1960 Knoxville College students initiated a massive protest outside Knoxville businesses that limited or disallowed Black customers. The pickets on Gay Street were not unlike sit-ins going on elsewhere (notably Greensboro, North Carolina, and Nashville), and many Black Knoxvillians were galvanized by Martin Luther King's visit to Knoxville College's late in May commencement.[40] One demonstration outside of Byerley's Cafeteria (located next to UT Law and one of the last bastions of segregation near campus) was led by future Washington DC mayor Marion Barry, a UT graduate student studying chemistry and co-founder of Knoxville's branch of the Student Non-Violent Coordinating Committee.[41] White UT faculty and students also participated in small numbers, including a student named Lee Butler and biology professors Joe Howell and Arthur Jones, all of whom tried to negotiate lunch counter desegregation with the manager of Rich's department store.[42] Like in other Southern cities, activists concentrated on downtown lunch counters until about seven storeowners promised to make the busy midday space open to all customers after a two-month summer campaign. Most other stores had followed suit within the next three years[43] In May alone Knoxville police reportedly arrested more than a hundred demonstrators, and white officers brutalized at least one student who was protesting segregated seating in the Tennessee Theatre.[44]

That same summer, young activist Theotis Robinson Jr., a recent graduate of all-Black Austin High School in east Knoxville (although Robinson lived much closer to all-white East High School but was not allowed to enroll even after *Brown v. Board*), applied to UT but was turned down. Robinson had originally planned to attend Knoxville College on scholarship, but his participation in the recent sit-ins inspired him to force UT to make good on a promise it had made in his boyhood.[45] UT denied Robinson's application, but the young man managed to schedule a meeting with Holt, informing the president that he had a right to attend UT by virtue of being a Tennessee citizen and a taxpayer (Robinson and his father were also season-ticket holders for "Section X," Shields-Watkins's segregated bleacher seats). Robinson asserted that he and his family were prepared to take legal action.[46] Holt did not immediately relent, but Robinson's assertive meeting was the beginning of the end of all-white education on the Knoxville campus. Soon thereafter state attorney general George McCanless told Holt that the school no longer had a legal basis for maintaining segregation.[47] In January 1961 Robinson enrolled as a UT student alongside two other Black classmates, Charles Blair and Willie Mae Gillespie. It was among the first such moments in the history of university integration, and (perhaps because the new students were unceremoniously enrolled in the middle of a school year) one not met with the level of notorious white resistance seen in Georgia (where there was anti-integration rioting on the very same winter day when Robinson, Blair, and Gillespie enrolled), Mississippi, and Alabama over the next three years.[48] But, like so many other places in the South, desegregation at UT resulted not from administrative benevolence but from the patient insistence of long-term agitation in the courts and in the streets. The following fall, many Black students, most of them Knoxville natives, became UT students. In 1964, Brenda Peel received UT's first bachelor's degree awarded to an African American student; she was a transfer student from Knoxville College.[49] In early 1965, UT became the second university in the country (after the University of Miami in Florida) to conduct desegregation training under Title IV of the Civil Rights Act, a move that reiterated the school's public service role envisioned by past presidents like Dabney and Morgan— although, in this case, UT had come a long way from advising Tennessee farmers on scientific crop selection. A permanent Race Desegregation Assistance Center [RDAC] was eventually formed under the aegis of the College of Education).[50]

Charles Blair (left) and Theotis Robinson (right), along with
Willie Mae Gillespie, enrolled as UTs first three African
American undergraduate students in 1961. Robinson held various
administrative jobs at UT for decades before retiring as vice
president of equity and diversity in 2014.

Dr. Robert H. Kirk joined UT's Health and Safety department in 1967, thus
becoming the school's first Black faculty member.[51]

While the RDAC worked to integrate Tennessee's primary and secondary
public schools, the university that housed it did not become an integrated
institution overnight. It would be years before African Americans made up more
than a small fraction of the growing student body, and years before desegregation
of Tennessee higher education started to look more like true integration.
Robinson, Blair, and Gillespie ate separately from other UT students and did
not live on campus.[52] Robinson later recollected that he in no way depended on
UT for a social life, and that, years later, Black students who did live in dorms

recounted "horror stories" of bigotry, and that Black men attending interracial off-campus parties had been arrested.[53] The following fall Jessie Lou Arnold became the first Black student at the Martin campus and lived in a dorm room with no roommate (it would be years before Black students would live on campus in Knoxville).[54] As the 1960s progressed, UT's first generation of Black students worked to make the university a more democratic space. In 1962 Marion Barry formed Students for Equal Treatment to further desegregation on and around campus.[55]

It was a tumultuous decade and, between 1964 and 1969, the student body increased from over fourteen thousand to more than twenty-three thousand.[56] As UT continued its rapid 1960s expansion, including building on to its one-building campus in north Nashville. Making UT-Nashville something larger than it had been so close to the TA&I campus established a possible conflict of interests for the two schools given the ongoing de-segregation of the UT system. African American attorney Rita Sanders Geier filed suit against the state of Tennessee in 1968 (the same year TA&I became TSU) alleging that its higher education system remained segregated despite a federal mandate ordering desegregation. She claimed that the opening of a University of Tennessee campus at Nashville would lead to the creation of another predominantly white institution that would strip TSU, the only state-funded historically Black university, of resources.[57] The suit was not settled until 2001 when it was decided that predominantly white UT–Nashville would be absorbed into TSU, an unprecedented decision, and one that was never duplicated in any other state.[58]

What became known as the UT System came into being including the Martin campus and a new consolidated UT campus in Chattanooga as of 1969. Andy Holt became the System's president and the UT campus was placed under the direct executive leadership of the school's first chancellor, UT engineering dean Charles Weaver. Hand-picked by Holt without consultation with the faculty, many professors saw the new governmental arrangement as a setback after two decades of increased faculty authority.[59]

Integration of the undergraduate student body was one thing, but doing same for UT athletics was another matter, especially under the gaze of UT's most famous administrator. In 1946 UT men's basketball coach John W. Mauer refused to let his team set foot on the court after traveling to Pennsylvania's Duquesne University because the latter's team included future Harlem Globetrotter Chuck Cooper (after playing for the Globetrotters, Cooper played guard and forward for the Boston Celtics as the first Black draftee to the National Basketball Association). It was a far cry from the transsectional "gentlemen's agreements" that had allowed the Vols football team to avoid playing against Black players in bowl games half a decade earlier, and it was clear that World War II had caused a considerable shift of attitudes among athletic programs outside the South (Cooper was himself a veteran). For the next two decades the national profile of Southern intercollegiate sports was tempered by schools like UT refusing to cross the color line.[60]

During the 1950s, however, UT quietly began playing away games against teams with Black competitors, although they still refused to host them in Knoxville. UT football coaches Harvey Robinson and Bowden Wyatt broached the subject of hosting integrated teams to the UT athletic board. Wyatt later remarked to the board that an integrated student body made integrated sports inevitable, but board members preferred that the SEC lead its teams rather than the other way around.[61] In 1961, Robert Neyland canceled an intercollegiate track meet because one of the opposing teams included Black athletes. That fall Neyland verbally abused men's basketball coach Johnny Sines and student Avon Rollins when the latter attempted to try out for the team.[62] Neyland died early the following year, shortly after being given an unprecedented lifetime contract by the trustees, but varsity integration was still slow in coming even as the size of the stadium surrounding Shields-Watkins increased to a capacity of more than 64,000.[63] Shortly after his death the athletic department tentatively scheduled home football games at the newly named Neyland Stadium against two integrated teams, UCLA and the University of Houston, for the 1965 season (UT won both games, 17–8 and 37–34, respectively).

UT and other major Southern state universities were desegregated under pressure from activists by students who were a few years older than the "baby boom" President Holt had accurately predicted and old enough to remember and understand *Brown v. Board*. However, most of these schools' sports teams were not integrated until after the passage of the Civil Rights Act (1964), a law that demonstrated federal will to discredit and end segregation once and for all by withholding federal funds from any institutions that received them (i.e., virtually every state university, especially land-grants like UT).[64] As late as 1965, Willie Dawson, an excellent sprinter, was denied a scholarship for the UT track team before being "snapped up" by a northern college.[65] Meanwhile, schools outside of the South were recruiting excellent athletes who happened to be Black, many of them from Southerners.[66] Still, the Act did not bring about change overnight. The nature of organized sports dictated that direct action such as marches and sit-ins were not readily available to potential athletes. Moreover, members of the civil rights movement did not consider college football and other sports as their primary targets. UT and other SEC schools' sports teams were ultimately the "Final citadel of segregation."[67]

That was soon to change, but only gradually. What brought about change was the athletes and coaches, and just in time for the most volatile years of the 1960s. In 1966 UT announced that race would no longer be a barrier to athletic scholarships.[68] The next year two runners, Memphis native Audry Hardy and Alabamian James Craig integrated the track & field team and excelled in the two-mile relay for a team that had already dominated the SEC for most of the decade (they were honored by the solidarity of their teammates who refused to eat at a Georgia restaurant that would not serve Hardy and Craig on a road trip).[69] Former University of Florida quarterback Doug Dickey took over the football coach's office in 1964, initiating what could be called the silver age of Volunteer football and ultimately reversing Neyland's unofficial policy on racial politics ahead of almost all other SEC schools. Dickey had coached an integrated team while in the army and, three years into his term as UT football coach, recruited Nashville halfback Lester McClain, the Vols' first Black player. McClain went on to play in four of the team's most storied seasons. Albert Davis, who grew up near Knoxville, signed a letter of intent in spring 1967 and would have been the first to integrate the team had he not been eliminated by standardized test scores.[70] McClain was the lone Black member of the team for two seasons before being joined by linebacker Jackie Walker, running back Andy Bennett, and kick returner Kevin Milam.[71] McClain remembered his teammates treating him as an equal on the field but "sarcastic" in social situations, while at least once coach hassled him for growing facial hair, calling him "boy."[72] Alabamian Condredge Holloway not only became the first Black quarterback in the SEC, but also integrated the Volunteer baseball team at shortstop in 1973, just after starting as the first black quarterback in the SEC's history.[73] In a 2011 interview, Holloway said he had been the target of racial hate speech while at UT, but dismissed its impact. "I'm not Martin Luther King. I'm just a former football player who loved his time at Tennessee."[74]

Collegiate sports, despite recent achievements, remained one of the more conservative institutions on campus, especially in contrast to the roiling nature of campus life in the Viet Nam War era. Nevertheless, McClain and other early UT athletes led the way toward integration of SEC sports with an undisputed national championship for the 1967 season (a respectable 26–6–1 run between 1967 and 1969 and two SEC championships left little for anyone but the most bigoted Vols fans to complain about).[75] In 1972 8 percent of the SEC conference's football players were Black, a number that grew to a third by 1980 and well over

As UT's first African American quarterback, Condredge Holloway took the Vols
to three bowls while also excelling on the baseball diamond as a shortstop.

half by 1990. Gains in basketball and track & field were even greater.[76] Sports
at UT, especially those that were great money-makers, remained a space for
African American students that remained a space subject to the scrutiny and
consent of white elites. However, they nevertheless provided a means to a greater
end, that end being a more diverse campus. The presence of black athletes in
stadium named for a man who had raged at their presence might have been
overshadowed by two of the most controversial events in the history of Vols
football: the installment of artificial turf on Shields-Watkins ("Doug's Rug," which
the team played on from 1968 through the 1993 season by which time Dickey had
returned as UT's fourth athletic director), and Dickey's sudden departure to the
University of Florida (along with three Vol assistant coaches) immediately after
a 14–13 loss to the Gators in the 1969 Gator Bowl.[77]

   Overall, UT's desegregation, along with the rest of the state's higher education
system, was more successful in Tennessee than in any other Southern state,
according to historian Bobby Lovett. But Holloway's statement of being "no

Martin Luther King" reflected his own satisfaction with his time as a UT student while also representing a more common desire at UT and other campuses to embrace integration without confronting the politics of race. By the end of the twentieth century, seven other former Jim Crow states were under observation by the Department of Education for failure to follow through with court decisions, four of them in ongoing court battles. There were no acrimonious bigoted politicians standing in front of the registrar's door or riots stirred by white hate as happened at other Southern state universities.[78] As of 1980 UT had forty black faculty members but as the university grew, the number only had a net increase to seventy-eight by 2017, less than four percent of the total faculty.[79] Despite leading by some metrics, the school's dedication to integration reached a decades-long holding pattern.

The growing Black student body was an active presence in the late 1960s not only on the playing fields but also on the hustings of campus politics. In 1969, Air Force veteran Jimmie Baxter won a run-off election for Student Government Association president, becoming one of the first African American student

Jimmie Baxter became UT's first African American
Student Government Association president in 1969.

government presidents at any white-majority school in the United States. Like his opponents, Baxter ran on a platform based on increasing the power of students on campus, an issue that united black and white students in one accord.[80]

Student government had been around in some form or another since the days of Charles Dabney, but students never felt it necessary or possible to challenge administrative authority until the 1960s. The sticking point for Baxter and his allies was an issue that had persisted since the 1950s when students had begun inviting controversial speakers to campus. In 1967 UT students allegedly invited controversial African American New York congressman Adam Clayton Powell to campus just months after Nashville had erupted in police attacks on private residences after Black activist Stokely Carmichael spoke at Vanderbilt.[81] After Powell, students invited LSD researcher Timothy Leary, journalist Max Lerner, crusading leftist attorney William Kunstler, and civil rights activist Julian Bond. Then came the turbulent summer of 1968 when the board of trustees, without provocation from the UT student body, authorized Holt "'to take any action which is necessary to maintain law and order' . . . if the need arises," with a coded warning that the board had "the belief and hope that such disruptions will never occur."[82] UT's student-run Issues Committee asked Chancellor Weaver for permission to invite Dick Gregory, an African American comedian who had played a flamboyant role in the street protests outside the Chicago Democratic Party convention. Weaver, who called Gregory an "extreme racist," balked, fearing that the comedian's presence on campus would anger Tennessee's conservative Democratic governor Buford Ellington and the legislature, a fear that President Holt apparently did not share.[83] Weaver went on to block Leary's appearance scheduled for the following year, while Bond refused to appear in protest of the ban on Gregory. The board of trustees refused to present the school with an official speaker policy, prompting students to take UT to court in early 1969 with representation by William Kunstler. That summer, a month after Jimmie Baxter's victory, UT settled on a fifteen-person committee that was probably the first governmental body on campus that included administrators, faculty, and students (in a three-five/seven/ratio, respectively). It was the first of many student victories, and a small vindication for the violations of free speech in the previous decade. That same month, Andy Holt announced his retirement as UT System president.[84] Gregory finally made it to campus in 1970. Within a few decades, controversial campus speakers had become commonplace, and future administrations knew better than to politicize their appearances. It is unlikely that the largely white demand for controversial black speakers at the end of the

UT was not known for campus radicalism in the late 1960s, but students
organized to protest the administration's heavy-handed attempt to keep
comedian Dick Gregory from speaking on campus.

1960s would have developed without the work of black students at the decade's
beginning.

Despite agitation on behalf of campus speakers, UT was not a hotbed of
protest when it came to Viet Nam. In American memory, the 1960s began with
a grassroots, multicampus effort to end Jim Crow, and ended amidst a larger
movement dedicated to ending the US military involvement in Viet Nam and
Cambodia, but UT did not fit easily into that mold. The campus was not fully
mobilized for war as had been the case in the 1940s, and college students were very
unlikely to be drafted, although UT students' contribution to the war effort was
notable. In 1962, UT ROTC's new commander Captain John Daniel organized
the first Ranger Training Program ever established at a civilian university. The
black-bereted Army Rangers played an integral role in the US occupation of Viet

Nam as it turned into a war over the course of the 1960s, and Daniel himself served multiple tours. In all, at least 159 UT students served in Viet Nam, with ten combat fatalities among them. Capt. Larry Taylor, a 1966 graduate, served with the Air Force and was decorated with three Distinguished Flying Crosses and a Silver Star. Navy medical corpsman David Ray, who attended UT from 1963–1966, was posthumously awarded the Congressional Medal of Honor for shielding a wounded Marine from an exploding grenade with his body.[85] UT's campus was not noted for large-scale protests against the war, especially in the early years of the conflict. Demonstrations against the US war effort in southeast Asia were muted in the South compared to those in coastal areas and the Great Lakes region, and many students supported the war effort.[86] UT Student editorials from the mid-1960s expressed perplexity and slight amusement at the marches and sit-ins taking place at campuses like Berkeley, and Knoxville politician John J. Duncan (by now a member of Congress) noted in early 1965 that his district's university lacked the "loud, protesting youth" seen on other campuses.[87] That same year a reported seven hundred UT students rallied in support of the war.[88] Even as late as fall 1969, with the war far less popular than it had been four years earlier, members of the school's Young Americans for Freedom chapter burned a Viet Cong flag in the newly constructed Circle Park area of campus.[89]

And yet, as the speaker controversy demonstrated, between 1968 and 1970 UT students shared the feeling of unrest felt on many other campuses largely because they did not consider their campus a democratic space. At the beginning of the 1968 fall semester, one student commented that the "change" sweeping over other campuses had "finally arrived in Big Orange Country."[90] The pronouncement was probably slightly premature. Something resembling a concerted antiwar movement probably could not have come into being at UT without circumstances specific to the campus itself, namely conflict over university leadership. Coming off of the free speaker movement, many students and faculty wanted more input on the matter of President Holt's replacement, and both parties were less than impressed with the board of trustees' choice of Edward Boling. The multifurcation between the Knoxville campus and the UT System was a new development, and the presidency was a different office than it had once been, but, unlike every UT president dating back to the nineteenth century, Boling did not have a professional background in education. Students and some faculty reasoned that the elevation of UT–Martin chancellor Archie Dykes, an educator by profession, would symbolize inclusion of the new campuses into the new system. "To the Board of Trustees meeting here to determine selection procedures, we ask that they again demonstrate the faith they showed in us concerning the open speaker

After the UT campus grew during the baby boomer years,
the university installed one of its most iconic pieces of
public art, the Torchbearer statue.

policy by including student and faculty representatives in the selection process," a
student editorial proposed at the beginning of the 1969 fall semester. "Let's avoid
the ugliness which accompanied the speaker policy before its adoption."[91]

The trustees quietly met during the Christmas holiday to appoint Boling in
a meeting that a later chancellor acknowledged was less than democratic.[92] In
January 1970, with tensions from the open-speaker fight still running high, and
national events like the beleaguered presidency of Richard Nixon exacerbating
matters, faculty and students attempted to forcibly occupy the Austin Peay
administration building. They were met with resistance from university police
and conservative students who tried to block the door, but the event ended
inconclusively even after one student, a Brazilian exchange student named

Peter Kami, farcically challenged Weaver to a duel.[93] Twenty-two protestors were arrested and, following his recent defense of the "Chicago Seven," Kunstler returned to represent the "Knoxville 22" in April—as it happened, the same month Dick Gregory finally visited. In late April student Carroll Bible was arrested in the Hess Hall dormitory for selling "Knoxville Legal Defense Record" raffle tickets, but with little fallout.[94] Despite the show of resistance, Boling went on to serve as UT System president for the next eighteen years.[95] For most of those years, he and his wife Carolyn were determined to be as visible on campus as possible, and their favorite way of doing so was as regular patrons of the arts at plays produced at the Clarence Brown Theatre (the Bolings were noted for always paying full price for tickets rather than accepting "comps").[96]

Feelings over the appointment were still raw that spring when Chancellor Weaver used the open-speaker policy himself, perhaps to show students and faculty that free speech was a double-edged sword. In 1969 he and Holt had been approached by a committee of religious Knoxville–area citizens who had recently secured a promised visit from Billy Graham. Two decades into an evangelical mission that had already circled the globe, Graham, a North Carolina native, was close to the zenith of his fame and had already become the unofficial pastor- for multiple White House administrations. His profile had increased far beyond the capacity for practically all churches, and the committee petitioned Holt and Weaver to rent Neyland Stadium for Graham's crusade. With one foot out the door toward retirement, Holt deferred to Weaver who, according to a later interview, believed the event would be good publicity for UT. Over the next few months, Weaver weighed his ability to invite speakers to campus without sponsorship from an organization (at one point UT's chapter of Fellowship of Christian Athletes was identified as a sponsor, but Weaver later denied it was one) and the proper amount to charge for Neyland's rental. What became known as the "East Tennessee Crusade" was finally settled at $20,000 (a fee not unlike those Graham had paid for other appearances of similar venues) for multiple nights in late May. Weaver stressed to students and faculty concerned over church/state separation that the event was not officially sanctioned by the university.

As May arrived, UT students had other things on their minds. Four students protesting the bombing of Cambodia in late April were shot dead at Kent State by the Ohio National Guard on May 4. Many UT students, along with those at Knoxville and Maryville Colleges, participated in a nationwide three-day student strike with the support of many of their professors. Jimmie Baxter warned an assemblage of three thousand that what happened in Ohio could happen in Tennessee, and Kunstler returned yet again to support the growing resistance.

Classes were cancelled. The protests were endorsed by the student government and even Weaver praised Baxter's characterization of the protest as antiviolence. The newly formed UT Black Student Union held its own protest against the killings of two students by policemen on the Jackson State University campus in Mississippi. Two buildings, including the Army Reserve National Center, were set on fire with homemade incendiaries but quickly extinguished.[97] Quite suddenly, the UT campus had seemingly become radicalized, but only after blood had been shed at other campuses that, only short years earlier, would have just been a faraway place somewhere up north or in the Deep South.

Billy Graham's crusade began later that month, the Friday evening of May 22, with no problems save student concerns that the expanded traffic would complicate the exam period.[98] The university was mostly uninvolved, save renting out its most famous space and Holt's delivering the offertory prayer on the opening day.[99] Things got complicated midway through the following week when local media announced the arrival of President Nixon to join Graham on "Youth night" six days later. It was a sudden announcement, only twenty-four hours before his Thursday arrival, and both Graham (who already had a close relationship with the president) and Congressman John Duncan were said to be the source of the invitation (there were also indications that Weaver had requested the president's presence for UT's 175th anniversary).[100] The strange abruptness of his addition to the festivities (particularly at a religious event) appeared to many a direct response to Baxter, Kunstler, and UT's agitated student body.

Whoever invited him, Nixon needed a friendly audience to kick off his midterm campaigning, preferably on a university campus in the most Republican part of the South.[101] By the 1960s the Solid South's old means of power, the Democratic Party, was losing ground to the Republicans in many parts of the region. Tennessee's Democratic potentate Edward "Boss" Crump, who ran a large part of the state by remote control from his Memphis headquarters, had been defeated by dissidents within his own party shortly before his death in 1954. Younger Democrats like Estes Kefauver and Al Gore Sr. did not want to use Jim Crow to maintain dominance. Meanwhile, Tennessee was beginning to see in-migration from places like Ohio and Michigan, states Tennesseans had moved to short years before. Soon after Kefauver's election to the US Senate in 1948 and Gore's in 1952, Tennessee Republicans saw a resurgence, including the 1966 election of Howard Baker (a 1949 graduate of UT Law), Tennessee's first elected Republican US Senator in ninety-six years. A white Memphis dentist named Winfield Dunn would soon (in fall of 1970) become Tennessee's first Republican governor in a half century; Chattanooga Republican Bill Brock would defeat Gore in a Senate race that same election day.[102] Of course much of East Tennessee had remained solidly Republican for that entire span of time, and the new success of Southern Republicans in the 1960s meant new clout for the area in the state capitol unseen since Reconstruction. Moreover, East Tennessee Republicans had not fought Jim Crow as hard as their party mates in the North and West, and created a safe space for former Democrats who were switching parties in the 1960s to protest passage of the Civil Rights Act (1964) and the Voting Rights Act (1965). Knoxville was a beachhead for Nixon's "Southern Strategy" or, at least, an opportunity to campaign for Brock (Gore was not invited to the Billy Graham event).[103] An appearance with a Southern minister, let alone the most-loved evangelist in America, would provide an extra layer of legitimacy. "Town, gown, bank, church and Crusade were of one mind" in Knoxville, wrote conservative commentator Garry Wills. "If this was not Nixon Country, then what is?"[104]

"Nixon Country," if UT was such, did not provide Nixon with the unalloyed welcome he hoped for. When word got out that Nixon had been added to the program, students and faculty quickly organized protests. John Smith, Baxter's (white) successor as SGA president met with the president aboard Air Force One, but others telegraphed Nixon asking him to cancel his speech.[105] On the afternoon of Nixon's appearance, religious studies professor Charles Reynolds and psychology professor Kenneth Newton led more than four hundred students, and about a dozen other faculty, into Neyland with signs saying, "Thou Shall Not Kill."[106] Their boos at Nixon were dampened by the cheers from the mainly non-UT throng of thousands as police photographed those they considered miscreants. One graduate student complemented his long hair and beard with a biblical gown (his alleged name, Carroll Bible, did not prove to be apocryphal).[107] The protestors left after Nixon finished to avoid disturbing Graham's subsequent sermon, but not before nine were arrested and many signs confiscated. The Knoxville police arrested forty-six of the protestors later, including Reynolds who was fined $20 for interrupting a religious gathering.[108]

Although Andy Holt condemned the protest, no one was fired, expelled, or suspended by UT, even after eighty faculty members issued a "statement of 'moral outrage'" stating that the Neyland Stadium gathering was political rather than religious.[109] In the aftermath, many protestors were pleased that they had managed to express their disapproval to the president without actually disturbing the original purpose of the gathering. Professor Ralph Norman, chair of the Religious Studies Department, concentrated his ire not so much on Nixon's manipulation of the faithful as he did the American complacency of faith he feared Graham would not address:

1970 Neyland Stadium was in the national spotlight when a 1970 Billy Graham crusade included an appearance by President Richard Nixon weeks after student protestors were killed in Ohio and Mississippi. Protests by UT faculty and students ensued. Left to right: UT President Andy D. Holt, Martha Chase Holt, Ruth Graham, Billy Graham, Richard Nixon.

East Tennesseans will drive to the Graham stadium in air-conditioned Dodges and Buicks, and they will return to comfortable suburban homes with lovely green lawns. They will be vaguely hoping for some word that reassures them they can keep these possessions free from inflation, war, and revolution and still have salvation too. Graham will tell them that their houses and cars will be worth nothing at the end of the world, which is coming in this very age. They will have trouble believing that he means this seriously, and have more trouble still knowing what to do with their possessions afterwards, other than to continue to protect them from the poor, the young, the black and the subversive. It is reasonably safe to predict that they will not sell what they have and give it to the poor.

Mr. Graham is sincere, has enormous charisma, and quite obviously does not want to leave Nixon's America as he found it. There are some things he could say to Knoxville, abrupt and jolting and vital things—but they are not the things you say to the leaders of a great civic festival replete with country ham breakfasts and marching bands and the keys to the city.[110]

Reynolds appealed his conviction on the grounds that his rights of free speech and equal protection had been violated by his arrest. In early 1974 the US Supreme Court voted 6–3 not to hear Reynolds's case, with all four of Nixon's appointees voting in the majority.[111] By that time, with the Watergate scandal in its final phase and Nixon months away from resignation, the presidential visit must have seemed a distant memory on the UT campus.

Other than sports events, the Billy Graham crusade at Neyland Stadium was UT's most famous encounter with national affairs, a memorable spectacle on a campus that many visitors would have considered sleepy and monotonous in contrast to the larger roiling campuses in New York, California, and elsewhere. But the crusade, and its attendant protest, were like many past events: larger national trends reflected on and around the Hill, combined with local peculiarities. Student unrest at UT in 1970 was exemplary of other contemporary campuses, but it would never have happened without leadership from a biracial coalition of student leaders who recognized that their campus's speaker policy was undemocratic (black student government presidents were rare on American campuses in the 1960s in any region, let alone the South). And said coalition would never have happened had Black Tennesseans not demonstrated, beginning no later than the 1930s, that the "separate but equal" doctrine was also a betrayal of democracy. The UT student's traditional deference to the authority of age and title crumbled after the old mandate of racial deference came under attack. It had been a long time since the Pride of the Southland Band had attempted a revival of blackface minstrelsy at a Volunteers halftime show. But even as the football team itself became Black majority, some all-white Greek organizations made blackface, mock lynchings, and (far more often) displays of the Confederate battle flag a regular feature of their yearbook photos well into the 1980s.[112] In 1989 Wade Houston became the first African American head coach in the SEC when he took over the Vols' basketball squad.[113] Before his five seasons (65–90) could even start, he also became the first UT coach to be denied membership in Knoxville's all-white Cherokee Country Club, a frequent locale for university recreation and society for decades. Doug Dickey (who had returned to UT to serve as athletic director) and football coach Johnny Majors both quit the club in protest.[114]

Between 1954 and 1972, Tennessee and its university put the official ties to the old days of racial politics behind them. Segregation of public facilities went from being forced upon the state by law to prohibited by law in less than a generation. UT students proved, as never before, that their voices would be heard both as part of their institution and as part of their democracy. Even if their majority was as dedicated to establishment values and "law and order" as Nixon suspected and hoped they were, a vocal minority proved that that change is rarely initiated by majority rule. The baby boom generation of Volunteers helped teach America that the progression of democracy required a vocal minority.

Racial equality proved to be a goal that could not be met absolutely but, like other elements of democracy, remains an ongoing struggle. However, the civil rights movement introduced the possibility that students, Black or white, had the right to make serious decisions as to how their school was run. For a time, scarcely outlasting the Viet Nam war, UT students insisted that their voices be heard on campus on a level equal with deans and chancellors—it so happened that a fair number of their faculty happened to be in agreement. The sudden influx of baby boomers that Andy Holt had foreseen in the early 1960s had impacts on UT other than just a drastic increase in size. It brought about a permanent change in the 1970s that twenty-first-century UT community members might consider a *sine qua non*: board meetings became open to the public and subject to petitions and protests from practically any interested party. The speaker controversy also led to greater student input when it came to showing controversial movies on campus, such as the film adaptation of James Joyce's *Ulysses* the following February (film committee chairperson Kitty Welch assured the *Beacon* that, despite furor over the show, viewers expecting a "dirty movie" were disappointed).[115] But mass student engagement did not persist far into the 1970s. Its brief duration during the early Nixon years (or the early Boling years as it were) was, in the approving words of UT psychology professor Howard Pollio, "a short-term 'period of empowerment.'"[116]

But the 1970s also brought about a relative complacency just in time for the lull in new construction and perhaps even a mellowing of student expectations. "Students returned to their books and other attractions," wrote one relieved obscurantist in the history department. "Dress became more conventional; males started to cut their hair and trim their beards., Student elections became less raucous and less interesting. Life looked more like the 1950s."[117] It was an observation reflecting a willful unwillingness to recognize what changes *had* been permanent (in the 1950s only a small number of African American graduate students walked among an otherwise lily-white student body; that was certainly not the case in the 1970s), as well as an omission of that which had become commonplace (i.e., controversial speakers). Near campus, if not on campus itself,

UT students and recent graduates participated in social justice movements organized by groups like Highlander and the Tennessee Council on Human Relations, targeting civil rights and the persistence of Appalachian poverty. In some respects, a "student movement" at UT had only begun in 1970 just as it was fizzling on campuses all over America.[118] However, at this writing, UT students have never assembled against a campus-wide or national status quo as they did in 1970. The school had its taste of 1960s idealism, and perhaps even a moment of true radicalism, but it did so on its own terms.

CHAPTER SIX

The Hardest Blow:
UT Sees the Future, 1970–2010

. . . .

"The great enemy of truth is very often not the lie—deliberate,
contrived and dishonest—but the myth—persistent, persuasive and
unrealistic. Too often we hold fast to the clichés of our forebears.
We subject all facts to a prefabricated set of interpretations. We enjoy
the comfort of opinion without the discomfort of thought."

—JOHN F. KENNEDY—
Commencement Address at Yale University, June 11, 1962

"I spent four years prostrate to the higher mind.
Got my paper and I was free."

—INDIGO GIRLS—
"Closer to Fine" (1989)

I n concluding his 1970 chronicle of twentieth-century campus culture, historian
Calvin Lee noted that, because of various recent societal changes, American
college students no longer cleaved to the traditions and rituals of the past, and
"the traditional 'rah rah' is hard to find" even during football season. "Loyalty to
an institution is not particularly part of this generation. One-fourth of every
graduating class began school in another college. A high percentage switch and
drop out before graduation. This is a mobile society—and the college students
are no different. Transfers from one college to another are much more prevalent
in the Sixties than before." Universities had grown large, bureaucratic, and
complex, and students did not view them as they had back in the "golden age of Joe
College." "How did one expect loyalty to a large corporate body such as Berkeley
or Columbia in this generation? No more than one expected this generation to
establish loyalties to a large corporation like IBM."[1]

In many ways UT was only beginning to codify its own peculiar institutional symbols and traditions when Lee made that observation. Since early in the twentieth century, the school had its share of seasonal dances and events, but few that did not have analogs at others of comparable size and age, especially in the "Joe College" Roaring Twenties. National Greek letter fraternities and sororities had grown on campus since before the first world war, many maintaining their own individual codes and rituals. In 1921 the university had started "Torch Night" as an initiation for freshmen (no doubt founded by the university to mitigate extracurricular hazing made evident by various yearbook entries) and followed it in 1926 with "Aloha Oe," an ambiguously Hawaiian-themed spring ceremony for departing seniors. Vic Davis, who served as alumni secretary from 1923 until 1948, devised a number of traditions for students to carry out, including the singing of the UT alma mater "Spirit of the Hill" (in previous years, UT students had inexplicably sung the Cornell University alma mater), and a designated student cheering section in Neyland Stadium briefly referred to as "the Cherokee Tribe."[2] The annual crowning of homecoming queen came to a farcical end in 1970 when *Beacon* humor writer Vince Staten won 3,500 votes over fifteen hundred cast for eleven other candidates with a campaign promise of having "something none of the other candidates have."[3] Staten campaigned with a paper grocery bag over his head and was eventually disqualified from the running because, as a graduate student, he was not qualified for a distinction officially awarded only to seniors. The prank was enough to permanently disrupt the crowning of homecoming "royalty"; four UT Homecoming Queens were crowned for four years in the 1980s, and "Miss Homecoming" and "Homecoming Highnesses" were attempted in the twenty-first century, but permanent demand for the old school tradition never rematerialized.[4]

But the university had the same problem as other schools with institutional anomie. "At this time, with the enrollment soaring into the thousands," a *Daily Beacon* editorial warned in 1967, "the school reflects an impersonal institution with countless members of this community walking trance-like through four years of their life and leaving UT with only a printed material to represent their achievements." "By grasping some meaning for traditions, students can realize more fully the spirit of the Hill, and unhappy memories of college and its impersonalness perhaps be softened."[5] Students suggested to President Holt some sort of physical addition to the campus that would symbolize an institutional daemon and a sense of historical continuity. In April 1968, the university unveiled the nine-foot Torchbearer at Circle Park, a statue whose design dated back to the early 1930s when a Yale University art student had won a national contest.

Unlike past castings, this one had a gas-burning "eternal flame" that became an eye-catching attraction for visitors' photographs.[6] That same year, a fountained sculpture, "Europa and the Bull" sculpted by Swedish artist Carl Milles was placed on the otherwise ascetic flat concrete area surrounding McClung Tower a few yards northwest of the Torchbearer.[7] Holt's own namesake building, Andy Holt Tower (nicknamed among faculty the "Power Tower"), was completed in 1973 on the southern edge of campus within view of the Tennessee River, giving UT's administrative center its first home away from Barbara Hill.[8] The Hill was still the most iconic section of campus, and the remnant of neo-Gothic architecture, but it was no longer UT's center-point.

Another new tradition was born with the Pride of the Southland Band's first-ever performance of "Rocky Top," as part of an instrumental medley of country songs during halftime for the 1972 Alabama game (Alabama, 17–10) in Neyland Stadium. The inaugural performance featured Nashville session saxophonist Boots Randolph. The performance was met with approval, and Randolph reprised the performance at the Astro-Blue Bonnet Bowl in Houston the following New Year's Eve during the Volunteers' 24–17 win over LSU. The song was written in 1967 by Felice and Boudleaux Bryant, a successful pop and country songwriting duo who had previously written for Carl Smith and the Everly Brothers (both acts had ties to Knoxville) and dozens of other musical acts. Gnomically named for a peak in the Great Smoky Mountains National Park, "Rocky Top" was a paean for a mythical mountain community devoid of modern nuisances like "smoggy smoke" and "telephone bills." First recorded with acoustic string instruments by Bobby and Sonny Osborne's bluegrass group, a polished, heavily produced "country-politan" cover by country singer Lynn Anderson hit the charts in 1970. The Bryants' company eventually granted UT perpetual license to use the song. Although "Rocky Top" never replaced "Down the Field" (also known as "Here's to Old Tennessee") as UT's official game time "fight song," it gained greater nationwide familiarity than any other song associated with a university, perhaps because, unlike most college-related songs, it was originally written and recorded for commercial purposes.

Part of the appeal of "Rocky Top" stemmed from in-state sectional politics. By describing a mountainous setting that could be imagined in the Blue Ridge or the Cumberland Plateau, the adoption of Rocky Top was a final statement on the eastern third of the state's unofficial ownership of Tennessee's state university and land-grant institution. As mentioned in a previous chapter, Knoxville city elites had resisted association with its rural surroundings for most of the twentieth century. And the ambivalence was felt in Nashville too; in 1943

Tennessee governor Prentice Cooper had scoffed at the Grand Old Opry and its star East Tennessee-native star Roy Acuff for making the capital city the "hillbilly capital of the United States."[9] But, by the 1970s, the Opry had become a national broadcasting institution, and country music had become a nationally consumed commodity. After a letter-writing campaign, "Rocky Top" became Tennessee's fifth official state song in 1982. "There is nothing wrong with having state songs to suit all tastes," opined a Nashville editor. "They don't cost the taxpayers anything, and instead of singing Rocky Top and voting on songs, the legislators could be doing something worse."[10] Even if UT's adoption of the song was a sectional statement, it still managed to ingratiate itself to the "flatlanders" in the rest of the state. In 2014, Lake City, a town north of Knoxville, voted to change its name to Rocky Top for entrepreneurial reasons.

Whatever associations Rocky Top had with the "hillbilly" concept had become an object of fun (and profitable!) derision urban and suburban Tennesseans wanted to appropriate for themselves rather than disparage in others. As Mark Banker observed in his Knoxville-centered historical memoir *Appalachians All,* "one would have to look hard among the 110,000 orange-clad fanatics who regularly fill Neyland Stadium to its brim to find the [stereotypical] gingham-clad lady. Vol partisans, at least those who attend games, are mostly successful folks."[11] It was an ironic public relations move considering the problem UT, and the UT System, had in the late twentieth century with their parochial national image, at least in the minds of leaders such as Edward Boling.[12] While the UT campus was never on the top of an isolated escarpment as described by "Rocky Top," it did have a wealth of exposed sedimentary substrata because of constant construction and excavation, including a ninety-seven-ton boulder on the southwest side of campus that students began "tagging" with spray paint around 1980. The university soon legitimized painting "the Rock" and even went to the trouble of moving it across Volunteer Boulevard in 2009 to make way for new construction and continue another latter-day tradition.

In 1973 the board of trustees selected UT's vice chancellor for Academic Affairs and former professor of English Jack Reese as the new chancellor, the first noninterim chancellor since the creation of the UT System during the Holt and Weaver years.[13] During sixteen years in office, the longest time in office for the Knoxville campus's executive since Charles Dabney, the "fatherly" Reese oversaw some of UT's most dramatic expansions in education.[14] The year of his appointment, UT earned its first designation from the Carnegie Classification of Institutions as a research university. The school had been in the top fifty colleges receiving federal funds for research and development since the growth decade of the 1960s, and the transition from land-grant to research institution was complete.[15] The university retained its prior mission of professional training, however. The College of Nursing was founded in 1971 after a social science study revealed Tennessee's shortage of nurses. In 1973 UT's social work program was given its own dean and was awarding Tennessee's first doctorates in social work a decade later. UT joined a small number of universities in founding a veterinary school in 1974. The College of Communications was created out of the journalism program in 1969.[16] Late in Reese's chancellorship he cajoled both the faculty senate and the board of trustees into one of the most dramatic, if not flamboyant, changes in practical teaching: a switch from the sixty-year-old quarter system to a two-semester format in 1985. It was a change initially decried by students who had to get used to a new school year and engineering professors who suddenly had a more complicated scheduling arrangement with the employers who typically hired students on a quarterly basis (most faculty in social sciences and humanities were very much in favor of the change). But the change was eventually taken as a given, and the controversy was forgotten except when examined by other land-grant universities considering making the change themselves.[17].

As chancellor and president, respectively, Jack Reese and Ed Boling oversaw the interlude years after the Baby Boom and withstood a new era of relative austerity and fiscal conservatism in the Tennessee state government.

The seemingly unfettered growth of the 1960s was being checked, partly by West Tennessee legislators who wanted a bigger piece of the pie for other schools in the UT System (as did these schools' own administrations), but also by a new voice for cutbacks in the person of Winfield Dunn, the state's first Republican governor since 1923.[18] Regardless, UT's Knoxville campus had its largest budget to date in 1973–74, just as the United States was beginning to recognize a problem with inflation coupled with slowed economic growth. Moreover, Dunn's successor as governor, Democrat Ray Blanton, wrote in federal contributions to the state along with state revenue numbers in a way that made the state look as if it was increasing expenditures at a rate far higher than was feasible in a time of slow economic growth. As a result, state colleges became a permanent target of growing antitax rhetoric.[19] During the governorship of Lamar Alexander (1979–1987), higher education was "starved" in Tennessee according to one dean, and Reese became the first chancellor or president in living memory forced to reduce student enrollment. In order to do so, UT heightened admissions requirements and encouraged students on the sheer borderline of acceptance to begin their educations at another resource that was growing in size and number: state community colleges.[20] Nationally, a record 59 percent of 1988 high school graduates enrolled in college, compared with forty-nine percent in the previous decade.[21] Over the course of the same decade, the Knoxville campus's student body fell from thirty thousand to 25,000.[22] The days of Keynesian largesse were slowly coming to a close, just as four-year degrees were becoming less a middle-class luxury and more a requirement to enter or even stay in the middle class. UT students began to sense an indifference in their (suddenly much larger) school's administrative demeanor, especially when bureaucratic oversights or snafus in Admissions, the Registrar's office, or various academic departments hindered their progress toward a degree or imposed unexpected expenses along the way. As early as the 1980s frustrated students spoke of falling victim to what they called the "Big Orange Screw," a colloquialism that persisted on and around campus well into the next century.[23]

The students' problem extended to the faculty as well. By the beginning of the 1980s, the AAUP reported that UT faculty pay was lower than any other southeastern university.[24] By the end of the decade budget cuts were leading to so many classes being dropped that Chancellor John Quinn had to ask departments to allow "liberal substitution" of classes in order to fulfill majors.[25] Quinn had been hired from Brown University in 1989 in order to bring "new blood" to change a 1960s campus culture that was running out of steam. Quinn was an eager academic. But, as a former Ivy League private university administrator, he had little experience dealing with the paucities of state funding and left after three years.[26] His successor as chancellor, former UT Dean of Engineering William Snyder, predicted to a University of Georgia vice president that the 1990s "will not be the best of times for higher education. . . ."[27]

By 1983 UT had thirteen colleges and a social mission inspired by the school's past experience with civil rights, which did not jibe easily with the conservative atmosphere of the late 1970s and 1980s.[28] Since the late 1960s Black students and faculty had discussed the formation of a Black Cultural Center, a development that finally came about in 1975 as part of the College of Liberal Arts (a Black Studies curriculum had been developed in the College in 1970).[29] The center absorbed some of the Office of Minority Affairs' mission of combating racism, but it also took on a more expansive role to promote Black History Month (first celebrated on the campus of Kent State University in 1970) and to bring elements of the Black Arts movement to the UT campus under the direction of educator and activist Dennis Littlejohn.

The center worked with a number of African American groups on the UT campus as well as Knoxville College, many of whom continued the sort of direct-action tactics that first brought desegregation to Knoxville. In 1978 four UT students were arrested for disrupting a UT board of trustees meeting to demand that the school withdraw investments from South Africa's Apartheid regime (the board rejected the demand at Boling's suggestion; "I don't think we have any business whatsoever using the funds of the university to cure social injustices," said Boling).[30] A local artist commemorated their act of civil disobedience with a painting two years later on Martin Luther King's birthday just briefly after, as it happened, the administration had rejected a demand by a group called the Afro-American Student Liberation Force to make King's birthday a campus-wide holiday. Soon after the painting was given to the Black Cultural Center, Littlejohn was removed from his position and transferred to UT's personnel office, and the center closed. Several hundred students rose up to occupy the building where the center was housed and boycott classes. Eleven students were arrested for trespassing. Reese denied that Littlejohn had been removed because of the painting or the King birthday holiday controversy and said that racism on campus was no worse than what could be found in "society in general," but he avowed that the arrests were the hardest thing he had ever had to do.[31] It was the largest student demonstration since 1970, but smaller and without the biracial cooperation seen under the leadership of student government president Jimmie Baxter. UT's Black Cultural Center was restored but, in 1980, Black students (who made up less than 7 percent of the student body at a time when Tennessee had a

Black population of over 15 percent) knew that desegregation had not translated into complete integration.

Over the following years the UT African American community grew, but never matching numbers at other campuses. At 5 percent of the UTK student body in 1995 (compared to 12 at the Chattanooga campus and 15 at Martin), the Black student body's relative deficiency was attributed by the administration to Knoxville's distance from urban centers like Nashville and Memphis (although UT System president Joe Johnson noted that much-improved Black graduation rates were higher than those of white students at any of the institutions).[32]

The 1970s brought with it a paradigmatic change in the status of women on campus. The speaker controversy of the late 1960s coincided with a reinvigorated women's movement on campus. In January 1969, UT's chapter of the Associated Women Students (AWS) began campaigning for an open hours policy for female students who were forced to keep curfew hours that were not imposed in male dormitories.[33] The new policy was adopted on a provisional basis for juniors and seniors despite protests from the Tennessee state legislature. Over the following spring and summer, twelve hundred women living on campus were allowed to stay out later on a trial basis, and fewer than fifteen reportedly used the privilege on weeknights.[34] State representative William Huettel complained to Andy Holt about what he considered the latter's "quick concession to student demands" and demanded that UT's administration try to "stick to their guns" on some issues.[35] The change was made permanent the following fall for students over twenty-one with over eighty completed class hours, although members of the Women's Action Movement had been charged with inciting ineligible students to break curfew in the meantime. Sophomore Madeline Hebert, one of the two accused, asserted that she should have the same rights as a man with her GPA (3.8) and that "girls [at UT] have to keep disobeying the rules if they want to have their freedom."[36] This achievement was no mean feat on a campus where curfew had been a controversial rule since the early nineteenth century. The old doctrine of *in loco parentis* (in which it was understood that schools held authority of discipline "in the place of the parent") was deteriorating, or, at least, receiving a heavy levelling between the sexes. And, like so many other democratizing forces at UT, it came about through the power of student civil disobedience.

As the students directed, the university followed. In 1970 UT alum Ann Baker Furrow became the first woman to serve on UT's oldest governing body, its board of trustees. Betsey Creekmore was appointed assistant vice chancellor for administration in early 1973, beginning a long administrative presence on the campus, much of it dedicated to architectural preservation amid years of razing and construction.[37] Around 1986 UT's Race Desegregation Assistance Center, which had been formed to assist Black students new to the campus in the 1960s, changed focus "from a center focusing on race desegregation to sex equity."[38] The following year Marilyn Yarborough became dean of UT Law, and the first African American woman to become dean of a major law school.[39] In 1979 UT graduate Nancy-Ann Min became the first UT graduate in fifty-one years to be offered a Rhodes scholarship for study at Oxford University, two years after the scholarship was extended to women. Min later became a deputy chief of staff in the Obama administration.[40] Nevertheless, well into the 1980s, according to one contemporary observer, the faculty was still dominated by "tall men with silver hair" graduated from East Coast elite universities, and there were departments that were "hell for women [professors]" and "toxic environments." For years female faculty supported one another with off-campus gatherings; eventually UT required that departments provide internal mentoring services.[41]

The 1970s was a revolution for women's athletics, and UT was in its vanguard. In 1972 Congress passed the Title IX addendum to the 1964 Civil Rights Act, protecting students from "discrimination under any education program or activity"

UT alum and long-time employee Betsey B. Creekmore has dedicated years to preserving the history and architecture of the Knoxville campus. The special collections in Hodges Library was named in her honor.

Marilyn Yarborough was an aerospace engineer before
becoming a law professor and eventually UT's first
African American dean, and one of the first Black
women to head a major American law school.

in any institution receiving federal assistance. Sports historian Welch Suggs
theorizes that institutions were inspired to support women's athletics during
the Cold War because of a national desire to beat the Soviet Union and the
Eastern Bloc (where women were practically coequal to men in almost all physical
education settings) in international competition, especially the Olympics, and
to demonstrate American democracy as superior to the Eastern Bloc's alleged
communist egalitarianism. Although intercollegiate women's sports had been
drastically defunded after World War II, by the 1960s women athletes were
growing in national and international popularity.[42] Closer to home, the Women's
Movement, both on campus and beyond, demanded an institutional equality of
the sexes unprecedented in American history. When institutions were slow to
make room for women's teams, pioneers made do with what was available; a half

decade before she served on UT's board of trustees, Ann Baker Furrow received a scholarship to play golf on the hitherto men's team.

UT–Martin graduate Pat Head arrived on campus in 1974 to work on a graduate degree in physical education and train for the 1976 Olympic basketball team. That same year she was asked to coach UT's women's basketball team. Head had been a standout at Martin and had made the West Tennessee campus's men's basketball coach feared "a women's movement on campus" in the age of Women's Liberation would motivate her to try out for his team.[43] After the Volettes were discontinued in 1926, the women's team had been renewed in 1960 and seen a measure of success under coach Margaret Hutson, who led the "Lady Vols" to a 60–18 record over eleven seasons (including a twenty-one-game winning streak) while sometimes having to sell doughnuts to fund her team.[44] Hutson's departure was unexpected, and Pat Head was obliged to build a coaching staff from scratch, choosing fellow phys ed graduate students Judy Wilkins Rose and Sylvia Rhyne Hatchell to be her assistant coach and junior varsity team coach, respectively. When the three women started, women's sports were overseen not by the NCAA but by the Association for Intercollegiate Athletics for Women (AIAW), an organization that tried to sustain an atmosphere of amateur student athletics the former organization had given up on years earlier. The AIAW placed limitations on athletic scholarships for women and encouraged women's sports to remain in scholastic physical education departments rather than the athletic departments that handled men's sports. Ironically, the organization did not conform to Title IX regulations, and ended up disbanding in 1982.[45]

By the end of that year, Coaches Head (now under her married name of Summitt), Rose, and Hatchell had established a dominant women's basketball program that elevated the sport nationally over the following decades with a record two hundred wins in seven seasons.[46] It helped also to have Tennessee Tech University, the only other women's program in Tennessee with a national profile, as a ready, nearby rival.[47] In her early years of coaching, Head's duties included hand washing her players' uniforms while being paid a standard graduate-student stipend and afforded funding for only four player scholarships.[48] Her team's home locker room in the basement of the Stokely athletic building was inconveniently shared by UT's wrestling team (which was often taken up by a visiting men's team of one sport or another), and practice courts were accessible only after the men's team already had their practice. The Lady Vols often travelled with the men for doubleheaders—although by van or bus while the latter flew in a chartered plane even after Title IX was expanded during the Ford administration. The same expansion had also forced UT to let the women's team use Stokely rather than the dilapidated court in Alumni and allowed Summitt to provide additional scholarships.[49] In 1976 the University of Kentucky tried to lure Head to Lexington with a $9,000 per year offer, a $100.00 raise from what she was getting from UT. She declined.[50]

That same year, a few months after her silver-medal appearance in the summer Olympics in Montreal, Head acted as an expert witness in a high school athlete's unsuccessful lawsuit against Tennessee's secondary school athletic association for limiting women's basketball to a complicated six-on-six player arrangement that required half-court play and forbade guards from shooting baskets.[51] In her testimony she predicted a future for women's sports that would include better funding and larger audiences thanks to the openings made by Title IX, and suggested that half-court games on the preparatory level were a poor grounding for the sport's future. Three years later Head announced that she would withhold recruitment of Tennessee high school players until the state's high school women were allowed to play a standard full-court game. Her clout was enough to cause a rapid change in policy within weeks.[52] Girls' high school basketball in Tennessee began full-court competition in the 1979–80 season, soon followed by public schools in Oklahoma and Iowa.[53] During the 1960s UT men's athletics had been a leader among moderates when it came to racial integration. But a decade later Summitt was making UT an undeniable national leader in bringing gender equality to college sports.

Summitt's contribution to gender equity in sports was matched by her coaching record over the next two decades. Women's college basketball became an increasingly popular sport while Summitt brought about change through, in her words, "finesse" rather than to "go right at it." "Especially in the South, a woman didn't make male allies by ranting or picking fights," she recalled in her autobiography, "There was an old saying, 'You don't cut what you can untie.'" Noting that, having grown up with three brothers, she knew that the best way to grow her program despite the "apprehension about what Title IX would mean for men's sports" was to assuage insecure men's fears. While lobbying for donations (many of which came from the city of Knoxville), Summitt and women's athletic director Gloria Ray "made a point of saying 'We are not a substitute for men's sports. We're an addition to them.'"[54]

It was a needed addition in the early years of her and Ray's leadership. After Doug Dickey's departure, UT's athletic department hired Bill Battle, a protégé of rival Alabama coach Bear Bryant, as the new head coach. After an overall 59–22–2 record, Battle was forced out after winning only two conference games in the 1976 season and replaced by University of Pittsburgh coach and former

Pat Summitt (pictured with star player and fellow Olympian
Patricia Roberts) made the Lady Vols a national powerhouse
while also actively for women's sports on the preparatory and
college level. By the time of her death in 2016 she had achieved an
international profile unmatched by anyone associated with UT.

Volunteers tailback Johnny Majors.[55] Despite being a favorite [he wasn't prodigal,
was he?] son, Majors got off to a slow start, winning twenty-one games in his
first four seasons with only ten wins in the SEC.[56] Meanwhile, longtime men's
basketball coach Ray Mears (said to be the originator of the phrase "Big Orange
Country") retired in 1977 and, after an unsuccessful one-season replacement, was
succeeded by Don Devoe who led the men's team to five straight appearances
in the NCAA national tournament. At the end of the 1970s, UT football was
no longer a monolith overshadowing all other sports. Track & field coach Terry

Hull Crawford led her team to an AIAW national title in 1981 just as Summitt's team was becoming competitive. Between 1974 and 2009, UT men's and women's track & field won a combined seven national championships, and alumnus Tyson Gay is tied for the honor of second-fastest athlete ever. In their first season of NCAA competition, the Lady Vols made it to the 1982 Final Four and, in 1984, lost the final championship 72–61 to the University of Southern California. That summer Summitt returned to the Olympics, this time as coach, and led the US women's basketball team to a gold medal after an 85–55 win over South Korea.[57]

Summitt coached the Lady Vols to twenty-eight consecutive tournament appearances, including eight championship wins between 1987 (over Louisiana Tech, 67–44) and 2008 (over Stanford, 64–48). Summitt's 1,098 combined wins (out of 1,306 games and thirty-eight seasons) as a coach in AIAW and NCAA competition surpassed all other Division I college coaches and earned her ten Coach of the Year awards between 1983 and 2011 from the SEC, NCAA, and other national organizations.[58] In 1987 the Lady Vols began playing in Thompson-Boling Arena as their popularity became comparable to Devoe's men's team. Lady Vols' fan-friendly attractions like the "guest coach" practice initiated in the 1980s ingratiated fans on campus and in town by allowing them to "help" courtside.[59] Lady Vols games were attracting hometown crowds of seven thousand or more by the end of the 1980s, and ticket sales continued to grow until they edged out the men's team in attendance by the end of the century. Only the University of Connecticut was comparable in women's team ticket sales.[60] In 1999 the Women's Basketball Hall of Fame was established in Knoxville because of UT and Summitt's centrality to the sport. After the end of the 2006 season and a record 913 career wins, long after million-dollar paychecks had become standard for male coaches in the higher echelons of Division I NCAA sports, Summit became the first female coach to negotiate a yearly salary over six figures and, in 2011, she was on hand for the merger of the men's and women's athletic departments.[61] After announcing an Alzheimer's disease diagnosis to her team and later to the public, she retired in 2012, handing coaching duties over to her former Lady Vols guard Holly Warlick, who had been on the Lady Vols coaching staff for twenty-seven years. That same year she was awarded the Presidential Medal of Freedom by Barack Obama.[62] Summitt passed away in 2016 at the age of sixty-four, easily the most famous UT employee in history, and hailed by sports sociologist Mary Jo Kane as one of two figures (along with professional tennis player Billie Jean King) whose visage belonged on the proverbial "Mount Rushmore of women's sports."[63]

Summitt's teams gave UT a national profile that surpassed what the football team had earned in the World War II era; the former had rivals—but few peers—in women's basketball until years into the twenty-first century. Further, Summitt's leadership was different from that of her predecessors in UT men's sports. Given the state of college sports by the end of the twentieth century, perhaps her prevailing accomplishment was a preservation of the old ideal of the student athlete. Summitt famously monitored her players' academic performances, insisting on players' attending team-mandated study halls and always sitting in the front three rows of all classrooms as a public demonstration of dedication. Summitt insisted on graduation for all players that played four seasons.[64] The beginning of the twenty-first century, more than two thirds of Lady Vols players were earning degrees at a rate more than twice that of the Volunteer men's team. The graduation rate for the school's football team bottomed out at a startling 11 percent in 1991 before improving substantially over the next few years.[65] With no rumors—let alone allegations—of bribery or cheating, Summitt's Lady Vols defied what sports historian Welch Suggs has called "a danger associated with the big time." the seemingly inevitable tendency of men's college sports to succumb.[66] Summitt's career proved that the fears of the Women's Division of the National Amateur Athletic Federation that women would be corrupted by intercollegiate sports were unfounded even in a program whose profitability approached that of many men's programs. The integrity and unprecedented overall success of the Lady Vols in the Summitt era had the unfortunately ironic effect of eclipsing women's athletics that came beforehand. University publications from 1993 mistakenly spoke of Summitt as UT's only women's basketball coach in the team's history.[67]

The federal intervention of Title IX insured that talents like Summitt's and her players would not be suppressed by patriarchal insecurities as they had been in the 1920s. However, that new mandate of equality did not extend to every element of life on an ever-growing campus. With the Sexual Revolution ongoing in the 1970s, the gay and lesbian community sought political and social solidarity, as well as protection from persecution under the law (the Civil Rights Act had addressed discrimination based on sex but not sexual orientation), through groups like the Gay Liberation Front and the Gay Activists Alliance. College campuses were an intuitive environment for the gay liberation movement since most schools, at least secular ones, claimed to be spaces of free expression by the 1970s. Attempts to stifle speech and assembly in the 1960s had exhausted UT's and other administrations in the previous decade, but they were still afraid to embrace all variety of official campus clubs and groups. Following the protests of spring 1970, a group calling itself the University of Tennessee Gay Liberation Front petitioned UT for recognition, group funding, and meeting places on campus in November, but were rejected by Dean of Students Thomas Scott on the grounds that "sex acts of homosexuals" were illegal by state statute so he doubted UT "should provide a base of operations which has results that are contrary to law."[68] During the 1973–1974 school year, representatives of the newly formed Gay People's Alliance petitioned Vice Chancellor Howard Aldmon and (after his refusal) the UT System's board of trustees to be recognized as a campus organization. The trustees followed an ad hoc committee's recommendation to reject the petition on the grounds that the Alliance planned to provide "an atmosphere conducive to the establishment of such homosexual acquaintances and social contacts includes providing homosexuals with a convenient and 'respectable' means of locating and becoming acquainted with individuals desiring to engage in homosexual sex acts," rather than the purportedly legitimate function "facilitate[ing] or permit[ting] the expression, discussion or exchange of ideas and opinions." The committee implicitly called the petitioners liars, casting doubt on their "candor and forthrightness" and, without giving examples, accused them of contradictory testimonies.[69] Further, UT's legal counsel had earlier organized with Edward Boling and Jack Reese, and UT's vice presidents to design a "de novo" meeting that would eliminate all prior evidence from consideration and keep petitioners out of earshot of one another during their respective testimonials.[70] After a court found in favor of a similar group at Austin Peay State University, UT was forced to bureaucratically accept the existence of a third group, Gay UT, in 1980, although with obstinacy. The school changed its policy language toward campus organizations from 'recognition' to 'registration', the better, said UT System counsel Beauchamp Brogan, to avoid the implication of "approval of the stated beliefs or purposes of the organization." "The party," Brogan assured the trustees, "has the same rights as when it was 'recognized.'"[71] The change in policy language saved UT from a bad public relations situation and a potential civil rights crisis, but it would be years to come before the school's LGBTQ community had a voice on campus that was consistently recognized by the administration.

In 1982, UT helped host one of Knoxville's most illustrious and eccentric, undertakings, the Knoxville International Energy Exposition, otherwise known as the 1982 World's Fair, the first such event held in Tennessee since Nashville had hosted the "Tennessee Centennial Exposition" in 1897, a year after the state's actual centennial (Knoxville had hosted an event called the Appalachian Exposition, the first industrial fair in the South, in 1910 that did not have a global theme). Knoxville's mayor and its leading banker were convinced that an international exposition was the cure for the city's ills, and the fair's energy theme addressed the recent international explosion in oil prices while also exploiting the closeness of Oak Ridge and the TVA. The fair lasted from May Day till Halloween and attracted more than two million visitors within its first four weeks, and nearly ten million more before the end. More than twenty countries were represented, including unique (during the Cold War, at least) contributions from communist Hungary and the People's Republic of China. Fiscally, the fair essentially broke even, while the city was thrown into debt that led to massive financial restructuring, and an East Tennessee banking empire collapsed.[72] The fair provided summer jobs for UT students, but the school was relatively uninvolved despite the fair's abutment to the eastern edge of campus on recently rezoned land surrounding Second Creek.[73] After the fair's conclusion, the iconic Sunsphere and a park were left behind to serve as an attractive special connection between UT's campus and Knoxville's downtown where the defunct Louisville & Nashville railyards had been. But, for years, World's Fair Park was instead an unattractive space of transience and vandalism, a reminder that urban decay could not be solved with a quick fix.[74] The park was in fine shape by the early twenty-first century, but even improved, the space that once hosted the fair continued to serve as a relatively empty gulf between the university and its city. Although well served by the Strip on Cumberland Avenue, town and gown were still as separate from each other as they ever had been.

Just across the river, UT initiated another eccentric undertaking, the establishment of the United States' first "body farm," a facility dedicated to the study of human corpse putrefaction subject to various physical factors. Professor William Bass became head of the Anthropology Department shortly after it broke off from the History Department in the early 1970s, and he quickly began organizing the study of human remains. Early examinations of bones began in Neyland Stadium after the department moved into the former dorm space on the south-facing outside of the structure. Although the Anthropology Department stayed in Neyland until well into the twenty-first century, Bass secured a three-acre area across the Tennessee River in 1981 to be run by UT's Forensic Anthropology Center. Many other universities have followed suit with their own "body farms" (including one founded by one of Bass's former students), but UT's facility remains a mecca for students of law enforcement and forensic science.[75]

Not long after the fair's conclusion, UT experienced another brush with censorship, although this time the administration was not obstinate to the students' and faculty's demand for freedom of expression. The male and female nudes displayed in the University Center were described as "depersonalized" and artistic attempts to "'divest' the human form as depicted on canvas 'of expressionism, romanticism and idealism.'" The exhibit drew fire from parents

The 1982 World's Fair left a physical imprint on Knoxville, namely
the iconic Sunsphere and a park that still serves as a half-mile stop
gap between the UT campus and downtown Knoxville.

(one of whom expressed concern for students' "teenage virgin minds") as well as
at least one local clergyman who called the art "'a disgrace to the ideals of the
university and the sense of propriety among the decent people.'"[76] Near the end
of the fall semester, the Pearlstein pieces were moved to the Frank McClung
museum, a move that campus free speech advocates deemed a retreat prompted
by a the arrival of "political and economic notables" who arrived at the Student
Center just before the last home football game against the University of Kentucky.
A lawsuit against the Office of Student Affairs by students and faculty was
ultimately dismissed but did lead to the reinstallation of the art pieces back
in the Student Union after the Kentucky game under orders from Chancellor
Reese.[77] The affair ended with relations between administration and faculty
bruised but unbroken, and multiple expressions of goodwill between Reese and
various professors.[78]

It took more to galvanize UT students by the 1980s, just as it took more to scandalize administrators and parents, even as the already conservative campus entered the 1980s. The forced austerity of the 1970s reflected a national turn toward fiscal conservatism and a dismantling or de-centralization of public sector institutions.[79] The core institutions of the New Deal were being left behind in government as the economy approached a new postindustrial status that troubled the professions as they troubled the working class. College students became more inclined toward what the *Chronicle of Higher Education* called "new vocationalism," a trend in which seemingly safer career paths were sought. Students who wanted to "start making it" immediately after graduation soared in number while those who planned to "work for political or social change" diminished considerably.[80] Accordingly, even the most idealistic faculty members who had marched with students in past decades became divided into bickering "leftist" and "liberal" camps, while both were lambasted by an insurgent right wing as "tenured radicals" and practitioners of (a phrase more often associated with the 1990s) "political correctness."[81] There was a new tendency to look askance at universities for being pockets of dissent even as the universities themselves took on the infrastructure of fictive corporations. And yet, in the last two decades of the twentieth century, a four-year college degree still remained a badge of middle-class attainment, so the students kept coming.

Along the way, the southeast started to join East Tennessee as friendly ground for the Republican Party and, accordingly, the UT campus became a popular visit for prominent party members in the 1980s. President Ronald Reagan had visited Knoxville for the 1982 World's Fair without really showing up on campus, but he returned three years later for an appearance at the UT University Center, arranged by his later chief of staff Senator Howard Baker (a UT Law alum) before travelling fifty miles south to Athens, Tennessee, to announce a simplification of the federal tax code.[82] Former president Gerald Ford appeared on campus the following month.[83] Lamar Alexander controversially replaced Edward Boling as UT System president in 1988 amid controversy a year after leaving the governor's office. UTK Students and faculty had protested Boling's appointment nearly two decades earlier because he was not an educator at a time when the UT System was brand new and the distinctions between university chancellor and university *system* president were just coming into being. By the 1980s it was nationally far more common for individuals with no teaching experience whatsoever to take over university helms, and the career politician Alexander fit that trend. Still, as governor, Alexander had appointed almost every single trustee serving on the board at the time he was selected, so there was some suspicion of an unprecedented *quid pro quo* at work.[84] Student governments on both the Knoxville and Martin campuses, protested Alexander's appointment by the board of trustees as a move based more on politics than ability.[85] Administrators disliked Alexander's micromanaging of affairs on the UTK campus, and his hiring of seemingly nonessential vice presidents (a superfluous combination, in the words of business school dean Warren Neel, "one vice president to say where the university was going" and another "to measure progress along the way").[86] Alexander resigned in 1991 to become US Secretary of Education under President George Herbert Walker Bush (who had, notably, visited campus in the winter of 1990) and was replaced by longtime UT vice president Joe Johnson, the first UT System president with classroom experience (earned while working on his EdD at UT in the late 1950s) and a role on campus since the Holt administration. Johnson resisted many of the board of trustees' efforts to continue Alexander's corporate university model that involved adding more levels to the administration (particularly at the vice presidential level).[87] After heading the Department of Education, Alexander remained in the public eye. After two unsuccessful campaigns for the Republican presidential nomination, he was elected in 2002 to the US Senate where he served three terms.[88]

Johnson's years as system president (1991–1999) were remarkable and eventful ones, partly because of the continuing question over the differences and similarities between the missions of UTK and its smaller campuses. At least at the Knoxville campus, one driving theme was the growth of partnerships with the private sector for the sake of innovation and in reaction to shrinking state largesse. In 1993 and 1995 UT firmed deals with Eastman Chemical and SOFTWARE AG, respectively, to exchange the school's research feedback and student labor for the latter's provision of cutting-edge technology and shop-level training on campus for engineers and business students. Chancellor William Snyder sought out such partnerships, calling them a "natural role for the 21st century land-grant university."[89] Although UT remained a public institution, during the 1990s it came to rely more and more on corporations, private equity, and private donations. Probably the most noticeable corporate presence on campus was the 1997 arrival of Aramark, a food services contractor that took over the campus's cafeterias, expanding the variety of foods available on campus while also relieving the university of labor costs for a large chunk of its staff. As the school took steps toward privatization it also played a role in the federal government's slivering of its own operations to private entities. In 2000 UT formed a limited liability company in partnership with Battelle, an Ohio-based nonprofit technology developer, to run Oak Ridge National Laboratories for the Department of Energy.

Late in the 1990s UT initiated a gigantic fundraising project dubbed the "21st Century Campaign," an effort to amass hundreds of millions of dollars from companies and individuals, including staff and faculty who were encouraged to donate via payroll deductions.[90] Demand for higher education had continued to soar since the 1960s while governments began to ease off funding in the 1970s and 1980s. By the 1990s, UT had adopted a business model very different from the virtually cost-free education offered in the first hundred years of land-grant status, and very different from the heavy research funding of the Cold War Keynesian era.[91] And even with support from private entities, tuition began to increase at rates far above the standard of inflation. In the 1992–1993 fiscal year, the UT System garnered 12 percent of its total resources from fees. By the end of 1996 the costs to students were on the rise even as the UT System was undergoing a full-on funding crisis that prompted a campus-wide hiring freeze.[92] "There is a financial crisis in the state of Tennessee," wrote a departing education professor at the end of the century.

Joseph E. Johnson presided over the UT System
as president during the 1990s and briefly as
an interim in the following decade after the
presidency changed hands quickly and the
position of chancellor was temporarily ended.

Higher education has taken the hardest blow—salaries are stagnant, lines are not being filled, and operating budgets are not big enough to cover expenses. The impact of this shortfall reverberates throughout the academic community. Students are hurt by fewer and bigger classes. Professors must put in more hours of work for less pay in real dollars. In this, the premier research institution in the state, the library has had a flat budget for several years. The number of periodicals ordered has been cut every year. At this point there seems to be no hope that this situation will improve in the near future.[93]

Despite lack of funding, Snyder also made the expansion of campus diversity one of his primary goals, a campaign he insisted was necessary not just for ethical reasons but for turning UT into what he termed a "University of Choice" (in an effort to popularize an unofficial university slogan, Snyder included the phrase "University of Choice" in most of his correspondence during his early chancellorship).[94] In spring 1994 he published a position paper that was later turned into a pamphlet extolling the virtues of campus diversity itself, but also its practical importance for being "a university of choice by being value driven, customer oriented, and learning focused":

> You've heard it all before: Powerful technological advances in communications, transportation, and manufacturing have drawn all of us into their vortex. The world is literally at our door. Our livelihoods no longer center on small rural communities of like folk, as they did two-hundred years ago, but rely, instead, on a huge interdependent, multinational community. As new industries move into Tennessee, the population of our state is becoming more diverse—our graduates are competing for jobs, and once they have jobs, competing for business in the world market. Practically speaking, the University's constituents look to us now, more than ever before, for social and economic leadership.[95]

Even though UT did not meet Snyder's goals by the end of his term in office, he established diversity as an ideal that future leaders had to pay homage to even when they did not actively embrace it. And during his time in office, the university did make strides toward the good if not the perfect. In 1994 the Lambda Student Union was founded as a resource for the gay, lesbian, and trans campus community, the fruition of a struggle for recognition that had started more than two decades earlier. In 2006 the university founded an advisory commission for LGBTQ concerns staffed by faculty, staff, and students.

Like most attempts at democratization in the school's history, UT's recognition—even embrace—of LGBTQ people and their lives happened because of student demand and faculty advocacy. But a "customer oriented" university was

Snyder's hint that calls for diversity were means to a commercial end and, for that matter, that UT had finally embraced a commercial identity. Higher education had become, by the 1990s, a commodity to be bought and sold and students were deemed customers. Diversity was a necessary element of a democratic education, but under late-twentieth-century conditions it had also become a shibboleth, and a virtual billboard advertisement. "Although Snyder should be commended for articulating a vision in which diversity should be embraced," anthropologist Faye Harrison wrote in 2008, "his attempt to accommodate diversity within a model of university development oriented toward corporate constituencies and the market values of customer orientation was problematic, to say the least."[96] In Snyder's defense, his neoliberal approach to promoting diversity as an ideal simply reflected the times he and his school lived in. Public universities like UT were under growing scrutiny and criticism for being costly sources of left-leaning propaganda. While conservatives of the early Cold War had tried to root radicalism out of campus, their descendants attacked universities as inherently subversive —the better to justify forced austerity.[97] And, like all UT presidents since before World War II, Snyder was also faced with publicly balancing scholastics with the school's main public ambassador: athletics. Snyder deflected one complaint from a local football fan with a bromide that seemed quaint by the 1990s. "This situation has attracted a lot of publicity. I only wish that those persons who have displayed so much focused passion about the coaching situation would manifest the same passion about the rest of the university, particularly the academic part of the university."[98]

In retrospect, Snyder's wish for a re-focus of passion toward academics seems tender and ingenuous since his years as president marked a new high-water mark for Volunteers football, as well as the team's final transition from scholar athletes to semiprofessional franchise. The complaint in question was the firing of Johnny Majors as head football coach at the end of the 1992 season. Majors had been a popular coach with ten bowl appearances (7–3), three SEC championships in 1985, 1989 (shared with Alabama and Auburn), and 1990, and a 116–62–8 record over the course of sixteen seasons. Majors was let go late in the 1992 season shortly after two losses that followed his midseason convalescence from heart surgery (the losses broke interim coach offensive coordinator Phil Fulmer's 3–0 streak). Majors had previously complained about his contract with UT and had even told a *Knoxville News Sentinel* reporter that he had spent his happiest years coaching at the University of Pittsburgh before returning to UT right after a national championship season. His firing by athletic director Doug Dickey and the eventual offer extended to Fulmer to replace him, came as little surprise but much outrage from fans with or without connections to the university. In his capacity as chancellor, William Snyder received a handful of letters complaining of Majors's dismissal, a decision chancellors of the day had little hand in (in fact it was likely that UT System president Joe Johnson was more involved in the decision to replace Majors with Fulmer).[99]

The Fulmer years, especially the first six seasons, were a storied period in the history of UT football, punctuated by the first national championship in a generation, won at the 1998 Fiesta Bowl. Fulmer began just as the Southeastern Conference expanded from ten to twelve member schools and divided into eastern and western divisions. Between 1997 and 2007 Fulmer coached the Volunteers to five eastern division championships and two consecutive conference titles in 1997 and 1998. Fulmer coached ten wins over traditional rival University of Alabama (as well as the last-ever tie between the two teams in 1993) and five victories over Florida, which had become Tennessee's primary division rival since the formation of the SEC-East. During the 1990s two UT quarterbacks, Heath Shuler and Peyton Manning, were runners-up for the Heisman Trophy, an accolade never earned by the program (Majors had been a runner-up in 1956). Manning earned more than eleven thousand yards of total offense before going on to a long and successful professional career with the Indianapolis Colts and Denver Broncos.[100] Manning's successor Tee Martin led the Volunteers to a national championship at the end of the 1998 season, their first since 1967 and the first with a head coach who was a former Volunteer player (Fulmer had played offensive guard between 1968 and 1971 under coaches Doug Dickey and Bill Battle). Demand for tickets caused UT to increase seating at Neyland Stadium to over 104,000 seats by 2000.[101] Tennessee football's national profile was higher than ever, and not only because of talent that equaled past teams. Nineteen Ninety-Eight was UT's first championship season in the Information Age, and the exposure paid to Fulmer's teams surpassed those of Neyland's and Dickey's because of cable sports television and a new communication utility called the "world wide web." But Fulmer's organization simultaneously hearkened back to a time when collegiate football was more local; when Fulmer was dismissed in 2008 he was the last coach in the SEC working in his home state and coaching the team for whom he had once played.[102]

It was also an era of college sports scandals, many of them involving grade inflation and fraud. Universities had been accused of fudging academics and taking money under the table for the sake of sports, especially football, since early in the twentieth century. But the NCAA became more vigilant in the last third of the century, leading to various infractions, fines, suspensions, and dismissals

With a series of star players, coach Phil Fulmer took Vols football
to new heights in the 1990s including the team's first national
championship of the cable television and digital media era.

in the SEC and other major conferences. NCAA sanctions in the SEC often
came soon after marked gridiron success, as when the University of Florida was
forced to vacate its 1984 conference title. In the 1980s and 1990s most scandals
involved money changing hands with team boosters and illegal recruitment
practices, infractions that highlighted how distant college sports had become from
academics by hardly ever involving scholastics in any direct way.[103] And yet the

NCAA mandated academic standards for athletes to maintain some semblance of the old scholar-athlete ideal and the officially amateur nature of college sports. The sacrosanct ideal was in direct paradox to the commercial realities of the day when even public sector entities were expected to act as profit-based competitors. Those who complained ran the risk of sounding naïve or behind the times.

In the 1980s and 1990s UT had remained relatively untouched by sports scandal compared to many other SEC schools, and Lamar Alexander's membership in the Knight Foundation on Intercollegiate Reform, an independent oversight committee on reforming college athletics, seemed to confirm UT's transcendence.[104] But this changed briefly after the national championship. In 1997 English professor Linda Bensel-Meyers sent a document to the faculty senate reporting papers submitted by athletes she believed to be "either co-written or entirely written" by tutors under the employ of the UT athletic department.[105] Four freshman football players were suspended from playing at the beginning of the 1999 season after Bensel-Meyers shared her findings with sports cable network ESPN (who reported on it a week before UT's opening game).[106] Eventually records that revealed 105 grade changes for 29 athletes between 1995 and 1999 were released, including two students who received eleven grade changes each.[107] The accusations led to an uproar on campus and division among the faculty. After the investigation closed, UT released the transcripts along with a report detailing Bensel-Meyers's accusations to UT's faculty senate.[108] J. Wade Gilley, Joe Johnson's successor as UT System president, denied any wrongdoing, and wrote her accusations off as products of a "big pregnant idea" calculated to deemphasize sports on the campus.[109] Bensel-Meyers reported harassment from UT employees and students, death threats, and the burglary of her office in McClung Tower.[110] She reported feeling unsafe in her home, and her husband was fired from his local job as a private-sector environmental auditor. The family eventually relocated to Colorado after her resignation from UT in 2003 (two years after Gilley resigned, citing health issues).[111] Bensel-Meyers later cofounded the National Alliance for College Athletic Reform (later renamed the Drake Group), an organization dedicated to monitoring the effects of college athletics on institutional integrity.[112] Four years after leaving Tennessee she told *The Nation* that her experience at UT reflected a larger problem in higher education: "The values of a commercialized and professionalized playing field, not the values of the university, have become dominant. They become our national values. Might makes right. Scapegoat women. Win at any cost."[113] The basis for the scandal was of a very different sort than the revelation (and subsequent cover-up) of Robert Neyland's slush fund in the 1950s. The latter suggested that money was changing hands in ways that violated the amateur sanctity of the "student athlete" ideal, an ideal that dominated Olympic and college sports for most of the twentieth century. It did not suggest what Bensel-Meyers's accusation did decades later, that campus athletics was directly impugning the university's mission of providing an education to all of its enrolled students. Plus, in an era of electronic media saturation, the revelation meant that the university, more than the coaches, administrators, and tutors, were indicted in the court of public opinion. Bensel-Meyers's exposé did not lead to tremendous reforms or a revitalization of the old scholar-athlete ideal. Tutor services for athletes were transferred from the athletic department to the provost's office, and the university threw up new barriers between faculty and student transcripts after it was cleared by an NCAA inquiry.[114] In 2016, when UT athletics was again the subject of a sexual harassment lawsuit by six women (which the university settled with a $2.48 million payment to the plaintiffs), Bensel-Meyers was scarcely remembered on campus, while athletic boosterism prevailed in the local press.[115]

UT began the 1970s with a new attention to equality between the sexes, partly due to the activism of faculty and students, but also because of the sheer talent and leadership ability of women like Pat Head Summitt. But the university concluded the twentieth century with a reminder that much improvement was still needed. The scandal ended inconclusively, but still laid bare one of the primary paradoxes of university life at the end of the twentieth century. Academic integrity has been sacrificed for sports victories since the pre-World War II days of "booster schools," even as public higher education became more and more accessible to a large segment of the American population. And, irrespective of the commercialization of college athletics, UT and many of its peers came to embrace diversity as an organizational ideal and a selling point. No measure of diversity training or other positive measures could prevent a woman professor from being ostracized and harassed for blowing a whistle on UT's failure to fulfill its mission for all of its students. As always, the school had a long way to go to live up to its own expectations.

Bensel-Meyer's exposé was playing out at the same time as a massive administrative restructuring that was meant to cut costs for the entire UT System and increase the Knoxville campus's prospects as a research-based destination.[116] President Gilley initiated a plan to streamline authority within the Knoxville campus while giving the Martin and Chattanooga campuses more autonomy. Aside from eliminating many vice presidencies, the plan also did away with the office of chancellor after William Snyder's departure and, in one observer's phrasing, change UT's "moral focus." Further, it would give Gilley and all later system presidents a secondary title as "chief executive officer"[117] But Gilley's ideas (which some observers considered good aims but poor execution) did not last long after his 2001 resignation. In less than four years the chancellor position was reestablished and tuition and fees raised (still in search of recovery for a budgetary shortfall that dated back to at least 1995).[118]

Like many American universities, UT began the twenty-first century under a cloud of uncertainty. A century earlier, Charles Dabney had provided the school with a new mission and pointed the school in a direction that led it from parochial land-grant to research university status, but only for white, mostly upper-class students. One hundred years later, the school was officially open to all, regardless of race, sex, sexual orientation, but tuitions and fees were always on the rise, and a college education was not the guarantor of success after graduation that it once had been, even for star athletes (fears circulating of a "Y2K" global computer crash in 2000 were answered not with technological failure but instead a burst "tech bubble" in which many graduates lost tech-based jobs advertised during the late 1990s). UT continued to attract talented students and educators in the new century. But like many similar universities, the school's expectations for the future—and its accompanying search for growth—were checked slightly. Even the capacity of Neyland Stadium (hardly a metric for UT's general health, but symbolic nonetheless at a school that had dedicated so much of its public identity to football) was reduced by nearly two thousand seats from its all-time maximum of just over 104,000 between 2004 and 2010.[119] It was not a moment of existential danger like earlier iterations of the school experienced in the early republic and the Civil War era. It was, however, a glum way to begin a new millennium.

The next few years were a frenzy at the administrative level. Gilley's successor John Shumaker was hired away from the University of Louisville in 2002 with a salary exceeding $700,000, the second highest of any public university president in the country at the time, in a process noted for being hurried and secretive.[120] Within months, Shumaker came under fire for questionable no-bid contracts to acquaintances, personal use of a UT airplane, and spending over a half-million dollars for renovations and parties at the UT president's house. An audit found his explanations "untruthful," and he resigned at the beginning of the 2003 school year.[121] After the chancellorship was reestablished in 2003, Loren Crabtree ran the Knoxville campus for nearly five years before conflicts with UT System president John Petersen led to his resignation. Petersen wanted to disperse resources to the other campuses of the UT System, while Crabtree resisted his attempts at levelling control centered on jurisdiction of university property just across the Tennessee River from the Knoxville campus. Eleven months later, in February

2009, Petersen announced his own resignation after a non-formal vote of no confidence from the faculty senate amid a system-wide budget crunch worsened by an immense national recession.[122]

The arrival of Jimmy Cheek as chancellor in 2009 and Joe DiPietro as president in early 2011 marked a return to some measure of stability and a sustained return to an understanding between the respective functions of campus chancellor and system president. Cheek was a vice president at the University of Florida at the time of his hire, while DiPietro was recruited from the UT College of Veterinary Science. "The UT family hopes [DiPietro's] ascension will end a period of turmoil," wrote a *Knoxville News Sentinel* editorial in 2010, noting the revolving door of "three presidents with no ties to UT and two in-house caretakers" that had filled the office since Johnson's resignation in 1999, as well as the state's recent budget slashing. The board of trustees' search for the replacement had been a public matter (especially in contrast to recent presidential hires), and it was suspected that some candidates had been scared off by the publicity.[123] DiPietro ended up having the longest presidency since Joseph Johnson, while Cheek held his office longer than every chancellor since Jack Reese.

DiPietro's and Cheek's challenges centered on a continuance of state budget-ary conservatism that UT had dealt with in some form or another since 1970s. In 2001, a tax protest orchestrated by Nashville talk radio personalities prevented

UT chancellor Jimmy Cheek served in the office for most of a decade, bringing a measure of stability after a tumultuous start (and a rapid series of leadership changes) to the twenty-first century at UT.

creation of a proposed state income tax. A state income tax blockage amendment has since been added to the state constitution. A few years later Democratic governor Phil Bredesen signed a bill from a Republican-majority General Assembly that tied university budgets to graduation rates, a metric that did not always favor four-year universities. Shortly after Cheek took office, and just before DiPietro, *US News and World Report* placed UT 104th among "national universities, significantly below neighbors like the Universities of Florida (53rd), Georgia (56th) and even Alabama (79th). Soon after taking office Cheek announced a campaign to propel UT into the "Top 25," an effort that bore fruit in fundraising within five years.[124] By 2019 the same magazine had been ranking UT in the top fifty among public universities for a number of years, after the school had increased in total enrollment past 29,000 for the first time since late in the last century.[125] Amongst a countless number of changes, there was some sign of success.

But the early years of the twenty-first century were also defined by a concurrent ideological distrust of universities in general among segments of the taxpaying population. Since the nineteenth century UT had been subject to political disputes, typically between opponents who differed on matters of expense and execution but who at least agreed on the value of public higher education itself. But in the new century, the very existence of higher education was under attack for ideological reasons. "Recently I have seen too many children sent to schools and universities by parents with traditional patriotic values," wrote one self-described 1962 UT graduate responding to the *News Sentinel*'s announcement of DiPietro's election. "The children turn out to be socialists with communistic view points and being brain washed by the liberal leftist professors in our schools and universities. Does government money mean more than our Republic? I am a potential donor, but not as long as this kind of destructiveness takes place in our shcools [*sic*]."[126]

The accusations were unfounded. Under DiPietro and Cheek, the UT administration was no more inclined toward "communistic viewpoints" than had been past leaders like Edward Boling and Andy Holt. On the contrary, in the first decade of the twenty-first century UT and other state campuses were under far greater sway from capitalist institutions than they ever had been before, and calls for further strides toward privatization and corporate partnership were louder than ever before. The very geography of the city blocks surrounding the UT campus changed drastically in the twenty-first century, reflecting a movement away from small business and toward massive student-targeted real estate. The stretch of campus-adjacent Cumberland Avenue called The Strip was radically changed between 2013 and 2019 to make the area more pedestrian friendly. The same was done for a long stretch of Volunteer Boulevard on the southwest side of campus near the Norfolk & Southern railyard. And yet UT students are probably more wedded to automobile travel than ever. Many drive daily from other parts of Knoxville or surrounding counties, while even some who live on campus drive around in expensive Brobdingnagian pickup trucks. Capitalism, in the form of school-days consumerism, is more than safe. Indeed, while UT students of the late twentieth century expressed a fashionable sense of semi-ironic alienation from the drudgery of organized education, twenty-first century students often express their role as customers.

It is easy to understand how current students might view themselves as participants in an economic exchange. Changes in policy and the American economy had seen to it that UT was not the publicly guaranteed affordable opportunity it had been in the days of Boling and Holt when students first started singing about an uncomplicated precapitalist past in a mythical place called Rocky Top. But UT had undergone concurrent changes since the 1970s, both institutional and cultural, that made it a public symbol of diversity and inclusiveness, traits that a core of white conservatives felt ran counter to "traditional patriotic values." Even if the symbol was occasionally more reputation than reality, it could only mean a better future. And yet, when it comes to the cost of education in real dollars, students have cause to yearn for some elements of the past.

Epilogue:
UT in the Twenty-First Century

"When everyone in the classroom, teacher and students, recognizes
that they are responsible for creating a learning community together,
learning is at its most meaningful and useful."

—bell hooks—
Teaching Critical Thinking: Practical Wisdom (2013)

"I think the responsibility of a university is to be thinking ahead
and sort of helping to set the pace for civilization. If universities are
blessed with so many thinking people as they are supposed to have,
they have a responsibility to be thinking ahead. That means
finding better ways to do things, developing new ideas,
then inspiring others to join in the thinking ahead."

—ANDY HOLT—
Going Fishing (1981)

In the middle of spring semester 2020, the University of Tennessee was con-
fronted with a strange, uncompromising challenge in the form of the "novel
COVID 19" virus, a potentially fatal illness that was well on its way to global
pandemic status before many students had begun studying for midterms. Classes
were hurriedly moved to remote electronic communications for the weeks of the
semester remaining after spring break. Faculty scrambled to adjust to new conditions and learn new skills that would enable them to teach from home (226 years
earlier Blount College began in a domestic environment when Reverend Samuel
Carrick began teaching in his parsonage). Campus staff either moved their tasks
off campus or continued doing vitally important work in maintenance, house-
keeping, and student services under circumstances that were suddenly hazardous
and life threatening. Students, most of whom had grown up with the internet

ever-present, responded to their sudden on-screen learning environment with aplomb, some of them juggling "essential" jobs in hospitals and grocery stores with their class work. When the fall semester began the following August, most classes were being held via remote learning, and the usual hustle and bustle of fall semester on the UT campus was missing—even with the controversial decision to allow a modified football season with distanced seating at Neyland Stadium (and, later, in Thompson-Boling Arena for the basketball season). The ensuing school year was a struggle to regain a modicum of curricular regularity and the twenty-first century college experience under conditions where everyone involved was maintaining "social distancing" from teachers, students, coworkers, and loved ones. It was, to say the least, difficult.

The events of 2020 suggest an uncertain future for higher education, but on the UT campus the sudden sea change was also a strange climax to a tumultuous twenty-year period. A look backward to the first fifth of the twenty-first century suggests a state of barely controlled chaos, a pressure cooker leaking steam. Since 2008, UT has had six chancellors and four system presidents (both these numbers include interims), not to mention a similar rate of turnover for the more visible positions in the athletic department (all of which get more regular press attention than the administration).[1] In 2016 the Tennessee state legislature defunded UT's Office of Diversity and threatened the annual student-run "Sex Week" event that had gained national attention on cable news a few years earlier.[2] The university relies more and more on nontenured and contingent faculty, and a reference to "de-tenure" in a 2015 board of trustees meeting raised alarms among faculty that tenure itself might have an endangered future.[3] Despite student and faculty protests, a 2018 "UT Focus Act" suggested greater state control over the UT System by decreasing the board from twenty-seven members down to eleven.[4] The state of the university feels tenuous, especially after one Tennessee legislator, Republican Kerry Roberts, mused on a radio show about eliminating public funding for higher education altogether in order to do away with what he called a "liberal breeding ground."[5]

The only parts of UT's history that seem anywhere near as tenuous are, well, the majority of the two centuries that came before. The school spent decades in the nineteenth century hanging from a proverbial spiderweb because of financial instability. After that, it was more a matter of a hectic search for identity with thousands of discordant tongues shouting out their own stories as to what a university should be, as well as what a university should be *in Tennessee*. Although UT is now a robust university, financial concerns remain—perhaps more for students than for the university itself. When looked at as a whole cloth, the decades of Keynesian comfort between World War II and the 1980s were the exception, while instability has been the rule for most of the span of UT's history.

Most of that instability has been caused by power struggles. The university is still, in the words of historian Johann Neem, the "critical conscience of a democratic society," and politics is the necessary consequence of democracy.[6] Public education necessitates that schooling be subject to the vicissitudes of politics, and UT has always had a peculiar relationship with politics and politicians. There were few institutional threats to academic freedom in 1800 because academia was a rare thing, affordable or desirable to a small segment of the population. That began to change once the United States slowly started to democratize, and the school that would become UT had to learn to manifestat democracy rather than serve as a barrier to it. After surviving a civil war, UT moved slowly toward becoming a vehicle of democracy, first through the intrigues of politicians and later via the hard work of activists. In the 20th and 21st centuries there were plenty, most coming from TN government. It would be better for public education to remain a public good, but also intellectually free from the vicissitudes of politics and the regime de jour. But in an age when public education is vilified as "government schools," public institutions like the University of Tennessee may have their greatest challenges ahead of them rather than behind.

A review essay on *To Foster Knowledge* published in 1986 noted that the book "does not end with the triumphant emergence of a leading university. Rather it ends with a yawn. The authors tell us that the University of Tennessee is after all in Tennessee, so what could one expect?"[7] It was a fair assessment. The book ended on a vague note with apparent derision for UT's students and lack of inspiration for the school's mission. The old book's dour take on its subject belies the fact that academia was relatively healthy at the time it came out, while now it is under attack, and professors cannot afford to hold their students or their institutions in contempt. My assessment of UT's recent history is more optimistic than that of the authors of *To Foster Knowledge*—because it needs to be. The only way to save public higher education from anti-education politics is to have a durable optimism of the will among educators despite their necessary pessimism of the intellect. Before, during, or after his presidency, Andy Holt's hopeful wish that his university always have many thinking people busy inspiring others has never been granted easily. "If universities are blessed with so many thinking people as they are supposed to have, they have a responsibility to be thinking ahead. That means finding better ways to do things, developing new ideas, then inspiring others to join in the thinking ahead."[8] Even on a campus with conservative leadership, conservative oversight, and corporate-minded strategies, new ideas are bound to rise to attention unless they are actively killed by revanchist politicians. At UT, public education continues that struggle.

NOTES

· ·

ABBREVIATIONS

BWP   William Bruce Wheeler Papers
ETC   East Tennessee College
ETHS   East Tennessee Historical Society
ETU   East Tennessee University
OUHC   Office of the University Historian Collection
UTSC   University of Tennessee Special Collections
UT   University of Tennessee

INTRODUCTION

1. "All Tennessee, as was Gaul, 'is divided into three parts.' In the parlance of her people the three parts are designated as 'East Tennessee,' 'Middle Tennessee' and 'West Tennessee.' They are recognized by her constitution and laws, and, in many respects, her oneness embraces the mystery of a trinity. No other State of the Union has such a peculiarity. It is a vestige of her peculiar development into statehood, and by it much of her history may be read and better understood. It has bred a sectional State pride among her people, which the sweep of a century has tended to deepen rather than efface." William A. Henderson, *East Tennessee: Historical and Biographical* (Chattanooga: A.D. Smith, 1893), 17.

2. John S. Whitehead, "Southern Universities: Are They Rising?" *History of Education Quarterly* 26, no. 4 (Winter 1986): 553–568.

3. James R. Montgomery, Stanley J. Folmsbee, and Lee S. Greene, *To Foster Knowledge: A History of the University of Tennessee, 1794–1970* (Knoxville: University of Tennessee [hereafter UT] Press, 1983), 392–407, 451.

4. Ibid., 366.

1. SLENDER BEGINNINGS, 1790–1860

1. The "Lost State of Franklin" existed in some legislative form from 1784 till 1787; John R. Finger, *Tennessee Frontiers: Three Regions in Transition* (Bloomington: Indiana University Press, 2001), 125–28, 208–9, 227; Kevin Barksdale, *The Lost State of Franklin: America's First Secession* (University Press of Kentucky, 2009), 22, 34, 58–71, 83–84, 130, 145–61, 241n11.

2. John R. Thelin, *A History of American Higher Education* (Baltimore: Johns Hopkins University Press, 2004), 46–47.

3. *Early History of the University of Tennessee: Address Before the Alumni Association* (Knoxville: University of Tennessee Board of Trustees, 1879), 23–29, in Moses White Papers, Box 1, Folder 3, University of Tennessee Special Collections (hereafter UTSC); Neal O'Steen, "Pioneer Education in the Tennessee Country," *Tennessee Historical Quarterly* 35, no. 2 (Summer 1976): 213q; Nathan O. Hatch, *The Democratization of American Christianity* (New Haven: Yale University Press, 1989), 30, 79; George M. Marsden, *The Soul of the American University: From Protestant Establishment to Established Nonbelief* (Oxford: Oxford University Press, 1994), 69; Colin G. Calloway, *The American Revolution in Indian Country: Crisis and Diversity in Native American Communities* (Cambridge: Cambridge University Press, 1995), 200–212; East Tennessee Historical Society (hereafter ETHS), *First Families of Tennessee: A Register of Early Settlers and Their Present-Day Descendants* (Knoxville: ETHS, 2000), 25–27; Cameron Addis, *Jefferson's Vision for Education: 1760–1845* (New York: Lang, 2003), 66. Richard Hofstadter and Walter Metzger, *The Development of Academic Freedom in the United States* (New York: Columbia University Press, 1955), 243. Hofstadter included Blount College among a small number of future state universities "launched before the tide of Enlightenment thought had receded and in advance of the establishment of the denominational schools," and aided "by the guidance of the declining generation of liberal aristocrats."

4. Edward T. Sanford, *Blount College and the University of Tennessee: An Historical Address Delivered Before the Alumni Association and Members of the University of Tennessee, by Edward T. Sanford, A. M., June 12th, 1894* (Knoxville: University of Tennessee, 1895), 16q, 101–5; Freeman Hansford Hart, *The Valley of Virginia in the American Revolution, 1763–1789* (Chapel Hill: University of North Carolina Press, 1942), 141; William MacArthur, *Knoxville, Crossroads of the New South* (Tulsa: Continental Heritage Press, 1982), 1–15; Theda Perdue, *Cherokee Women: Gender and Culture Change, 1700–1835* (Lincoln: University of Nebraska Press, 1998), 74, 91, 109–13; Barksdale, *Lost State of Franklin*, 117; Richard Gildrie, "Tennessee in the American Revolution: A Reconsideration," in *Before the Volunteer State: New Thoughts on Early Tennessee, 1540–1800*, ed. Kristofer Ray (Knoxville: University of Tennessee Press, 2014), 118–24; Finger, *Tennessee Frontiers*, 117–20.

5. James G. Leyburn, *The Scotch-Irish: A Social History* (Chapel Hill: University of North Carolina Press, 1962), 285q–86.

6. "Notes from the History of Knoxville," Hoskins Collection (Addendum) AR-76, Box 1, Folder 5, UTSC; First Board of Trustees Minutes, East Tennessee College (hereafter ETC), April 7, 1808–March 5, 1849, 1, UTSC; *Early History, of the University of Tennessee*, 31–34; Fletcher M. Green, *The Role of the Yankee in the Old South* (Athens: University of Georgia Press, 1972), 48.

7. Hofstadter and Metzger, *Development of Academic Freedom*, 229.

8. Daniel Dorchester, *Christianity in the United States from the First Settlements down to the Present Time* (New York: Hunt & Eaton, 1889), 294–95; John Edminston Alexander, *Brief History of the Synod of Tennessee, from 1817 to 1887* (Philadelphia: MacCalla, 1890), 92; Sanford, *Blount College and the University of Tennessee*, 11, 14, 16, 21–23, 39; *The Scotch-Irish in America: Proceedings of the Scotch-Irish Congress* (Nashville: Barbee & Smith, 1895), 7:101–5; Charles Sydnor, *The Development of Southern Sectionalism: 1819–1848* (Baton Rouge: Louisiana State University Press, 1966), 65, 66; O'Steen, "Pioneer Education in the Tennessee Country," 200, 206, 207, 210–11, 212, 213, 216; James Patrick, *Architecture in Tennessee, 1768–1897* (Knoxville: University of Tennessee Press, 1981), 50–51q; Joe L. Kincheloe, "The Battle for the Antebellum Southern Colleges: The Evangelicals vs. the Calvinists in Tennessee," *Journal of Thought* 18, no. 3 (Fall 1983): 124–25; Walter T. Durham, *Before Tennessee: The Southwest Territory, 1790–1796: A Narrative History of the Territory of the United States South of the River Ohio* (Piney Flats, TN: Rocky Mount Historical Association, 1990), 242; Ira Read, "The Church College in Central Appalachia," in *Christianity in Appalachia: Profiles in Regional Pluralism*, ed. Bill J. Leonard (Knoxville: University of Tennessee Press, 1999), 75; Craig Steven Wilder, *Ebony & Ivy: Race, Slavery, and the Troubled History of American Universities* (New York: Bloomsbury Press, 2013), 102–10; Montgomery, Folmsbee, and Greene, *To Foster Knowledge*, 10–11, 13–14.

9. "Admission of Women," Hoskins Collection (Addendum) AR-76, Box 1, Folder 3, UTSC.

10. Thelin, *History of American Higher Education*, 97.

11. Carrick's tacit admission of female students contrasts starkly with schools that opened in the South later, but it is not necessarily without parallel in the three decades that followed the American Revolution. In schools where missionaries (many of them Presbyterian like Carrick) taught Cherokee children, boys outnumbered girls considerably, but education of girls was nonetheless common. In the decades after Indian removal from Tennessee and other Southern states, white society became stratified for the purpose of maintaining subservience from Black Americans, a process that also discouraged formal education for girls and women. *Early History of the University of Tennessee*, 55, Moses White Papers, Box 1, Folder 3, UTSC; "Admission of Women"; Amy Thompson McCandless, "Maintaining the Spirit and Tone of Robust Manliness: The Battle against Coeducation at Southern Colleges and Universities, 1890–1940," *National Women's Studies Association Journal* 2, Issue 2 (Spring 1990): 199–216; Linda K. Kerber, *Toward an Intellectual History of Women* (Chapel Hill: University of North Carolina Press, 1997), 230–32; Christine D. Myers, *University*

Coeducation in the Victorian Era: Inclusion in the United States and the United Kingdom (New York: Palgrave MacMillan, 2010), 21–22; Sanford, *Blount College and the University of Tennessee*, 23; Montgomery, Folmsbee, and Greene, *To Foster Knowledge*, 12–13, 88q; Perdue, *Cherokee Women*, 172–74.

   For the Barbara Blount Literary Society, see Lizzie Williams and Annie McKinney to UT President and Board of Trustees, June 12, 1894, Humes and Dabney Papers, Box 1, Folder 14, UTSC.

12. Sanford, *Blount College and the University of Tennessee*, 20, 21.

13. Durwood Dunn, *Cades Cove: The Life and Death of a Southern Appalachian Community, 1818–1937* (Knoxville: University of Tennessee Press, 1988), 84–85, 125.

14. First Board of Trustees Minutes, East Tennessee College, April 7, 1808–March 5, 1849, p. 1, UTSC; Moses White, *Early History of the University of Tennessee: Address Before the Alumni Association* (Knoxville: University of Tennessee Board of Trustees, 1879), 22, 63–65, Moses White Papers, Box 1 Folder 3, University of Tennessee Special Collections, Hodges Library, Knoxville, TN (hereafter UTSC); James Edmonds Saunders, *Early Settlers of Alabama, Part 1* (New Orleans: L. Graham & Son, 1899), 283; *Annual Report of the State Superintendent of Public Instruction for Tennessee* (Nashville: Foster & Webb, 1899), 216–19; Rachel Caroline Eaton, *John Ross and the Cherokee Indians* (Menasha, WI: George Banta, 1914), 47; Kate White, "Knoxville's Old Educational Institutions," *Tennessee Historical Magazine* 8, no. 1 (April 1924): 3; Jonathan M. Atkins, *Parties, Politics, and the Sectional Conflict in Tennessee, 1832–1861* (Knoxville: University of Tennessee Press, 1997), 26–54; Lormen Ratner, *Andrew Jackson and His Tennessee Lieutenants: A Study in Political Culture* (Westport, CT: Greenwood Press, 1997), 73–82; Sean Wilentz, *The Rise of American Democracy: Jefferson to Lincoln* (New York: W. W. Norton, 2005), 448–49, 451, 453; Anna Rosina Gambold and John Gambold, *The Moravian Springplace Mission to the Cherokees: 1814–1821* (Lincoln: University of Nebraska Press, 2007), 524n7; Walter Brownlow Posey, *Frontier Mission: A History of Religion West of the Southern Appalachians to 1861* (Lexington: University Press of Kentucky, 1966), 163–64, 267; Montgomery, Folmsbee, and Greene, *To Foster Knowledge*, 11, 18–19. Regardless of its official name, ETC was already referred to as "the University of Tennessee," at least among alumni living in Alabama; see *Alabama State Intelligencer* (Tuscaloosa), February 9, 1831.

15. Entry, January 17, 1852, First Board of Trustees Minutes, ETC, May 15, 1849–February 13, 1877, 39–40; First Board of Trustees Minutes, April 7, 1808–March 5, 1849, 51, 53–54, 64–65, 76–77, 81–82, 112–21, UTSC; Donald Ratcliffe, "The Right to Vote and the Rise of Democracy, 1787–1828," *Journal of the Early Republic* 33 (Summer 2013): 237; Montgomery, Folmsbee, and Greene, pp. 19–20; *Annual Report of the State Superintendent of Public Instruction for Tennessee*, p. 217

   For white Southern squatters on Cherokee land or Tennessee land in the early republic, see Malcolm J. Rohrbaugh, *The Land Office Business: The Settlement and Administration of American Public Lands* (New York: Oxford University Press, 1968), 32, 118; Keri Leigh Merritt, *Masterless Men: Poor Whites and Slavery in the Antebellum South*

(New York: Cambridge University Press, 2017): 43–45; Finger, *Tennessee Frontiers*, 128, 161–62, 203, 253–56, 269–70; Wilder, *Ebony & Ivy*, 137–38.

16. Stanley F. Horn, "Thomas Jefferson on Lotteries and Education," *Tennessee Historical Quarterly* 3, no. 3 (September 1944): 273–74; Neal O'Steen, "The University of Tennessee: Evolution of a Campus," *Tennessee Historical Quarterly* 39, no. 3 (Fall 1980): 259.

17. Jefferson continued: "These separate buildings, too, might be erected successively and occasionally, as the number of professorships and students should be increased, or the funds become competent. I pray you to pardon me if I have stepped aside into the province of counsel; but much observation and reflection on these institutions have long convinced me that the large and crowded buildings in which youths are pent up, are equally unfriendly to health, to study, to manners, morals and order; and, believing the plan I suggest to be more promotive of these, and peculiarly adapted to the slender beginnings and progressive growth of our institutions, I hoped you would pardon the presumption, in consideration of the motive which was suggested by the difficulty expressed in your letter, of procuring funds for erecting the building. But, on whatever plan you proceed, I wish it every possible success, and to yourselves the reward of esteem, respect and gratitude due to those who devote their time and efforts to render the youths of every successive age fit governors for the next." Thomas Jefferson to Hugh White et al., May 6, 1810, Miscellaneous Files 1688–1951, Box 7, Item J-84, Tennessee Historical Society, Nashville, TN. Despite his earlier personal rejection of lotteries, Jefferson and his family attempted a similar plan in order to settle his debts shortly before his death in 1826.

18. Wilder, *Ebony & Ivy*, 137–38.

19. Thomas Jefferson to Hugh White et al., May 6, 1810, THS.

20. David C. Hsiung, *Two Worlds in the Tennessee Mountains: Exploring the Origins of Appalachian Stereotypes* (Lexington: University Press of Kentucky, 1997), 92–93.

21. *First Board of Trustees Minutes, East Tennessee College, April 7, 1808–March 5, 1849,* 8, UTSC; "East Tennessee Journalism: Address of Col. Moses White at the Recent Meeting of the Tennessee Press Association" (1877?), 10, Moses White Papers, Box 1, Folder 2, UTSC; J. W. Caldwell, "History of Knoxville, Tennessee," in *East Tennessee, Historical and Biographical* (Chattanooga: A. D. Smith, 1893), 468–69; Finger, *Tennessee Frontiers*, 200–201, 226–28.

22. *First Board of Trustees Minutes, East Tennessee College, April 7, 1808–March 5, 1849,* 37, 146, UTSC; "East Tennessee Journalism: Address of Col. Moses White at the Recent Meeting of the Tennessee Press Association" (1877?), 6–7, Moses White Papers, Box 1, Folder 2, UTSC.

23. *First Board of Trustees Minutes, East Tennessee College, April 7, 1808–March 5, 1849,* 84–87, UTSC; Kate White, "Knoxville's Old Educational Institutions," *Tennessee Historical Magazine* 8, no. 1 (April 1924): 6; O'Steen, "The University of Tennessee: Evolution of a Campus," 259–60; Patrick, *Architecture in Tennessee*, 99–100.

24. Atkins, *Parties, Politics, and Sectional Conflict*, 26–55; Wilentz, *Rise of American Democracy*, 218–329.

25. Ratner, *Andrew Jackson and His Tennessee Lieutenants*, 73–82; Craig Brashear, "The Market Revolution and Party Preference in East Tennessee: Spatial Patterns of Partisanship in the 1840 Presidential Election," *Appalachian Journal* 25, no. 1 (Fall 1997): 8–29.

26. First Board of Trustees Minutes, East Tennessee College, April 7, 1808–March 5, 1849, 13, 45, UTSC.

27. Clipping, "Old College," Office of the University Historian Collection (hereafter OUHC), AR.0015, Box 15, Folder 12, UTSC; Moses White to Pryor Lea, April 27, 1879, Moses White Papers (Correspondences), Box 1, Folder 1, UTSC; Moses White, *Early History of the University of Tennessee: Address Before the Alumni Association* (Knoxville: University of Tennessee Board of Trustees, 1879), 131–43, 132–33q, 135q, Moses White Papers, Box 1, Folder 3, UTSC; White, 27; Montgomery, Folmsbee, and Greene, 29–30. Congressman David "Davy" Crockett levelled a similar complaint against another land-beneficiary school in Nashville; Richard Hofstadter, *Anti-Intellectualism in American Life* (New York: Vintage, 1966), 162–64; Scott Gelber, *The University and the People: Envisioning American Higher Education in an Era of Populist Protest* (Madison: University of Wisconsin Press, 2011), 20.

28. First Board of Trustees Minutes, *East Tennessee College*, April 7, 1808–March 5, 1849, 137, UTSC.

29. *Alabama State Intelligencer* (Tuscaloosa), February 9, 1831.

30. *First Board of Trustees Minutes, East Tennessee College*, April 7, 1808–March 5, 1849, 210, 221–23, 224–26, 237, 241–42, 243–44, 252, 253–54, 255, UTSC.

31. Statute laws of the State of Tennessee of a general character: passed since the compilation of the statutes by Caruthers and Nicholson in 1836 : and being a supplement to that work, 1847–1848, (Nashville: James G. Shepard, 1848), 21–22; Moses White, *Early History of the University of Tennessee: Address Before the Alumni Association* (Knoxville: University of Tennessee Board of Trustees, 1879), 145–49; Moses White Papers, Box 1, Folder 3, UTSC; Sanford, *Blount College and the University of Tennessee*, 59–61; Finger, *Tennessee Frontiers*, 306–313.

32. First Board of Trustees Minutes, East Tennessee College, April 7, 1808–March 5, 1849, 170, UTSC; *Fifteenth Annual Report of the Directors of the American Education Society* (Boston: Perkins & Marvin, 1831), 76; Fletcher M. Green, *The Role of the Yankee in the Old South* (Athens: University of Georgia, 1972), 48; Montgomery, Folmsbee, and Greene, *To Foster Knowledge*, 38q.

33. First Board of Trustees Minutes, East Tennessee College, April 7, 1808–March 5, 1849, 103, 139, 145, 159–65, 167, UTSC; Edwin Mims, *The South in the Building of the Nation: History of the Literary and Intellectual Life* (1909; repr. Gretna, LA: Pelican, 2002), 303. The native New Englander seemed to have been a supporter of Andrew Jackson by the midpoint of the latter's presidency, but a critical one. In an 1835 letter to a relative he complained of Jackson's selection of Martin Van Buren over former ETC trustee Hugh Lawson White, and complained that Jackson had spoiled his previous popularity in Tennessee; Joseph Estabrook to John Wood, December 25, 1835, MS.3494, Box 1 Folder 1, UTSC.

34. Joseph Estabrook to John Wood, December 25, 1835, MS.3494, Box 1 Folder 1, UTSC.

35. Clinton B. Allison, "Training Dixie's Teachers: The University of Tennessee, a Case Study," in *Three Schools of Education: Approaches to Institutional History* (SPE Monograph Series, 1984), 9–10.

36. An act passed in 1830 laid out districts for publicly funded schools in Tennessee, and the new state constitution of 1834 called for a perpetual common-school fund protected from legislative appropriations; Lucius Salisbury Merriam, *Higher Education in Tennessee* (Washington, DC: Government Printing Office, 1893), 283.

37. "Popular Education. An Address Delivered at the Annual Commencement of East Tennessee College, September 12, 1838," UTSC.

38. A. P. Whitaker, "The Public School System of Tennessee, 1834–1860," *Tennessee Historical Magazine* 2, no. 1 (March 1916): 1–30.

39. "House of Representatives," *Republican Banner* (Nashville, TN), October 25, 1839; *Acts of the Tennessee General Assembly, 1839–1840*, Chapter 98, 186; Montgomery, Folmsbee, and Greene, *To Foster Knowledge*, 40–45.

40. "East Tennessee Journalism: Address of Col. Moses White at the Recent Meeting of the Tennessee Press Association" (1877?), 24, Moses White Papers, Box 1, Folder 2, UTSC; Clinton B. Allison, *Teachers for the South: Pedagogy and Educationists in the University of Tennessee, 1844–1995* (New York: Peter Lang, 1998), 2; Edwin Mims, *The South in the Building of the Nation: History of the Literary and Intellectual Life of the Southern States, Volume 7* (Gretna, LA: Pelican Publishing, 2002), 303–4; Montgomery, Folmsbee, and Greene, *To Foster Knowledge*, 34–38q, 45.

41. "East Tennessee University (hereafter ETU)," *Abbeville* (South Carolina) *Banner*, August 25, 1847.

42. Warren A. Nord, *Religion & American Education: Rethinking a National Dilemma* (Chapel Hill: University of North Carolina Press, 1995), 84.

43. *First Board of Trustees Minutes, East Tennessee College, April 7, 1808–March 5, 1849*, 287–88, UTSC.

44. *First Board of Trustees Minutes, East Tennessee College, April 7, 1808–March 5, 1849*, 460, 488–93, UTSC; "East Tennessee Journalism: Address of Col. Moses White at the Recent Meeting of the Tennessee Press Association" (1877?), 35q–36, Moses White Papers, Box 1, Folder 2, UTSC.

45. Richard B. Drake, "Slavery and Antislavery in Appalachia," *Appalachian Heritage* 14, no. 1 (Winter 1986): 30; Dunn, *Cades Cove*, 124–25; Read, "Church College in Central Appalachia," 75.

46. *First Board of Trustees Minutes, East Tennessee College, May 15, 1849–February 13, 1877*, 19–20, UTSC; "East Tennessee Journalism: Address of Col. Moses White at the Recent Meeting of the Tennessee Press Association" (1877?), 21–22, Moses White Papers, Box 1, Folder 2, UTSC; *Early History of the University of Tennessee: Address Before the Alumni Association* (Knoxville: University of Tennessee Board of Trustees, 1879), 165–69, Moses White Papers, Box 1, Folder 3, UTSC; Montgomery, Folmsbee, and Greene, *To Foster Knowledge*, 49–54; Kincheloe, "Battle for Antebellum Southern Colleges," 123, 124–30.

47. Lacy K. Ford, Jr., "Making the 'White Man's Country' White: Race, Slavery, and State-Building in the Jacksonian South," *Journal of the Early Republic* 19, no. 4 (Winter 1999): 713–37; Atkins, *Parties, Politics, and Sectional Conflict*, 18–21, 280n9; Paul Bergeron, *Antebellum Politics in Tennessee* (Lexington: University Press of Kentucky, 2015), 38–40 (quote from 39); Dunn, *Cades Cove*, 14–17.

48. Atkins, *Parties, Politics, and Sectional Conflict*, 170–71.

49. *Port Gibson Herald, and Correspondent* (Port Gibson, MS), July 11, 1851.

50. Clipping, "Old College"; OUHC, AR.0015, Box 15, Folder 12, UTSC

51. *First Board of Trustees Minutes, East Tennessee College, April 7, 1808–March 5, 1849*, 106, 281–82, 284–85, UTSC; Entry, February 14, 1856, *First Board of Trustees Minutes, East Tennessee College, May 15, 1849–February 13, 1877*, 111, UTSC; Moses White, *Early History of the University of Tennessee: Address Before the Alumni Association* (Knoxville: University of Tennessee Board of Trustees, 1879), 165, Moses White Papers, Box 1, Folder 3, UTSC; Clipping, "Old College"; OUHC, AR.0015, Box 15, Folder 12, UTSC; James Patrick, *Architecture in Tennessee*, 36, 99–101.

52. Quotation from Biographical and Genealogical Material, Box 1, Folder 1, Crutchfield Family Papers, 1828–1886, Tennessee State Library and Archives, Nashville, Tennessee (hereafter TSLA); Will of Samuel Cleage, February 23, 1828: "Slave Deeds, 1828, 1855, 1856," Box 1, Folder 9, Crutchfield Family Papers, 1828–1886, TSLA.

53. Biographical and Genealogical Material, Box 1, Folder 1, Crutchfield Family Papers, 1828–1886, TSLA; Will of Thomas Crutchfield, September 17, 1831: Crutchfield Papers—Wills—Thomas Crutchfield Sr., 1831—Thomas Crutchfield, Jr. 1867–1881, and other legal papers; Box 1, Folder 10, Crutchfield Family Papers, 1828–1886, TSLA; Oliver Perry Temple, *Notable Men of Tennessee: From 1833 to 1875, Their Times and Their Contemporaries* (New York: Cosmopolitan Press, 1912), 109; William Harold Broughton, *The Cleggs of Old Chatham: the Ancestry, Family, Descendants of Thomas A. Clegg & Bridget Polk: their kin & events of interest* (Charlotte, NC: Clegg Family Association, 1977), 393; Patrick, *Architecture in Tennessee*, 99; S. E. Grose, ed., *Botetourt County, Virginia, Heritage Book, 1770–2000* (Summersville, WV: Shirley Grose & Associates, 2001), 104.

54. Dunn, *Cades Cove*, 64, 65; Robert Tracy McKenzie, *Lincolnites and Rebels: A Divided Town in the American Civil War* (Oxford University Press, 2006), 38; Mark T. Banker, *Appalachians All: East Tennesseans and the Elusive History of an American Region* (Knoxville: University of Tennessee Press, 2010), 58–59.

55. Merton L. Dillon, "Three Southern Antislavery Editors: The Myth of the Southern Antislavery Movement," *The East Tennessee Historical Society Publications* no. 42 (1970): 48–51.

56. Durwood Dunn, *An Abolitionist in the Appalachian South: Ezekiel Birdseye on Slavery, Capitalism, and Separate Statehood in East Tennessee, 1841–1846* (Knoxville: University of Tennessee Press, 1997), 34, 45–46, 47, 103n23; Wilma Dunaway, *Women, Work and Family in the Antebellum Mountain South* (Cambridge: Cambridge University Press, 2008), 114.

57. *First Board of Trustees Minutes, East Tennessee College, April 7, 1808–March 5, 1849*, 269, 274–75, UTSC; "East Tennessee Journalism: Address of Col. Moses White at the Recent Meeting of the Tennessee Press Association" (1877?), 24, Moses White Papers, Box 1, Folder 2, UTSC; Dunn, *An Abolitionist in the Appalachian South*, 17q, 95–96n29.

58. "University of Tennessee," *Knoxville Daily Chronicle*, May 6, 1882.

59. McKenzie, *Lincolnites and Rebels*, 36–38.

60. *Dr. Newton's Columns on the Position of the Old School Presbyterian Assembly on the Subject of Slavery* (Jackson, MS: Purdom, 1859), 54–55; Herman Albert Norton, *Religion in Tennessee, 1777–1945* (Knoxville: UT Press, 1981), 42–61; Elizabeth Fox-Genovese and Eugene Genovese, *The Mind of the Master Class: History and Faith in the Southern Slaveholders' Worldview* (Cambridge: Cambridge University Press, 2005), 498; Kincheloe, "Battle for Antebellum Southern Colleges," 127–30. Tennessee Baptists, Methodists, and Presbyterians debated slavery throughout the three decades leading to the Civil War, and all three denominations were torn asunder along the border between North and South before 1860. Before Estabrook's resignation, ETU became embroiled in a war of words between Methodist firebrand William Brownlow and Presbyterian minister Frederick Ross, who happened to be a nationally known apologist for the Biblical efficacy of slavery. Brownlow was no abolitionist, and his criticisms of Ross veered away from theology toward accusations of rape and miscegenation. Brownlow's lambasting of Ross probably reflected the attitude of eastern Tennesseans who despised slaveowners and slaves alike. In any case, it is very likely that East Tennessee's denominational quarrels had slavery as a constant backdrop.

61. Entry, August 27, 1853, *First Board of Trustees Minutes, East Tennessee College, May 15, 1849–February 13, 1877*, 72–73, UTSC; *Loudon Free Press*, September 2, 1853; "East Tennessee University," *Brownlow's Knoxville Whig*, March 13, 1867.

62. Entry, February 25, 1853, *First Board of Trustees Minutes, May 15, 1849–February 13, 1877*, 60–61, UTSC.

63. "East Tennessee University," Athens (TN) *Post*, September 13, 1850; Entry, February 19, 1853, *First Board of Trustees Minutes, East Tennessee College, May 15, 1849–February 13, 1877*, 19, UTSC; Entry, August 20, 1853, *First Board of Trustees Minutes, East Tennessee College, May 15, 1849–February 13, 1877*, 70–71, UTSC; Entry, July 7, 1857, *First Board of Trustees Minutes, East Tennessee College, May 15, 1849–February 13, 1877*, p. 129, UTSC; Entry, February 12, 1857, *First Board of Trustees Minutes, East Tennessee College, May 15, 1849–February 13, 1877*, p. 123, UTSC; "East Tennessee University," *Brownlow's Knoxville Whig*, March 13, 1867; Moses White, *Early History of the University of Tennessee: Address Before the Alumni Association* (Knoxville: University of Tennessee Board of Trustees, 1879), 169; Moses White Papers, Box 1, Folder 3, UTSC; Montgomery, Folmsbee, and Greene, *To Foster Knowledge*, 53–54. Clement Eaton, *The Mind of the Old South* (Baton Rouge: Louisiana State University Press, 1976), 305–6; Merritt, *Masterless Men*, 157q. There is no evidence that the Knoxville public objected to Northerners like Samuel Carrick or Joseph Estabrook for sectional reasons in previous decades. Cooke's dismissal was very possibly part of a multistate impulse to rid Southern schools of Northern "itinerate adventurers" in the late 1850s.

64. "East Tennessee University," *Brownlow's Knoxville Whig*, March 13, 1867.

65. Earl J. Hess, *The Knoxville Campaign: Burnside and Longstreet in East Tennessee* (Knoxville: University of Tennessee Press, 2012), 1.

66. Green, *Role of the Yankee*, 48; Hsiung, *Two Worlds*, 78–79; McKenzie, *Lincolnites and Rebels*, 21–22. Green asserts that Cooke openly spoke out against slavery, but does not

cite his source, nor does he cite his contention that Estabrook had, in contrast to Cooke, "sanctioned slavery."

The rail connection to the Deep South was soon joined by one to the north and east. The East Tennessee & Virginia Railroad (later renamed the Virginia & Tennessee Railroad) was completed between Knoxville and the Virginia state line in 1858; Biographical and Genealogical Material, Box 1, Folder 1, Crutchfield Family Papers, 1828–1886, Tennessee State Library and Archives, Nashville, Tennessee; Mary Rothrock, ed., *The French Broad-Holston Country: A History of Knox County, Tennessee* (Knoxville: ETHS, 1972), 101–11, 223–31; Kenneth W. Noe, *Southwest Virginia's Railroad: Modernization and the Sectional Crisis in the Civil War Era* (Tuscaloosa: University of Alabama Press, 1994), 29–30, 68, 69, 82. See also William L. Ketchersid, "Major Campbell Wallace: Southern Railroad Leader," *Tennessee Historical Quarterly* 67, no. 2 (Summer 2008): 90–105; David C. Hsiung, *Two Worlds*, 135, 138, 154–61.

67. Entry, February 12, 1857, *First Board of Trustees Minutes, East Tennessee College, May 15, 1849–February 13, 1877*, 123, UTSC; Moses White, *Early History of the University of Tennessee: Address Before the Alumni Association* (Knoxville: University of Tennessee Board of Trustees, 1879), 169; Moses White Papers, Box 1, Folder 3, UTSC.

68. "East Tennessee University," *Nashville Union and American*, January 12, 1859.

69. "Franklin College," *Nashville Union and American*, August 24, 1860. Franklin College, a school associated with the Restorationist Christian Church, turned out to be short-lived.

70. Entries, February 22, 1855, April 23, 1860, *First Board of Trustees Minutes, East Tennessee College, May 15, 1849–February 13, 1877*, 96–97, 154, UTSC.

71. Quotation from Rod Andrew, Jr., *Long Gray Lines: The Southern Military School Tradition, 1839–1915* (Chapel Hill: University of North Carolina Press, 2004), 13. For the connections between military training and slavery, see John Hope Franklin, *The Militant South: 1800–1861* (Urbana: University of Illinois Press, 1956).

72. Merriam, *Higher Education in Tennessee*, 66; Montgomery, Folmsbee, and Greene, *To Foster Knowledge*, 61.

73. Montgomery, Folmsbee, and Greene, *To Foster Knowledge*, 66.

2. MEANS AND OPPORTUNITIES, 1860–1890

1. Stanley F. Horn, *The Army of Tennessee* (1941; repr., Wilmington, NC: Broadfoot, 1987), 47, quoted in Sam Davis Elliott, *Isham G. Harris of Tennessee: Confederate Governor and United States Senator* (Baton Rouge: Louisiana State University Press, 2010), xi.

2. Charles F. Bryan, Jr., "A Gathering of Tories: The East Tennessee Convention of 1861," *Tennessee Historical Quarterly* 39, no. 1 (Spring 1980): 27–48; Martha L. Turner, "The Cause of the Union in East Tennessee," *Tennessee Historical Quarterly* 40, no. 4 (Winter 1981): 366–80.

3. James M. McPherson, *Battle Cry of Freedom: The Civil War Era* (New York: Ballantine, 1988), 283; Atkins, *Parties, Politics, and Sectional Conflict*, 3, 246–52; McKenzie, *Lincolnites and Rebels*, 63–70.

4. McKenzie, *Lincolnites and Rebels*, 192–95, 226q.

5. Moses White, *Early History of the University of Tennessee: Address Before the Alumni Association* (Knoxville: University of Tennessee Board of Trustees, 1879), 171, Moses White Papers, Box 1, Folder 3, UTSC.

6. Amy Murrell Taylor, *The Divided Family in Civil War America* (Chapel Hill: University of North Carolina Press, 2005), 13–16.

7. Obituary for Capt. John M. Brooks, *Confederate Veteran Magazine* 30, no. 1 (January 1922): 111; Montgomery, Folmsbee, and Greene, *To Foster Knowledge*, 66.

8. *The Papers of Andrew Johnson*, ed. Paul Bergeron, vol. 10, *February–July 1866* (Knoxville: University of Tennessee Press, 1992), 279n6; McKenzie, *Lincolnites and Rebels*, 117–18; Montgomery, Folmsbee, and Greene, *To Foster Knowledge*, 66–67.

9. "East Tennessee Journalism: Address of Col. Moses White," at the Recent Meeting of the Tennessee Press Association (1877?), 14, Moses White Papers, Box 1, Folder 2, UTSC.

10. M. C. Butler to America (sister), May 14, 1861, UTSC; *Biographical Record of the Alumni of Amherst College During Its First Half Century, 1821–1871* (Amherst: J. E. Williams, 1883), 246.

11. "East Tennessee University," *Brownlow's Knoxville Whig*, March 13, 1867; Thomas William Humes, *The Loyal Mountaineers of Tennessee* (Knoxville: Ogden Brothers, 1888), 180; Dan R. Frost, *Thinking Confederates: Academia and the Idea of Progress in the New South* (Knoxville: University of Tennessee Press, 2000), 39.

12. McKenzie, *Lincolnites and Rebels*, 101–5.

13. Entry February 3, 1862, *First Board of Trustees Minutes, East Tennessee College, May 15, 1849–February 13, 1877*, 19, UTSC; McKenzie, *Lincolnites and Rebels*, 116–17, 145–46, 151–59.

14. Entry, January 29, 1863, *First Board of Trustees Minutes, East Tennessee College, May 15, 1849–February 13, 1877*, 178, UTSC; McKenzie, *Lincolnites and Rebels*, 164.

15. Entry, January 29, 1863, *First Board of Trustees Minutes, East Tennessee College, May 15, 1849–February 13, 1877*, 178, UTSC.

16. Mark H. Dunkelman, "Blood Marked Their Tracks: A Union Regiment's Hard March to the Relief of Knoxville in 1863," *Tennessee Historical Quarterly* 63, no. 1 (Spring 2004): 2–17; Humes, *Loyal Mountaineers*, 180.

17. McPherson, *Battle Cry of Freedom*, 677, 681; Alexander Mendoza, *Confederate Struggle for Command: General James Longstreet and the First Corps in the West* (College Station: Texas A&M University Press, 2008), 126–37; McKenzie, *Lincolnites and Rebels*, 159–71; Hess, *Knoxville Campaign*, 151–74; Montgomery, Folmsbee, and Greene, *To Foster Knowledge*, 66–67.

18. Hess, *Knoxville Campaign*, 270.

19. Hess, *Knoxville Campaign*, 270–74.

20. Eric Foner, *Reconstruction: America's Unfinished Revolution, 1863–1877* (New York: Harper & Row, 1988), 44–45, 439–40; McKenzie, *Lincolnites and Rebels*, 207–8.

21. James E. Bond, *No Easy Walk to Freedom: Reconstruction and the Ratification of the Fourteenth Amendment* (Westport, CT: Praeger, 1997), 15–26; Gordon McKinney, *Southern Mountain Republicans: Politics and the Appalachian Community* (Chapel Hill: University of North Carolina Press, 1978), 31–41.

22. Entry, March 19, 1864, *First Board of Trustees Minutes, East Tennessee College, May 15, 1849–February 13, 1877*, 19, UTSC.

23. Called Meeting, July 10, 1865, *First Board of Trustees Minutes, May 15, 1849–February 13, 1877*, 180–81, UTSC; *Acts of the State of Tennessee Passed at the General Assembly*, vol. 34 (Nashville: S. C. Mercer, 1866), 77–78; *Brownlow's Knoxville Whig*, March 21, 1866; "East Tennessee University," *Brownlow's Knoxville Whig*, March 13, 1867; *Brownlow's Knoxville Whig*, January 15, 1868; Moses White, *Early History of the University of Tennessee: Address Before the Alumni Association* (Knoxville: University of Tennessee Board of Trustees, 1879), 173, Moses White Papers, Box 1, Folder 3, UTSC; "President Thomas W. Humes," *The University of Tennessee Record* no. 5 (July 1898): 220–21.

24. Stanley J. Folmsbee, "The Early History of the University of Tennessee: An Address in Commemoration of its 175th Anniversary," *The East Tennessee Historical Society's Publications*, no. 42 (1970): 3n1.

25. "Prominent Tennessean Is Dead at Knoxville," (Nashville) *Tennessean*, November 26, 1922.

26. 43 Cong. Rec., 1317–1319 (1874), 1317–1319.

27. Montgomery, Folmsbee, and Greene, *To Foster Knowledge*, 70–71.

28. "University of Tennessee," *Knoxville Daily Chronicle*, May 6, 1882.

29. *Index to the Reports of the Committees of the Senate of the United States, for the Second Session of the Forty-Second Congress (1871–'72)* (Washington, DC: Government Printing Office, 1872), 41q; "The University Claim," *Knoxville Chronicle*, April 10, 1872; "Trustees' Meeting," *Knoxville Chronicle*, April 12, 1872; *Nashville Union and American*, April 12, 1872; "Forty-Second Congress, Third Session: Senate," *Baltimore Sun*, February 1, 1873.

 ETU probably also sustained some damage from an 1867 torrential flood that left much of Knoxville underwater and destroyed a bridge over the river; Martha Munzer, *Valley of Vision* (New York: Alfred A. Knopf, 1969), 22.

30. Banker, *Appalachians All*, 98.

31. *Chicago Tribune*, February 1, 1873.

32. *Congressional Globe*, Third Session, Forty-Second Congress (Washington: Office of the Congressional Globe, 1873) 697, 701, 715, 722, 855, 991q, 1039–41; *A Hand-book of Politics for 1874: Being a Record of Important Political Actions, National and State, from July 15, 1872, to July 15, 1874* (Washington, DC: Solomons & Chapman, 1874), 139.

33. Clippings, "South College," OUHC, AR.0015, Box 15, Folder 28, UTSC; Carroll Van West, *Tennessee's Historical Landscapes: A Traveler's Guide* (Knoxville: University of Tennessee Press, 1995), 77, 79. At this writing, South College is the only extant nineteenth-century building on the UT campus.

34. Quoted in Anne B. Effland, "The Evolution of a Public Research System: The Economic Research Service and the Land-Grant Universities," in *Service as Mandate: How American Land-Grant Universities Shaped the Modern World, 1920–2015*, ed. Alan I. Marcus (Tuscaloosa: University of Alabama Press, 2015), 165. See also Thelin, *History of American Higher Education*, 74–83.

35. Arthur F. McClure, James Riley Chrisman, and Perry Mock, *Education for Work: The Historical Evolution of Vocational and Distributive Education in America* (London: Associated University Presses, 1985), 42–46.

36. Laurence R. Veysey, *The Emergence of the American University* (Chicago & London: University of Chicago Press, 1965), 14–15.

37. Joseph P. Wilson to Andrew Johnson, May 4, 1864, *The Papers of Andrew Johnson*, ed. Leroy P. Graf and Ralph Haskins, vol. 6, *1862–1864* (Knoxville: University of Tennessee Press, 1983), 688.

38. Sanford, *Blount College and the University of Tennessee*, 65; Montgomery, Folmsbee, and Greene, *To Foster Knowledge*, 81.

39. Stanley J. Folmsbee, "East Tennessee University, 1840–1879: Predecessor of the University of Tennessee," *University of Tennessee Record* 62, no. 3 (May 1959): 57.

40. "East Tennessee University," *Brownlow's Knoxville Whig*, March 13, 1867.

41. "Our State Universities," *Knoxville Commercial*, November 24, 1867; *Journal of the House of Representatives of the Fiftieth General Assembly of the State of Tennessee* (Nashville: Franc. M. Paul, 1897), 735; Moses White, Early History of the University of Tennessee: Address Before the Alumni Association (Knoxville: University of Tennessee Board of Trustees, 1879), 174, Moses White Papers, Box 1, Folder 3, UTSC; Folmsbee, "Early History of the University of Tennessee: An Address in Commemoration of its 175th Anniversary," *The East Tennessee Historical Society's Publications*, no. 42 (1970): 4; Fred Bailey, "Oliver Perry Temple and the Struggle for Tennessee's Agricultural College," *Tennessee Historical Quarterly* 36, no. 1 (Spring 1977): 45.

42. Folmsbee, "East Tennessee University, 1840–1879: Predecessor of the University of Tennessee," *University of Tennessee Record* 62, no. 3 (May 1959): 58–59. As anti-Catholic feeling grew in the following decade, the national Republican Party pushed for stringent barriers between public funds and any schools with church-based education; Paul D. Moreno, *The American State from the Civil War to the New Deal: The Twilight of Constitutionalism and the Triumph of Progressivism* (Cambridge: Cambridge University Press, 2013), 21.

43. *Memphis Public Ledger*, December 18, 1868; *Athens* (TN) *Post*, January 22, 1869; *Athens Post*, February 19, 1869; "Visit to East Tennessee University," *Nashville Union and American*, December 11, 1869; "East Tennessee University," *Republican Banner* (Nashville, TN), March 10, 1871; "East Tennessee University: A Memorial to Congress from the Board of Trustees," *Republican Banner* (Nashville, TN), February 29, 1872; Thomas Humes to T. W. Kearney, August 18, 1869, University of Tennessee President's Papers, Box 11, Folder 6, UTSC.

44. Jack Love to Thomas W. Humes, January 12, 1884q, University of Tennessee President's Papers, Box 11, Folder 5, UTSC; H. P. Wilkes to Dr. Humes, October 6, 1884q, University of Tennessee President's Papers, Box 11, Folder 7, UTSC.; "Students for the Agricultural College," *Nashville Union and American*, January 18, 1870; Connie L. Lester, *Up from the Mudsills of Hell: The Farmers' Alliance, Populism, and Progressive Agriculture in Tennessee, 1870–1915* (Athens: University of Georgia Press, 2006), 142–44.

45. Robert Tracy McKenzie, "Civil War and Socioeconomic Change in the Upper South: The Survival of Local Agricultural Elites in Tennessee, 1850–1870," in *Tennessee History: The Land, the People, and the Culture*, ed. Carroll Van West (Knoxville: University of Tennessee Press, 1998), 209–12.

46. The act also added members the board of trustees, insuring representation from all parts of the state; *Acts of the State of Tennessee, Passed at the Second Session of the Thirty-Fifth Assembly (1868–69)* (Nashville: S. C. Mercer, 1869), 13–14. See also Samuel H. Shannon, "Land-Grant College Legislation and Black Tennesseans: A Case Study in the Politics of Education," *History of Education Quarterly* 22, no. 2 (Summer 1982): 139–57.

47. William E. Hardy, "'Fare well to all Radicals': Redeeming Tennessee, 1869–1870" (PhD diss. (University of Tennessee, 2013); McKinney, *Southern Mountain Republicans*, 37–38.

48. "The Legislature Yesterday," *Nashville Union and American*, February 8, 1870; "Note From Mr. Thomas," *Nashville Union and American*, July 1, 1870; *Nashville Union and American*, January 19, 1871; *Memphis Daily Appeal*, January 19, 1871; *Knoxville Daily Chronicle*, January 21, 1871; Folmsbee, "Early History of the University of Tennessee," Lester, *Up from the Mudsills of Hell*, 143.

49. "The Agricultural College Fund," *Knoxville Chronicle*, August 17, 1870.

50. *Knoxville Daily Chronicle*, February 3, 1871.

51. "Governor Senter's Veto," *Knoxville Chronicle*, February 1, 1871 (quote); Folmsbee, "Early History of the University of Tennessee: An Address in Commemoration of its 175th Anniversary," *The East Tennessee Historical Society's Publications*, no. 42 (1970): 4.

52. "The Meeting Last Saturday," *Sweetwater Enterprise*, April 7, 1870; "Personal," *Nashville Union and American*, September 10, 1870; Hunter Nicholson to Thomas Humes, December 10, 1872, University of Tennessee President's Papers, Box 11, Folder 6, UTSC; "Organization at the University this Morning," *Knoxville Daily Chronicle*, July 2, 1881; *The Papers of Andrew Johnson*, ed. Leroy P. Graf and Ralph Haskins, vol. 3, *1858–1860* (Knoxville: Univ. of Tennessee Press, 1972), 392n2.

53. "University of Tennessee," *Knoxville Daily Chronicle*, August 5, 1880; "Organization at the University this Morning," *Knoxville Daily Chronicle*, July 2, 1881; Montgomery, Folmsbee, and Greene, *To Foster Knowledge*, 94q.

54. Hughes Bros. to Thomas Humes, July 5, 1876, University of Tennessee President's Papers, Box 11, Folder 6, UTSC.

55. "The Political Line Drawn in our Schools," *Knoxville Daily Chronicle*, December 13, 1882.

56. Charles Lee Lewis, *Philander Priestly Claxton: Crusader for Public Education* (Knoxville: University of Tennessee Press, 1972), 19–20q, 22.

57. Folmsbee, "East Tennessee University, 1840–1879: Predecessor of the University of Tennessee," *University of Tennessee Record* 62, no. 3 (May 1959): 103–4.

58. *Knoxville Tribune*, April 18, 1877.

59. Montgomery, Folmsbee, and Greene, *To Foster Knowledge*, 90.

60. *Knoxville Chronicle*, July 7, 1877; "Southern Intolerance: A Vague Feminine Chronology, *New York Times*, August 3, 1877"; "East Tennessee University," *Nashville Daily American*, August 15, 1877.

61. "A Southern Blunder," *Hartford* (CT) *Daily Courant*, July 14, 1877.

62. "Northern Teachers in the South," *Nashville Daily American*, August 15, 1877.

63. "Knoxville: The True Inwardness of the East Tennessee University," *Nashville Daily American*, September 20, 1877.

64. "University of Tennessee," *Knoxville Daily Chronicle*, August 5, 1880; "Organization at the University this Morning," *Knoxville Daily Chronicle*, July 2, 1881; Hunter Nicholson to Robert Craighead, September 18, 1883, University of Tennessee President's Papers, Box 11, Folder 7, UTSC.

65. Theodore Hymowitz, "The History of the Soybean," in *Soybeans: Chemistry, Production, Processing, and Utilization*, ed. Lawrence A. Johnson, Pamela J. White, and Richard Galloway Elsevier (Urbana, IL: AOCS Press, 2015), 19.

66. Bailey, "Oliver Perry Temple and the Struggle for Tennessee's Agricultural College," *Tennessee Historical Quarterly* 36, no. 1 (Spring 1977): 54.

67. *The National Cyclopaedia of American Biography*, vol. 3 (New York: James T. White, 1893), 172; Frost, *Thinking Confederates: Academia and the Idea of Progress in the New South* (Knoxville: University of Tennessee Press, 2000), 83; Montgomery, Folmsbee, and Greene, *To Foster Knowledge*, 98q.

68. Walter J. Fraser, Jr., "Black Reconstructionists in Tennessee," *Tennessee Historical Quarterly* 34, no. 4 (Winter 1975): 363.

69. Shannon, "Land-Grant College Legislation and Black Tennesseans," 140–41; Montgomery, Folmsbee, and Greene, *To Foster Knowledge*, 80, 101.

70. Debra A. Reid, *Science as Service: Establishing and Reformulating American Land-Grant Universities, 1865–1930* (Tuscaloosa: University of Alabama Press, 2015), 162.

71. John S. Reynolds, *Reconstruction in South Carolina, 1865–1877* (Columbia, SC: State Publishers, 1905), 236; Stephen Kantrowitz, *Ben Tillman & the Reconstruction of White Supremacy* (Chapel Hill: University of North Carolina Press, 2000), 49.

72. *Catalogue of the Officers and Students of East Tennessee University, 1876–7* (Knoxville: Whig & Chronicle, 1877), 34; "Campus Life, 1879–1887," Hoskins Collection (Addendum) AR-76, Box 1, Folder 11, UTSC; Michael Dennis, *Lessons in Progress: State Universities and Progressivism in the New South, 1880–1920* (Urbana: University of Illinois Press, 2001), 113n76.

73. James R. Montgomery, *The Volunteer State Forges Its University: The University of Tennessee, 1887–1919* (Knoxville: University of Tennessee, 1966), 4; Gerald H. Gaither and James R. Montgomery, eds., "Letters of Samuel Henry Lockett: Professor and Commandant at the University of Tennessee," *The East Tennessee Historical Society's Publications* no. 42 (1970): 116q.

    Immediately before accepting a position at ETU, Lockett had served with the Army Corps of Engineers in Egypt; "A Southern Blunder," *Hartford* (CT) *Daily Courant*, July 14, 1877; An Able and Interesting Lecture," *Nashville Daily American*, February 20, 1881.

74. "The Legislative Solons," *Knoxville Chronicle*, February 16, 1881.

75. Bobby L. Lovett, *The Civil Rights Movement in Tennessee: A Narrative History* (Knoxville: University of Tennessee, 2005), 336.

76. Shannon, "Land-Grant College Legislation and Black Tennesseans," 141q.

77. "Meeting of Colored Men on the University," *Knoxville Chronicle*, August 26, 1881.

78. "Colored Cadetships: A Knotty Question Before the Trustees of the University of Tennessee," *Washington Post*, August 14, 1881; "No Negroes," (Memphis) *Public Ledger*, August 18, 1881q.

79. "Action of the Board of Trustees on the Color Question," *Knoxville Daily Chronicle*, August 18, 1881; Clipping from *Chi-Delta Crescent*[?], University of Tennessee President's Papers, Box 11, Folder 8, UTSC; Thomas Humes to Robert Craighead, November 6, 1883, University of Tennessee President's Papers, Box 11, Folder 7, UTSC; Shannon, "Land-Grant College Legislation and Black Tennesseans," 142; Bobby L. Lovett, *Civil Rights Movement in Tennessee*, 336.

80. Montgomery, *Volunteer State Forges Its University*, 158–59, 210; Cynthia Griggs Fleming, "A Survey of the Beginnings of Tennessee's Black Colleges and Universities, 1865–1920," *Tennessee Historical Quarterly* 39, no. 2 (Summer 1980): 201–2.

81. Thomas Humes to W. W. Rule, February 1, 1872, University of Tennessee President's Papers, Box 11, Folder 6, UTSC (quote); Montgomery, Folmsbee, and Greene, *To Foster Knowledge*, 89.

82. Shannon, "Land-Grant College Legislation and Black Tennesseans," 142–47; Montgomery, *Volunteer State Forges Its University*, 101; Merriam, *Higher Education in Tennessee*, 274–78.

83. James A. Atkins, *The Age of Jim Crow* (New York: Vantage Press, 1964), 112.

84. *Atlanta Constitution*, June 22, 1878; "Commencement Day," *Knoxville Daily Chronicle*, June 19, 1879q; "University of Tennessee," (Memphis) *Public Ledger*, March 18, 1879; *Knoxville Chronicle*, November 2, 1879; "The State University," *Nashville Daily American*, July 15, 1880; Montgomery, Folmsbee, and Greene, *To Foster Knowledge*, 96.

85. "Our State University," *Knoxville Chronicle*, January 5, 1879.

86. Montgomery, Folmsbee, and Greene, *To Foster Knowledge*, 88.

87. Clipping from *Chi-Delta Crescent*[?], University of Tennessee President's Papers, Box 11, Folder 8, UTSC; Montgomery, Folmsbee, and Greene, *To Foster Knowledge*, 110.

88. Christine A. Ogren, *The American State Normal School: "An instrument of Great Good"* (New York: Palgrave MacMillan, 2005), 250n5.

89. Allison, "Training Dixie's Teachers," 10, 16q.

90. Bailey, "Oliver Perry Temple," 53.

91. Oliver Perry Temple Correspondence Regarding the University of Tennessee, AR.0453. University of Tennessee Libraries, Knoxville, Special Collections UTSC; Alison Vick, "'We Are A Distinct and Peculiar People': Oliver Perry Temple and the Knoxville Industrial Association Address of 1869," *Journal of East Tennessee History* 84 (2012): 87–100; Montgomery, *Volunteer State Forges Its University*, 5–10; Bailey, "Oliver Perry Temple," 44–61; McKinney, *Southern Mountain Republicans*, 84–85; William E. Hardy, "Fare Well to All Radicals," 156.

92. Clipping from *Chi-Delta Crescent*[?], University of Tennessee President's Papers, Box 11, Folder 8, UTSC.

93. Hugh B. Rice to Board of Regents of the E.T. University, August 7, 1883, University of Tennessee President's Papers, Box 11, Folder 7, UTSC; "Report of the Special Committee on the Appeal of Cadet Humes," University of Tennessee President's Papers, Box 11, Folder 8, UTSC; *Clarksville Chronicle*, August 11, 1883; H. E. Harris to George Andrews, August 15, 1883, University of Tennessee President's Papers, Box 11, Folder 7, UTSC; W. Latham to University of Tennessee Board of Trustees, August 20, 1883; W. G. McAdoo to Judge Moses, November 24, 1883, University of Tennessee President's Papers, Box 11, Folder 7, UTSC.

94. Thomas Humes to Board of Trustees, August 24, 1883, University of Tennessee President's Papers, Box 11, Folder 8, UTSC; (Memphis) *Public Ledger*, August 27, 1883; Rodes Massie to Robert Craighead, September 8, 1883, University of Tennessee President's Papers, Box 11, Folder 7, UTSC; James Dimwiddie to Robert Craighead, September 10, 1883, University of Tennessee President's Papers, Box 11, Folder 7, UTSC; T. O. Deaderick to Robert Craighead, September 17, 1883, University of Tennessee President's Papers, Box 11, Folder 7, UTSC; Hunter Nicholson to Robert Craighead, September 18, 1883, University of Tennessee President's Papers, Box 11, Folder 7, UTSC; Thomas Humes to Robert Craighead, November 6, 1883, University of Tennessee President's Papers, Box 11, Folder 7, UTSC; McDearmon & Tyree, attorneys at law to R. Craighead, May 19, 1884, University of Tennessee President's Papers, Box 11, Folder 5, UTSC; Bailey, "Oliver Perry Temple," 54.

95. (Memphis) *Public Ledger*, August 27, 1883.

96. Thomas Humes to Robert Craighead, November 6, 1883, University of Tennessee President's Papers, Box 11, Folder 7, UTSC.

97. H. P. Wilkes to Dr. Humes, October 6, 1884q, University of Tennessee President's Papers, Box 11, Folder 7, UTSC.

98. Merriam, *Higher Education in Tennessee* (Washington: Government Printing Office, 1893), 87–88.

99. Papers of O. P. Temple, UTSC; *The National Cyclopaedia of American Biography*, vol. 3 (New York: James T. White, 1893), 172.

100. "Dr. Harcourt A. Morgan," Hoskins Collection (Addendum) AR-76, Box 1, Folder 1, UTSC; Papers of Oliver Perry Temple, UTSC; Lester, *Up from the Mudsills of Hell*, 144.

101. Montgomery, Folmsbee, and Greene, *To Foster Knowledge*, 128–31. McBryde ended up running afoul of Governor Ben Tillman, who arranged to remove South Carolina's land-grant from South Carolina College and transfer it to Clemson University; Veysey, *Emergence of the American University*, 15.

102. *Pulaski* (TN) *Citizen*, September 1, 1887; for Dabney as part of a new generation of progressive Southern university heads, see Thelin, *History of American Higher Education*, 140–41.

103. "Endowment Fund," *Chattanooga News*, June 27, 1919.

104. Joel Williamson, *The Crucible of Race: Black-White Relations in the American South since Emancipation* (Oxford University Press, 1984), 275; Luke E. Harlow, *Religion, Race, and the Making of Confederate Kentucky, 1830–1880* (Cambridge: Cambridge University

Press, 2014), 196–97, 206; Frank J. Smith, "Robert Lewis Dabney" in *Religion and Politics in America: An Encyclopedia of Church and State in American Life* (New York: ABC-CLIO, 2016), 225–26.

105. John Latane, quoted in Dennis, *Lessons in Progress*, 69.

106. "With the Magazines," *Atlanta Constitution*, September 18, 1892.

107. Mary S. Hoffschwelle, *Rebuilding the Southern Community: Reformers, Schools, and Homes in Tennessee, 1900–1930* (Knoxville: University of Tennessee Press, 1998), 16; Frost, *Thinking Confederates*, 112q.

108. "Filipino Students," *Evening Bulletin* (Maysville, KY), May 25, 1904; "Filipinos as Students," *Lawrence [KS] Democrat*, June 3, 1904; "Don't Like Filipinos," *Daily Press* (Newport News, VA), February 24, 1905 (quote).

109. "Don't Like Filipinos," *Daily Press* (Newport News, VA), February 24, 1905; "Filipinos Ostracized," *Evening Star* (Washington, DC), February 24, 1905; "Filipino Students Not Made Welcome," *Columbia Herald*, March 3, 1905 (quote).

110. Shannon, "Land-Grant College Legislation and Black Tennesseans," 143; Reid, *Science as Service*, 158.

111. Hoffschwelle, *Rebuilding the Southern Community*, 20–21.

112. Dennis, *Lessons in Progress*, 77.

113. McClure, Chrisman, and Mock, *Education for Work*, 43–44; Natalie J. Ring, *The Problem South: Region, Empire, and the New Liberal State, 1880–1930* (Athens: University of Georgia Press, 2012), 122, 161–62.

114. H. Leon Prather, *Resurgent Politics and Educational Progressivism in the New South, North Carolina, 1890–1913* (Cranbury, NJ: Fairleigh Dickinson University Press, 1979), 121.

115. McKenzie, 224–25.

116. Humes, *Loyal Mountaineers*, 8, 10.

117. Folmsbee, "East Tennessee University," 135.

118. Humes, *Loyal Mountaineers*, 31; Oliver P. Temple, *East Tennessee and the Civil War* (Cincinnati: Robert Clarke, 1899) 557. See also Noel Fisher, "Definitions of Loyalty: Unionist Histories of the Civil War in East Tennessee," *Journal of East Tennessee History* 67 (1995): 58–88; McKenzie, *Lincolnites and Rebels*, 32.

3. THE UNIVERSITY OF TENNESSEE IN THE NEW SOUTH, 1890–1930

1. Joseph M. Stetar, "In Search of a Direction: Southern Higher Education after the Civil War," *History of Education Quarterly* 25, no. 3 (Autumn 1985): 361.

2. Veysey, *Emergence of the American University*, 73–76, 104–9, 174–176, 200–201.

3. Frost, *Thinking Confederates*, 109.

4. Ring, *Problem South*, 162–74.

5. Veysey, *Emergence of the American University*, 125–33.

6. Frost, *Thinking Confederates*, 109.

7. Gelber, *The University and the People*, 119.

8. Quoted in Dennis, *Lessons in Progress*, 70.

9. Fred Hobson, *Tell About the South: The Southern Rage to Explain* (Baton Rouge: Louisiana State University Press, 1983), 163–64, 172; Gelber, *The University and the People*, 37q.

10. Dennis, *Lessons in Progress*, 71–72.

11. Untitled, Hoskins Collection (Addendum) AR-76, Box 1, Folder 4, UTSC; Gelber, *The University and the People*, 136–37.

12. Dennis, *Lessons in Progress*, 76–77.

13. "Memorial Address for Cooper Davis Schmitt delivered by George F. Mellen, May 29, 1911," *University of Tennessee Record* 14, no. 5 (August 1911): 17.

14. Montgomery, *Volunteer State Forges Its University*, 209–10.

15. Gelber, *The University and the People*, 69.

16. Paul Conkin, *Gone with the Ivy: A Biography of Vanderbilt University* (Knoxville: University of Tennessee Press, 1985), 109–10; Dennis, *Lessons in Progress*, 75–76, 92, 112–13n68.

17. "Students Coming," *Atlanta Constitution*, September 13, 1895.

18. Daniel Merritt Robison, *Bob Taylor and the Agrarian Revolt in Tennessee* (Chapel Hill: University of North Carolina Press, 1935), 118.

19. Montgomery, Folmsbee, and Greene, *To Foster Knowledge*, 142–44.

20. Lester, *Up from the Mudsills of Hell*, 145–146.

21. T. C. Karns, *History of the University of Tennessee* (Washington, DC: Government Printing Office, 1893), 91, UTSC.

22. Robison, *Bob Taylor and the Agrarian Revolt*, 118–19; Montgomery, Folmsbee, and Greene, *To Foster Knowledge*, 144.

23. *Maryville (TN) Times*, December 20, 1893; *Savannah Courier*, December 21, 1893.

24. UT Board of Trustees to Governor Turney, February 10, 1894, Humes and Dabney Papers, Box 1, Folder 17, UTSC; "An Outrage," *Maryville (TN) Times*, October 24, 1894; "The State's Educational Institutions," *Bolivar (TN) Bulletin*, May 17, 1895.

25. (Jonesborough, TN) *Herald and Tribune*, December 20, 1893.

26. "An Outrage," *Maryville (TN) Times*, October 24, 1894.

27. Board of Trustees to Governor Peter Turney, February 27, 1894, Humes and Dabney Papers, Box 1, Folder 17, UTSC.

28. Quoted in Dennis, *Lessons in Progress*, 99.

29. Robert H. Wiebe, *The Search for Order, 1877–1920* (New York: Hill & Wang, 1967), xiii; Thelin, *History of American Higher Education*, 147.

30. "The Old College and the New: An Address Delivered at the Commencement of the Virginia Polytechnic Institute, Blacksburg, Virginia, June 24, 1896," 10, UTSC.

31. "Estabrook Hall Demolition Allows Engineering Department Growth," *Daily Beacon*, January 19, 2018.

32. Montgomery, *Volunteer State Forges Its University*, 33.

33. F. L. Coleman to Dr. Chas. Dabney, September 11, 1889, Humes and Dabney Papers, Box 1, Folder 15, UTSC.

34. "At the University," "University of Tennessee," *Knoxville Daily Chronicle*, November 8, 1878; Charles Howard Hopkins, *History of the Y.M.C.A. in North America* (New York: Association Press, 1951), 289; "'To Promote No Creed': Religion at the University

of Tennessee" *Context*, 12 (November 1995): 5–10, AR-0647, University Historian's Vignettes, box 2, folder 23, UTSC.

35. "To Make Strong Men," *Atlanta Constitution*, December 23, 1895; Conkin, *Gone with the Ivy*, 136–37.

36. Robert Thomas Epling, "Seasons of Change: Football Desegregation and the University of Tennessee and the Transformation of the Southeastern Conference, 1963–67" (PhD diss., University of Tennessee, 1994), 52; Myers, *University Coeducation*, 154.

37. William Bruce Wheeler, "The Founding, 1897–1920" (unpublished manuscript), William Bruce Wheeler Papers (hereafter BWP), 4.

38. "Memorial Services," *Bolivar* (TN) *Bulletin*, November 18, 1898; "To Instruct Young Cubans," *Atlanta Constitution*, January 12, 1899; "Will Educate One Cuban," *Bolivar Bulletin*, January 20, 1899.

39. Wheeler, "The Founding, 1897–1920," BWP, 4.

40. Montgomery, Folmsbee, and Greene, *To Foster Knowledge*, 377.

41. Reid, *Science as Service*, 14.

42. McCandless, "Battle against Coeducation" (Spring 1990), 200, 216; Kerber, *Toward an Intellectual History of Women*, 230–232; Myers, *University Coeducation*, 19–20; Thelin, *History of American Higher Education*, 97–98.

43. David Gold and Catherine L Hobbs, *Educating the New Southern Woman: Speech, Writing, and Race at the Public Women's Colleges, 1884–1945* (Carbondale: Southern Illinois University Press, 2014), 24–26.

44. "Admission of Women," Hoskins Collection (Addendum) AR-76, Box 1, Folder 3, UTSC.

45. "Admission of Women," Hoskins Collection (Addendum) AR-76, Box 1, Folder 3, UTSC.

46. "To the Women of Tennessee," *Bolivar* (TN) *Bulletin*, June 9, 1893.

47. "Admission of Women"; Hoskins Collection (Addendum) AR-76, Box 1, Folder 3, UTSC; Tiffany Cantrell, "East Tennessee's Hidden History: The Beginnings of Co-Education at UT," *Daily Beacon*, November 23, 2017.

48. *Knoxville Sentinel*, November 2, 1906.

49. *Knoxville Journal*, March 19, 1913.

50. Thelin, *History of American Higher Education*, 137–38.

51. Montgomery, *Volunteer State Forges Its University*, 16–17; O'Steen, "The University of Tennessee: Evolution of a Campus," 262q.

52. Myers, *University Coeducation*, 10–13.

53. "Schools for Girls," *Maryville* (TN) *Times*, June 1, 1892; *Savannah* (TN) *Courier*, June 2, 1892.

54. "In Women's Behalf," *Savannah* (TN) *Courier*, July 28, 1892.

55. Hoffschwelle, *Rebuilding the Southern Community*, 29.

56. "Admission of Women," Hoskins Collection (Addendum) AR-76, Box 1, Folder 3, UTSC.

57. *Maryville* (TN) *Times*, December 24, 1919; *Crossville* (TN) *Chronicle*, December 20, 1922q.

58. "A Prosperous Year—Women Admitted to the State University" (Jonesborough, TN) *Herald and Tribune*, June 22, 1893; "Admission of Women," Hoskins Collection (Addendum) AR-76, Box 1, Folder 3, UTSC.

59. "Committee of Lady Students Protest," June 1894, Humes and Dabney Papers, Box 1, Folder 14, UTSC.

60. "Admission of Women," Hoskins Collection (Addendum) AR-76, Box 1, Folder 3, UTSC; Tiffany Cantrell, "East Tennessee's Hidden History: The Beginnings of Co-Education at UT," *Daily Beacon*, November 23, 2017; Montgomery, Folmsbee, and Greene, *To Foster Knowledge*, 160–61.

61. "Admission of Women," Hoskins Collection (Addendum) AR-76, Box 1, Folder 3, UTSC.

62. *Savannah* (TN) *Courier*, December 14, 1900; Montgomery, Folmsbee, and Greene, *To Foster Knowledge*, 381; William L. Holt, "A Statistical Study of Smokers and Non-Smokers at the University of Tennessee," *Journal of the American Statistical Association* 18, no. 142 (June 1923): 766–72; Sarah Cansler, "Stamp Out This Awful Cancer: The Fear of Radicals, Atheists, and Modernism at the University of Tennessee in the 1920s," *Journal of East Tennessee History* 85 (2013): 64.

63. "Education in the South," *Nashville American*, January 3, 1902.

64. "Summer School of the South," Hoskins Collection (Addendum) AR-76, Box 1, Folder 4, UTSC; "A College for Teachers in the University of Tennessee," *The Journal of Education* 56, no. 21 (November 27, 1902): 355; Allison, "Training Dixie's Teachers," 11–14.

65. "For Southern Teachers," *Indianapolis Journal*, March 29, 1903; John David Smith, "Ulrich B. Phillips: Dunningite or Phillipsian Sui Generis?," in *The Dunning School: Historians, Race, and the Meaning of Reconstruction*, ed. John David Smith and J. Vincent Lowery (Lexington: University Press of Kentucky, 2013), 145q; Merton L. Dillon, *Ulrich Bonnell Phillips: Historian of the Old South* (Baton Rouge: Louisiana State University Press, 1985), 48–49.

66. Glenda Gilmore, "Which Southerners? Which Southern Historians? A Century of Southern History at Yale," *Yale Review* 99, no. 1 (January 2011): 236.

67. Untitled, Hoskins Collection (Addendum) AR-76, Box 1, Folder 4, UTSC; Lewis, *Philander Priestly Claxton*, 19–20q, 22; Prather, *Resurgent Politics*, 224; C. Vann Woodward, *Origins of the New South* (Baton Rouge: Louisiana State University Press, 1981), 403–4; Hoffschwelle, *Rebuilding the Southern Community*, 2, 19, 20, 28–29; Aaron Purcell, "'The Greatest Event Since the Civil War': Progressivism and the Summer School of the South at the University of Tennessee," *Journal of East Tennessee History* 76 (2004): 1, 10–22; *The Centennial Alumni of the University of Tennessee* (Knoxville: Tennessee Alumnus, 2017), 64.

68. Woodward, *Origins of the New South*, 403–4; Richard F. Teichgraeber III, *Building Culture: Studies in the Intellectual History of Industrializing America, 1867–1910* (Columbia: University of South Carolina Press, 2010), 121–25.

69. Quoted in James D. Anderson, *The Education of Blacks in the South, 1860–1935* (Chapel Hill: University of North Carolina Press, 2010), 85. See also Robert J. Norrell, *Up from History: The Life of Booker T. Washington* (Cambridge: Harvard University Press, 2009), 194–95, 313–14; Ring, *Problem South*, 165–73.

70. Untitled, Hoskins Collection (Addendum) AR-76, Box 1, Folder 4, UTSC; Hoffschwelle, *Rebuilding the Southern Community*, 19–20.

71. McClure, Chrisman, and Mock, *Education for Work*, 43–44; Thelin, *History of American Higher Education*, 135–37.
72. Lovett, *Civil Rights Movement in Tennessee*, 336–37.
73. Ibid, 337.
74. Quotes from James D. Anderson, *The Education of Blacks in the South*, 85 and "Education in the South," *Nashville American*, January 3, 1902.
75. Todd L. Savitt, "Money versus Mission at an African-American Medical School: Knoxville College Medical Department, 1895–1900," *Bulletin of the History of Medicine* 75, no. 4 (Winter 2001): 680–716; Phoebe Ann Pollitt, *African American and Cherokee Nurses in Appalachia: A History, 1900–1965* (Jefferson, NC: McFarland, 2016), 111–15.
76. Jacqueline Burnside, "A 'Delicate and Difficult Duty': Interracial Education at Maryville College, Tennessee, 1868–1901," *American Presbyterians* 72, no. 4 (Winter 1994): 235–38; Lovett, *Civil Rights Movement in Tennessee*, 337.
77. "Investigations of Committee," *Nashville Globe*, January 10, 1908.
78. "Bills for Normal Schools," *Nashville Globe*, February 5, 1909.
79. Hoffschwelle, *Rebuilding the Southern Community*, 20–21.
80. Shannon, "Land-Grant College Legislation and Black Tennesseans," 148–49.
81. Montgomery, *Volunteer State Forges Its University*, 101, 158–59, 210; Fleming, "Beginnings of Tennessee's Black Colleges and Universities," 195–207.
82. Shannon, "Land-Grant College Legislation and Black Tennesseans," 150.
83. "University Commission Studies Race Question," *Richmond Times-Dispatch*, May 6, 1915; "The University Commission on Southern Race Questions," *Fisk University News* 9, no. 10 (June 1919): 12–16; Josiah Morse, "The University Commission on Southern Race Questions," *The South Atlantic Quarterly* 19, no. 2 (April 1920): 302–10.
84. Quoted in Montgomery, *Volunteer State Forges Its University*, 86. It is unknown if Dabney counted among this group Booker T. Washington, who lamented that the Southern Education Board neglected Black education; Norrell, *Up from History*, 313–14.
85. Ring, *Problem South*, 4.
86. "Takes Dabney's Place," *Columbia Herald*, August 5, 1904; "New Head for University of Tennessee," *New York Times*, April 26, 1905; "Dr. Harcourt A. Morgan," Hoskins Collection (Addendum) AR-76, Box 1, Folder 1, UTSC; "Sketch of Dr. Brown Ayres," Hoskins Collection (Addendum) AR-76, Box 1, Folder 10, UTSC.
87. Betty Bean, "A Consequential Man: Brown Ayres Remembers," Knox TN Today, November 14, 2018, https://www.knoxtntoday.com/a-consequential-man-brown-ayres-remembers/.
88. "Want $50,000 Appropriated," *Bolivar* (TN) *Bulletin*, December 23, 1904; "University of Tennessee," *Commercial* (Union City, Tennessee), May 28, 1909; James R. Montgomery, "John R. Neal and the University of Tennessee: A Five-Part Tragedy," *Tennessee Historical Quarterly* 38, no. 2 (Summer 1979): 217; Lewis, *Philander Priestly Claxton*, 298.
89. Montgomery, Folmsbee, and Greene, *To Foster Knowledge*, 161–65.
90. "Tennessee Calf Club Will Show at All Big Fairs," *Jackson County Sentinel* (Gainesboro, TN), October 14, 1920.

91. *Lawrence* (KS) *Democrat*, June 2, 1905; "Middle Tennessee Farmers to Meet," (Gainesboro, TN) *Jackson County Sentinel*, June 13, 1918.

92. "Soy Beans Will Endure Cold," *Fayette Falcon* (Somerville, TN), April 30, 1920; Aaron Purcell, "'The Greatest Event Since the Civil War,'" 25–26; Allison, "Training Dixie's Teachers," 13–14.

93. "Doctor Brown Ayres," *Chattanooga News*, January 29, 1919.

94. "Taylor Law School," OUHC, AR.0015, Box 15, Folder 38, UTSC; Front matter, *Tennessee Law Review* 1, no. 1 (November 1922).

95. Robert Stevens, *Legal Education in America from the 1850s to the 1980s* (Union, NJ: Lawbook Exchange, 2001), 201n31.

96. "Dental Department of the University of Tennessee," *Nashville Daily American*, October 3, 1880; Mary H. Teloh and James Thweatt, "Tennessee Medical Imprints of the Nineteenth Century," *Tennessee Historical Quarterly* 53, no. 3 (Fall 1994): 208–17.

97. F. Garvin Davenport, "Scientific Interests in Kentucky and Tennessee, 1870–1890," *Journal of Southern History* 14, no. 4 (November 1948): 511, 512.

98. Montgomery, Folmsbee, and Greene, *To Foster Knowledge*, 325–42.

99. "Detailed to New Duty," *Chattanooga News*, September 30, 1918.

100. Wheeler, "The Founding," 13–14; Montgomery, *Volunteer State Forges Its University*, 204.

101. Carole Stanford Bucy, *Tennessee Through Time, the Later Years* (Layton, UT: Gibbs, Smith, 2007), 166.

102. "Construction to Begin," *Chattanooga News*, December 30, 1918; "Campus Life, 1879–1887," Hoskins Collection (Addendum) AR-76, Box 1, Folder 11, UTSC; O'Steen, "The University of Tennessee: Evolution of a Campus," 268.

103. *Fayette Falcon* (Somerville, TN), January 17, 1919; *Polk County News* (Benton, TN), January 23, 1919; *McNairy County Independent* (Selmer, TN), January 24, 1919.

104. "Deplores Death of Dr. Ayres," *Chattanooga News*, January 28, 1919q; "Death Claims One of Leading Educators," *Chattanooga News*, January 28, 1919; "Dr. Brown Ayres Dead; President of University of Tennessee Dies in Knoxville at 62," *New York Times*, January 29, 1919.

105. "Consider Twenty-Two Names for President," *Chattanooga News*, May 7, 1919; "Endowment Fund," *Chattanooga News*, June 27, 1919; "University of Tennessee," (Cookeville, Tennessee) *Putnam County Herald*, July 31, 1919; H. A. Morgan Oath of Office, Harcourt Alexander Morgan Papers, MS.0522, Box 1, Folder 9, UTSC; "Information secured from the Federal Court regarding Dr. H. A. Morgan," Hoskins Collection (Addendum) AR-76, Box 1, Folder 1, UTSC.

106. "Co-ed Chosen Sponsor," *Chattanooga News*, November 25, 1919q; "Campus Life, 1879–1887," Hoskins Collection (Addendum) AR-76, Box 1, Folder 11, UTSC; Clipping, "Old College," OUHC, AR.0015, Box 15, Folder 12, UTSC.

107. *McNairy County Independent* (Selmer, TN), December 8, 1922.

108. William Bruce Wheeler, *Knoxville, Tennessee: A Mountain City in the New South*, 3rd ed. (Knoxville: University of Tennessee Press, 2020), 45.

109. Robert J. Booker, "Old Newspapers Reveal Church Membership Numbers in Knoxville," *Knoxville News Sentinel*, October 22, 2018.

110. "Race Riot Rages in Knoxville," *Chattanooga News*, September 1, 1919; "Knoxville Has Riot," *Maryville* (TN) *Times*, September 3, 1919; Wheeler, *Knoxville, Tennessee*, 34; Cameron McWhirter, *Red Summer: The Summer of 1919 and the Awakening of Black America* (New York: Henry Holt, 2011), 170–82.

111. "Riot Situation Now Thought to be Well in Hand," *Greeneville Daily Sun*, September 1, 1919

112. Wheeler, *Knoxville, Tennessee*, 34–36; McWhirter, *Red Summer*, 176–79.

113. *Greeneville Daily Sun*, September 2, 1919.

114. James A. Burran, "Labor Conflict in Urban Appalachia: The Knoxville Streetcar Strike of 1919," *Tennessee Historical Quarterly* 38, no. 1 (Spring 1979): 62–78.

115. Wheeler, *Knoxville, Tennessee*, 33; Wheeler, "The Founding," 8.

116. Eric R. Lacy, "Tennessee Teetotalism: Social Forces and the Politics of Progressivism," *Tennessee Historical Quarterly* 24 (1965): 219–41; Grace Leab, "Tennessee Temperance Activities, 1870–1899," *The ETHS's Publications* 21 (1949): 52–68; Leslie F. Roblyer, "The Fight for Local Prohibition in Knoxville, Tennessee, 1907," *The ETHS's Publications* 26 (1954): 27–37; Thomas H. Winn, "Liquor, Race, and Politics: Clarksville During the Progressive Period," *Tennessee Historical Quarterly* 49 (1990): 207–17; Margaret Ripley Wolfe, "Bootleggers, Drummers, and National Defense: Sideshow to Reform in Tennessee, 1915–1920," *The ETHS's Publications* 49 (1977): 77–92.

117. Quoted in Calvin B. T. Lee, *The Campus Scene, 1900–1970: Changing Styles in Undergraduate Life* (New York: David McKay, 1970), 33–34.

118. "To Fight Liquor at Games," *New York Times*, October 30, 1929; Al Browning, *Third Saturday in October: Tennessee versus Alabama* (Nashville: Rutledge Hill Press, 1987), 28–34.

119. Paula Fass, *The Damned and the Beautiful: American Youth in the 1920s* (Oxford University Press, 1977), 13.

120. James C. Prude, "William Gibbs McAdoo and the Democratic National Convention of 1924," *Journal of Southern History* 38 (November 1972): 621–28; *Biographical Dictionary of the United States Secretaries of the Treasury, 1789–1995* (1996), 231–32, s.v. William Gibbs McAdoo.

121. Wheeler, *Knoxville, Tennessee*, 49–52.

122. Myers, *University Coeducation*, 122–123.

123. Wheeler, *Knoxville, Tennessee*, 52.

124. Wiley L. Morgan, "The University of Tennessee," *The T. P. A. Magazine: Official Organ of the Travelers' Protective Association of America*, 1920, 32.

125. Davenport, "Scientific Interests in Kentucky and Tennessee," 515–19; Hofstadter and Metzger, *Development of Academic Freedom*, 131; Paul Conkin, *When All the Gods Trembled: Darwinism, Scopes, and American Intellectuals* (New York: Rowman & Littlefield, 1998), 60–63.

126. Thomas Cary Johnson, ed., *The Life and Letters of Robert Lewis Dabney* (Richmond, VA: Whittet & Shepperson, 1903), 340–50; Monte Harrell Hampton, *Storm of Words: Science, Religion, and Evolution in the Civil War Era* (Tuscaloosa: University of Alabama Press, 2014), 195–237.

127. "The Old College and the New: An Address Delivered at the Commencement of the Virginia Polytechnic Institute, Blacksburg, Virginia, June 24, 1896," p. 16, UTSC.

128. Dan R. Frost, p. 81.

129. Alexander Edmond Cance, "The Legal Status of Religious Instruction in the Public Schools" (Master's thesis, University of Wisconsin, 1906), 29.

130. Robert Ewing Corlew, Stanley J. Folmsbee, and Enoch L. Mitchell, *Tennessee, A Short History*, 2d ed. (Knoxville: University of Tennessee Press, 1990), 397.

131. Charles A. Israel, *Before Scopes: Evangelicalism, Education, and Evolution in Tennessee, 1870–1925* (Athens: University of Georgia Press, 2004), 163; Hofstadter and Metzger, *Development of Academic Freedom*, 320–322.

132. Entry, April 9, 1923, Philip M. Hamer Diary (April 19–August 20, 1923), MS.0526, Box 1, Folder 1, UTSC; Edward J. Larson, *Summer of the Gods: The Scopes Trial and America's Continuing Debate over Science and Religion* (Cambridge: Harvard University Press, 1997), 60–61.

133. Entries, April 9, 13, 1923, Philip M. Hamer Diary (April 19–August 20, 1923), MS.0526, Box 1, Folder 1, UTSC; "Dr. Harcourt A. Morgan," Hoskins Collection (Addendum) AR-76, Box 1, Folder 1, UTSC; Michael J. McDonald and John Muldowny, *TVA and the Dispossessed: The Resettlement of Population in the Norris Dam Area* (Knoxville: University of Tennessee Press, 1982), 15–17, 134.

134. Charles B. Davenport, "The University of Tennessee and Professor Schaeffer," *Science* 58, no. 1492 (August 3, 1923): 86; Wheeler, *Knoxville, Tennessee*, 88; Hofstadter and Metzger, *Development of Academic* Freedom, 468–506.

135. Entry, July 4, 1923, Philip M. Hamer Diary (April 19–August 20, 1923), MS.0526, Box 1, Folder 1, UTSC.

136. Entry, July 14, 1923, Philip M. Hamer Diary (April 19–August 20, 1923), MS.0526, Box 1, Folder 1, UTSC; Allison, *Teachers for the South*, 114.

137. Entries, July 3, 4, 1923, Philip M. Hamer Diary (April 19–August 20, 1923), MS.0526, Box 1, Folder 1, UTSC; Montgomery, "John R. Neal and the University of Tennessee," 222–26; Kimberly Marinucci, "God, Darwin, and Loyalty in America: The University of Tennessee and the Great Professor Trial of 1923," *History of Intellectual Culture* 1, Issue 1 (January 2001): 6; Larson, *Summer of the Gods*, 56; Wheeler, *Knoxville, Tennessee*, 54.

138. Entries, April 16, May 8, 1923, Philip M. Hamer Diary (April 19–August 20, 1923), MS.0526, Box 1, Folder 1, UTSC.

139. Marinucci, "God, Darwin, and Loyalty," 4, 7.

140. James W. Garner et al., "Report on the University of Tennessee," *Bulletin of the American Association of University Professors* 10, no. 4 (April 1924): 21–68.

141. W. T. Laprade, John Kuiper, and Claiborne G. Latimer, "Academic Freedom and Tenure: University of Tennessee," *Bulletin of the American Association of University Professors* 25, no. 3 (June 1939): 311.

142. John Longwith, *Light Upon a Hill: The University at Chattanooga, 1886–1996* (University of Chattanooga, 2000), 86–87.

143. Conkin, *Gone with the Ivy*, 324; Wheeler, *Knoxville, Tennessee*, 54.

144. H. A. Morgan to Governor Peay, March 18, 1925, Harcourt Alexander Morgan Papers, MS.0522, Box 1, Folder 12, UTSC.

145. Larson, *Summer of the Gods*, 57, 58, 59, 99; Cansler, "Stamp Out This Awful Cancer," 64.

146. Neal had been an early public critic of the Butler Act and had run unsuccessfully for

the Democratic nomination for governor in 1924. Entries, April 9, July 3, 1923, Philip
M. Hamer Diary (April 19–August 20, 1923), MS.0526, Box 1, Folder 1, UTSC;
Montgomery, "John R. Neal and the University of Tennessee: A Five-Part Tragedy,"
Tennessee Historical Quarterly 38, no. 2 (Summer, 1979): 230; Adam R. Shapiro, *Trying
Biology: The Scopes Trial, Textbooks, and the Antievolution Movement in American Schools*
(University of Chicago Press, 2013), 85.

147. Conkin, *When All the Gods Trembled*, 108.

148. Telegram, Harcourt Alexander Morgan Papers, MS.0522, Box 1, Folder 1, UTSC.

149. Montgomery, Folmsbee, and Greene, *To Foster Knowledge*, 278–79.

150. Homer Croy, "Atheism Rampant in Our Schools: How Propaganda Works on the
Youthful Mind," *World's Work* 54 (June 1927): 142–44.

151. Cansler, "Stamp Out This Awful Cancer," 67–68.

152. "'To Promote No Creed,'" 5–10, AR-0647, University Historian's Vignettes, Box 2,
Folder 23, UTSC

153. Earl J. Hess, *Lincoln Memorial University and the Shaping of Appalachia* (Knoxville:
University of Tennessee Press, 2011), 153.

154. Wassell Randolph to H. A. Morgan, July 7, 1933, Harcourt Alexander Morgan Papers,
MS.0522, Box 1, Folder 1, UTSC; "Dr. Harcourt Morgan," Hoskins Collection
(Addendum) AR-76, Box 1, Folder 1, UTSC; McDonald and Muldowny, *TVA and
the Dispossessed*, 15–17, 19–23, 125, 129–36; Erwin C. Hargrove, *Prisoners of Myth: The
Leadership of the Tennessee Valley Authority, 1933–1990* (Princeton, NJ: Princeton
University Press, 1994), 24–30.

155. "Refugee Tennesseans Find Hearts Clinging to T.V.A. Land," *Washington Star*, March
17, 1941; "Harry Curtis Confirmed as TVA Director," *Washington Star*, February 9, 1949;
"Morgan Quits TVA; H.A. Curtis Named," *New York Times*, May 5, 1948; McDonald
and Muldowny, *TVA and the Dispossessed*, 129–136; Erwin C. Hargrove and Paul Keith
Conkin, *TVA: Fifty Years of Grass-Roots Bureaucracy* (Urbana: University of Illinois
Press, 1983), 45, 95–98; Montgomery, "John R. Neal and the University of Tennessee,"
231–32.

156. Harcourt Morgan, "Tentative Definition of the Common Mooring," Harcourt
Alexander Morgan Papers, MS.0522, Box 3, Folder 1, UTSC.

157. H. A. Morgan to James Hoskins, December 14, 1936, Harcourt Alexander Morgan
Papers, MS.0522, Box 1, Folder 1, UTSC.

158. Laprade, Kuiper, and Latimer, "Academic Freedom and Tenure," 310–19.

159. Montgomery, Folmsbee, and Greene, *To Foster Knowledge*, 187.

160. "University of Future Will Have No Campus," *Midland Journal* (Rising Sun, MD),
February 23, 1940.

4. A UNIVERSITY FINDS A NEW PURPOSE, 1930–1955

1. Lee, *The Campus Scene*, 23, 46. See also Thelin, *History of American Higher Education*, 211–14.

2. Thelin, *History of American Higher Education*, 211–17.

3. Brian M. Ingrassia, *The Rise of Gridiron University: Higher Education's Uneasy Alliance with Big-Time Football* (Lawrence: University Press of Kansas, 2012), 171–99.

4. "Campus Life, 1879–1887." Hoskins Collection (Addendum) AR-76, Box 1, Folder 11, UTSC.

5. "Out at Vanderbilt," *Nashville American*, March 20, 1898; Clipping, "Residence Halls," OUHC, AR.0015, Box 15, Folder 23, UTSC; "Campus Life, 1879–1887." Hoskins Collection (Addendum) AR-76, Box 1, Folder 11, UTSC.

6. Michael Oriard, *Reading Football: How the Popular Press Created an American Spectacle* (Chapel Hill: University of North Carolina Press, 1993), 25–26.

7. "A Foot Ball Sensation," (Nashville) *Tennessean*, November 23, 1895; Oriard, *Reading Football*, 127.

8. Montgomery, *Volunteer State Forges Its University*, 172–73.

9. W. Burlette Carter, "The Age of Innocence: The First 25 Years of The National Collegiate Athletic Association, 1906 to 1931," *Vanderbilt Journal of Entertainment and Technology Law* 8, no. 2 (Spring 2006): 225–29; Daniel J. Flynn, *The War on Football: Saving America's Game* (New York: Simon & Schuster, 2013), 166; S. C. Gwynne, *The Perfect Pass: American Genius and the Reinvention of Football* (New York: Simon & Schuster, 2017), 21–23.

10. "Bennett Jared Injured," *Putnam County Herald* (Cookeville, TN), November 4, 1915; Untitled Item, *Carthage* (TN) *Courier*, July 18, 1917; James R. Montgomery, *The University of Tennessee Builds for the 20th Century: A History of the University of Tennessee during the Administration of Brown Ayres, 1904–1919* (Knoxville: University of Tennessee Record, 1957), 75.

11. "Vol Schedule is Tentative—Bender," *Chattanooga News*, December 22, 1920; Carter, "The Age of Innocence," 225; Ingrassia, *The Rise of Gridiron University*, 168.

12. "Admission of Women" Hoskins Collection (Addendum) AR-76, Box 1, Folder 3, UTSC; "Notable Woman Award 1998: Dr. Mary Douglas Ayres Ewell," UT, accessed July 1, 2018, http://web.utk.edu/~cfw/awards/notable_woman/winners/notable-1998 .shtml; Brad Austin "'College Would Be a Dead Old Dump Without It: Intercollegiate Athletics in East Tennessee during the Depression Era," *Journal of East Tennessee History* 69, Issue 1 (January 1997): 52–53.

13. Eric John Kloiber, "True Volunteers: Women's Intercollegiate Athletics at the University of Tennessee, 1903 to 1976," (Master's thesis, University of Tennessee, 1994), 20

14. Eric John Kloiber, "True Volunteers," 16–21, 128.

15. Browning, *Third Saturday in October*, 17–20; Ingrassia, *The Rise of Gridiron University*, 147.

16. "O. K. Tennessee Statement," *Washington Star*, December 14, 1930; Ronald A. Smith, *Pay for Play: A History of Big-Time College Athletic Reform* (Urbana: University of Illinois Press, 2011), 67–68.

17. Michael Oriard, *King Football: Sport and Spectacle in the Golden Age of Radio and Newsreels, Movies and Magazines, the Weekly and the Daily Press* (Chapel Hill: University of North Carolina Press, 2005), 65; Browning, *Third Saturday in October*, 14.

18. Knoxville's first radio station began broadcasting in 1922; "Notes from the History of Knoxville." Hoskins Collection (Addendum) AR-76, Box 1, Folder 5, UTSC. For

the centrality of the Scopes Trial as a region-wide redefining moment, see George
B. Tindall, "Southern Mythology," in *The South and the Sectional Image: The Sectional
Theme Since Reconstruction,* ed. Dewey Grantham (New York: Harper & Row, 1967), 13.

19. "Tennessee Berth Beckons Bierman," *Washington Star,* December 2, 1934; David
Turpie, "From Broadway to Hollywood: The Image of the 1939 University of Tennessee
Football Team and the Americanization of the South," *Journal of Sport History* 35, no. 1
(Spring 2008): 125; Epling, "Seasons of Change," 55–56.

20. Montgomery, Folmsbee, and Greene, *To Foster Knowledge,* 357.

21. "Vols Keep Trio of Grid Coaches," *Washington Star,* January 4, 1931.

22. Tom Siler, *The Volunteers* (Knoxville: Archer & Smith, 1950), 73–74.

23. *University of Tennessee Record* 74, Issue 6 (1971): 339; Tom Siler, *Tennessee's Dazzling
Decade, 1960–1970* (Knoxville: Hubert E. Hodge, 1970), 75.

24. "Its Own Punishment," *Washington Star,* December 9, 1930; "Conference Confab
Likely to be Tame," *Washington Star,* December 10, 1930; "O. K. Tennessee Statement,"
Washington Star, December 14, 1930.

25. Smith, *Pay for Play,* 84–88. The founding of the Southeastern Conference predated
the other organization often shorthanded as the "SEC": the Securities and Exchange
Commission, formed by the federal government in 1934.

26. Ray Glier, *How the SEC Became Goliath: The Making of College Football's Most Dominant
Conference* (New York: Simon & Schuster, 2013), 31.

27. John Sayle Watterson, *College Football: History, Spectacle, Controversy* (Baltimore: Johns
Hopkins University Press, 2000), 184–185.

28. Browning, *Third Saturday in October,* 84–89.

29. Gwenda Young, *Clarence Brown: Hollywood's Forgotten Master* (Lexington: University
Press of Kentucky, 2018), 330; Turpie, "From Broadway to Hollywood," 125q–126, 133.

30. The first UT/Alabama football game was played in 1901, but for the first quarter of
the twentieth century Vanderbilt was arguably UT's primary rival. Robert Neyland
apparently considered Alabama his most challenging yearly game because of the latter
team's head coach Wallace Wade's leadership, which began with the 1923 season. By the
end of the 1930s, the two teams and their respective fan bases had come to regard one
another as unparalleled conference rivals; Blake Toppmeyer, "A controversial call. A
mob. A halted game. How Tennessee vs. Alabama football series began," *Knoxville News
Sentinel,* November 25, 2020; Browning, *Third Saturday in October,* 3–20.

31. J. Douglas Toma, *Football U.: Spectator Sports in the Life of the American University* (Ann
Arbor: University of Michigan Press, 2003), 133–38, 147–49.

32. "It Was a Conference with Character," *New York Times,* December 3, 1995.

33. Siler, *Tennessee's Dazzling Decade,* 113.

34. Watterson, *College Football,* 213.

35. "Columnist Was Early, Angry Voice against Sports Color Line," *Los Angeles Times,*
March 23, 2008; Lane Demas, *Integrating the Gridiron: Black Civil Rights and American
College Football* (New Brunswick: Rutgers University Press, 2011), 28–48; Epling,
"Seasons of Change," 59.

36. Andy Holt, *Going Fishing* (Knoxville: University of Tennessee, 1981), 22–24; O'Steen, "The University of Tennessee: Evolution of a Campus," 271.

37. Montgomery, Folmsbee, and Greene, *To Foster Knowledge*, 180–181.

38. Entry, July 31, 1933, Board of Trustees Minutes, UTSC.

39. Jack Neely, "How Alumni Memorial Changed Knoxville," *Torchbearer*, June 21, 2019, https://torchbearer.utk.edu/2019/06/how-alumni-memorial-changed-knoxville/.

40. Montgomery, Folmsbee, and Greene, *To Foster Knowledge*, 183.

41. "Colleges to Co-operate with Valley Authority," (Washington, DC) *Evening Star*, October 24, 1933.

42. H. A. Morgan to James Hoskins, December 14, 1936, Harcourt Alexander Morgan Papers, MS.0522, Box 1, Folder 1, UTSC.

43. *Progress and Problems: A Time for Building (Central Report; Self Study)*, (Knoxville: University of Tennessee Press, 1970); Clinton B. Allison Department of Education Collection AR.0574, Box 1, Folder 37, UTSC; Holt, *Going Fishing*, 9–12; Montgomery, Folmsbee, and Greene, *To Foster Knowledge*, 241–42.

44. David H. Dye, "Trouble in the Glen: The Battle over Kentucky Lake Archaeology," in *Shovel Ready: Archaeology and Roosevelt's New Deal for America*, ed. Baernard K. Means (Tuscaloosa: University of Alabama Press, 2013), 129–46.

45. Montgomery, Folmsbee, and Greene, *To Foster Knowledge*, 239–41.

46. Montgomery, Folmsbee, and Greene, *To Foster Knowledge*, 242–43.

47. "Refugee Tennesseans Find Hearts Clinging to T.V.A. Land," *Washington Star*, March 17, 1941.

48. "American Dies Under Jap Fire," *Wilmington* (NC) *Morning Star*, October 31, 1940.

49. Patricia Brake Howard, "Tennessee in War and Peace: The Impact of World War II on State Economic Trends," *Tennessee Historical Quarterly* 51, no. 1 (Spring 1992): 62; Wheeler, *Knoxville, Tennessee*, 68.

50. Betsey B. Creekmore, *Tennessee: A Celebration of 200 Years of the University* (Cincinnati: Scripps Howard, 1994), 19; Milton M. Klein, *Volunteer Moments: Vignettes of the History of the University of Tennessee, 1794–1994* (Knoxville: University of Tennessee, 1996), 212.

51. Montgomery, Folmsbee, and Greene, *To Foster Knowledge*, 202–3.

52. Allison, *Teachers for the South*, 172.

53. "Colleges Okehed For War Training," *Wilmington* (NC) *Star*, March 7, 1943; Kurt Vonnegut, *Palm Sunday: An Autobiographical Collage* (New York: Random House, 2009), 65.

54. Allison, *Teachers for the South*, 162–163.

55. Interview with Michael Kennedy, February 1, 2020.

56. Wheeler, *Knoxville, Tennessee*, 68.

57. Howard, "Tennessee in War and Peace," *Tennessee Historical Quarterly* 51, no. 1 (Spring 1992): 51–58.

58. Geoffrey Norris, *Rachmaninoff* (Oxford: Oxford University Press, 2000), 75; Alan Sherrod, "Rachmaninoff's Last Performance," *Classical Journal* (blog), updated February 13, 2013, https://classicaljournal.wordpress.com/2010/08/17/rachmaninoffs-last-performance/.

59. David M. Kennedy, *Freedom from Fear: The American People in Depression and War, 1929–1945* (New York: Oxford University Press, 1999), 786–787; Ira Katznelson, *When Affirmative Action Was White: An Untold History of Racial Inequality in Twentieth-Century America* (New York: W. W. Norton, 2006), 113–21; Thelin, *History of American Higher Education*, 262–68.

60. John B. Boles, *The South Through Time: A History of an American Region*, 3rd ed. (Upper Saddle River, NJ: Prentice Hall, 2004), 2:507; O'Steen, "The University of Tennessee: Evolution of a Campus," 273.

61. O'Steen, "The University of Tennessee: Evolution of a Campus," 272.

62. O'Steen, "The University of Tennessee: Evolution of a Campus," 273.

63. Interview with Dr. Graham Leonard, February 21, 2018.

64. Allison, *Teachers for the South*, 173.

65. Interview with Dr. Graham Leonard, February 21, 2018

66. S. A. Cain and L. R. Hesler, 1940, "Harry Milliken Jennison, 1885–1940," *Journal of the Tennessee Academy of Science* 15, no. 2 (1940): 173–76.

67. Holt, *Going Fishing*, 13–32.

68. Hoskins to McCord, June 22, 1945, quoted in James R. Montgomery, *Threshold of a New Day: The University of Tennessee, 1919–1946* (Knoxville: University of Tennessee Record, 1971), 398–99.

69. Allison, *Teachers for the South*, 173.

70. Montgomery, Folmsbee, and Greene, *To Foster Knowledge*, 223.

71. O'Steen, "The University of Tennessee: Evolution of a Campus," 272.

72. Milton Klein, "Academic Freedom at UT: The Crisis Years," *Context*, March 3, 1995, 11.

73. John Egerton, *Speak Now against the Day: The Generation before the Civil Rights Movement in the South* (Chapel Hill: University of North Carolina Press, 1994), 528.

74. Aaron D. Purcell, *White Collar Radicals: TVA's Knoxville Fifteen, the New Deal, and the McCarthy Era* (Knoxville: University of Tennessee Press, 2009), 17–18.

75. Klein, "Crisis Years," 11; Shelly Romalis, *Pistol Packin' Mama: Aunt Molly Jackson and the Politics of Folksong* (Urbana: University of Illinois Press, 1999), 102–3.

76. George A. Reisch, *How the Cold War Transformed Philosophy of Science: To the Icy Slopes of Logic* (Cambridge: Cambridge University Press, 2005), 266.

77. Klein, "Crisis Years," 11–12.

78. Baron, Samuel H., History Department Papers, 1938–1987, AR-365, Box 11, Folder 6, UTSC.

79. *Knoxville Journal*, October 6, 7, 1952; Milton Klein, "Academic Freedom at UT: The McCarthy Era," *Journal of East Tennessee History* 69 (January 1997): 66–69.

80. *Orange & White*, October 9, 1952.

81. Klein, "McCarthy Era," 69–70.

82. Wheeler, *Knoxville, Tennessee*, 88.

83. *Orange & White*, May 7, 1953; Klein, "McCarthy Era," 70–74.

84. Thelin, *History of American Higher Education*, 274–77.

85. For Keynesian economics at work in twentieth century East Tennessee, see Banker, *Appalachians All*, 228.

86. Entry, November 10, 1961, Board of Trustees Minutes, 39–40, UTSC; Klein, "McCarthy Era," 77–79.

87. *Knoxville News Sentinel*, November 8, 1958; Marvin West, *Legends of the Tennessee Vols* (Champaign, IL: Sports Publishing, 2005), 108.

88. Quoted in Purcell, *White Collar Radicals*, 165–66q.

89. University of Tennessee Office of the President Records, AR.0006, Box 2, Folder marked "Employment of Bowden Wyatt as Football Coach," UTSCq (partially missing); Smith, *Pay for Play*, 126–27.

5. RACE, RIOT, AND ROCKY TOP, 1955–1970

1. O'Steen, "The University of Tennessee: Evolution of a Campus," 274.

2. Folmsbee, "Early History of the University of Tennessee," 3n1.

3. Joseph A. Fry, *The American South and the Vietnam War: Belligerence, Protest, and Agony in Dixie* (Lexington: University Press of Kentucky, 2015), 290.

4. John W. Prados, interview by William Bruce Wheeler June 6, 2006, BWP.

5. Montgomery, Folmsbee, and Greene, *To Foster Knowledge*, 270.

6. Wheeler, *Knoxville, Tennessee*, 136–37; O'Steen, "The University of Tennessee: Evolution of a Campus," 275.

7. O'Steen, "The University of Tennessee: Evolution of a Campus," 275–80.

8. Longwith, *Light Upon a Hill*, 140–158.

9. Warren Neel, *The Accidental Dean* (Warren Neel, 2010), 25.

10. Interview with Michael Kennedy, February 1, 2020; Ralph Dosser and Ann Wilson, *A History of the University of Tennessee Computing Center* (Knoxville: UTCC, 1992), 15q–18.

11. William T. Snyder to Craig Fabian, December 7, 1992, Office of the Chancellor Records, AR.0541, box 1, folder December 1992, UTSC; Weldon Payne, *Web to the Stars: A History of the University of Tennessee Space Institute* (Dubuque, IA: Kendall-Hunt, 1992), 35–44; O'Steen, "The University of Tennessee: Evolution of a Campus," 273–74.

12. "Did You Know? 9 Astronauts Are UTSI Alumni," Department of Mechanical, Aerospace, and Biomedical Engineering, UT, October 2, 2014, https://mabe.utk.edu /did-you-know-10-current-and-former-astronauts-have-a-utsi-background/; *Volunteer Leaders: A Bicentennial Directory of Some Notable Alumni of The University of Tennessee, Knoxville, 1794–1994* (Knoxville: Office of the University Historian, 1995), 37–38, 39, 76; *Centennial Alumni*, 15, 25, 45, 70.

13. Banker, *Appalachians All*, 182–83.

14. Cormac McCarthy, *Suttree* (New York: Vintage, 1979), 4.

15. Wilma Dykeman, "Rural Areas are Misrepresented," *Knoxville News Sentinel*, January 14, 1965; Jim Stokely, "The Roles of Wilma Dykeman," *Appalachian Heritage* 41, no. 2 (Spring 2013): 32.

16. Quote from Allen Batteau, *The Invention of Appalachia* (Tucson: University of Arizona Press, 1990), 13.

17. Don Graham, "Remembering the Alamo: The Story of the Texas Revolution in Popular Culture," *Southwestern Historical Quarterly* 89, no. 1 (July 1985): 35–66.

18. Thomas J. Mattingly and Earl C. Hudson, *Smokey: The True Stories behind the University of Tennessee's Beloved Mascot* (Knoxville: University of Tennessee, 2013), 55.

19. "Smokey Trainer Earl Hudson Remembered for His Dedication to Dogs and Vols," *Knoxville News Sentinel*, June 27, 2017.

20. Egerton, *Speak Now against the Day*, 363–65, 393–97.

21. UT, *The Volunteer* (Knoxville: 1950), 133.

22. "UT's 'Pride of the Southland' Marching Band Has a History Much Older Than Its Name," *Knoxville Mercury*, January 11, 2017.

23. Clippings, Traditions and Football Slide Collection AR.0577, box 1, folder 16, UTSC.

24. "Student Sues University of Tenn.," *Detroit Tribune*, May 9, 1936; "Suit Filed against University of Tennessee," *The Crisis*, June 1936, p. 183; "Scholarships for Out-of-State Study," *Detroit Tribune*, September 25, 1937; Diana Crisp Lopez, *Graduate Education at Tennessee: An Historical Perspective* (Knoxville: Graduate School, University of Tennessee, 1990), 213–14; Richard Kluger, *Simple Justice: The History of Brown v. Board of Education and Black America's Struggle for Equality* (New York: Vintage, 2004), 199–200.

25. "Tennessee Supreme Court Decision, April 16, 1937," President's papers, AR.0006, UTSC; Crystal Renée Chambers, *Law and Social Justice in Higher Education* (New York: Taylor & Francis, 2016), 75–76.

26. "Scholarships for Out-of-State Study," *Detroit Tribune*, September 25, 1937q; Lovett, *Civil Rights Movement in Tennessee*, 339.

27. Wheeler, Knoxville, Tennessee, 69.

28. Quoted in Jack Neely, "Surveying a Few Hundred Years of Knoxville's Everchanging Public Image," (Knoxville) *Metro Pulse*, March 29, 2012.

29. John H. Roper, *C. Vann Woodward, Southerner* (Athens: University of Georgia Press, 1987), 167–70; *Context*, March 29, 1996; Wheeler, *Knoxville, Tennessee*, 93.

30. Lovett, *Civil Rights Movement in Tennessee*, 360.

31. Ibid, 344.

32. Ibid, 345–46.

33. "National Affairs, Report Card," *Time*, September 19, 1955.

34. "First Degree to Negro," *New York Times*, August 14, 1954; Lopez, *Graduate Education at Tennessee*, 215–217; Lovett, *Civil Rights Movement in Tennessee*, 24, 346–47; Chambers, *Law and Social*, 99.

35. Quoted in Montgomery, Folmsbee, and Greene, *To Foster Knowledge*, 229.

36. Egerton, *Speak Now against the Day*, 623–24.

37. Lovett, *Civil Rights Movement in Tennessee*, 43q; Michael J. Klarman, *From Jim Crow to Civil Rights: The Supreme Court and the Struggle for Racial Equality* (Oxford University Press, 2006), 385, 389.

38. Klarman, *From Jim Crow to Civil Rights*, 350–51, 397; Michael J. Klarman, *Brown v. Board of Education and the Civil Rights Movement* (Oxford: Oxford University Press, 2007), 260q.

39. June N. Adamson, "Few Black Voices Heard: The Black Community and the Desegregation Crisis in Clinton, Tennessee, 1956," *Tennessee Historical Quarterly* 53 (1994): 30–41; Lovett, *Civil Rights Movement in Tennessee*, 43–53.

40. Merrill Proudfoot, *Diary of a Sit-In* (Urbana: University of Illinois Press, 1990), 120–121; Lisa L. Zagumny, "Sit-Ins in Knoxville, Tennessee: A Case Study of Political Rhetoric," *Journal of Negro History* 86, no. 1 (Winter 2001): 52.

41. "University of Tennessee," *Detroit Tribune*, March 9, 1963; Interview, Theotis Robinson, October 7, 1992, OUHC, 1819–1997, AR.0015, Box 63, Folder 21, UTSC; Interview, Avon Rollins, October 14, 1992, OUHC, 1819–1997, AR.0015, Box 63, Folder 22, UTSC; Interview with Michael Kennedy, February 1, 2020; Bob Zellner with Constance Curry, *The Wrong Side of Murder Creek: A White Southerner in the Freedom Movement* (Montgomery: New South Books, 2008), 112.

42. Proudfoot, *Diary of a Sit-In*, 9–15, 22, 102, 181.

43. Zagumny, "Sit-Ins in Knoxville," 48–49.

44. "Knoxville Students Beaten by Police," *Detroit Tribune*, May 25, 1963.

45. Interview, Theotis Robinson, October 7, 1992, OUHC, 1819–1997, AR.0015, Box 63, Folder 21, UTSC; Cynthia Griggs Fleming, "White Lunch Counters and Black Consciousness: The Story of the Knoxville Sit-ins," *Tennessee Historical Quarterly* 49, no. 1 (Spring 1990): 49; Zagumny, "Sit-Ins in Knoxville," 49; Chambers, *Law and Social*, 99–100.

46. Interview, Theotis Robinson, October 7, 1992, OUHC, 1819–1997, AR.0015, Box 63, Folder 21, UTSC

47. Chambers, *Law and Social Justice*, 99–100.

48. Lovett, *Civil Rights Movement in Tennessee*, 347.

49. Chambers, *Law and Social Justice*, 100.

50. Materials on Desegregation Center, C. Glennon Rowell to Milton Klein, OUHC, 1819–1997, AR.0015, Box 23, Folder 6, UTSC.

51. "Race and Opportunity in the University: Report of the Task Force on Race Relations," 7, OUHC, 1819–1997, AR.0015, Box 23, Folder 9, UTSC.

52. Lovett, *Civil Rights Movement in Tennessee*, 347.

53. Interview, Theotis Robinson, October 7, 1992, OUHC, 1819–1997, AR.0015, Box 63, Folder 21, UTSC

54. "UT's Martin Branch Opens Door to 2 Negro Students" (Nashville) *Tennessean*, June 16, 1961.

55. Interview, Theotis Robinson, October 7, 1992, OUHC, 1819–1997, AR.0015, Box 63, Folder 21, UTSC; Marion Barry, Omar Tyree, *Mayor for Life: The Incredible Story of Marion Barry, Jr.* (New York: Strebor Books, 2014), 43–45.

56. Ruth Anne Thompson, "'A Taste of Student Power': Protest at the University of Tennessee, 1964–1970," *Tennessee Historical Quarterly* 57, no. 1 (Spring/Summer 1998): 84.

57. "At Black Campus, Desegregation vs. Dismantling," *New York Times*, May 29, 1991.

58. Norman C. Amaker, *Civil Rights and the Reagan Administration* (Washington, DC: Urban Institute Press, 1988), 49–50; Jeffrey A. Raffel, *Historical Dictionary of School Segregation and Desegregation: The American Experience* (Westport: Greenwood Press, 1998), 111–12; J. T. Snipes and Carl Darnell, "Non-Black Student Recruitment at Historical Black Colleges and Universities," in *Black Colleges Across the Diaspora: Global Perspectives on Race and Stratification in Postsecondary Education*, ed. M. Christopher Brown II and T. Elon Dancy II (Bingley, UK: Emerald Publishing, 2018), 56–57; Ron

Leadbetter, *Big Orange, Black Storm Clouds and More: A History of the University of Tennessee* (self-pub., CreateSpace, 2015), 222–23; Lovett, *Civil Rights Movement in Tennessee*, 349–96, 401.

59. Montgomery, Folmsbee, and Greene, *To Foster Knowledge*, 279–284.

60. Charles H. Martin, *Benching Jim Crow: The Rise and Fall of the Color Line in Southern College Sports, 1890–1980* (Urbana: University of Illinois Press, 2010), 55–57, 86–89; Epling, "Seasons of Change," 60–61.

61. Epling, "Seasons of Change," 84–86.

62. Interview, Theotis Robinson, October 7, 1992, OUHC, 1819–1997, AR.0015, Box 63, Folder 21, UTSC; Interview, Avon Rollins, October 14, 1992, OUHC, 1819–1997, AR.0015, Box 63, Folder 22, UTSC; Epling, "Seasons of Change," 63.

63. Epling, "Seasons of Change," 71–72.

64. Martin, *Benching Jim Crow*, 218.

65. Simon Henderson, *Sidelined: How American Sports Challenged the Black Freedom Struggle* (Lexington: University Press of Kentucky, 2013), 169.

66. Smith, *Pay for Play*, 153.

67. Henderson, *Sidelined*, 176, 169q.

68. Martin, *Benching Jim Crow*, 262.

69. Marvin West, *Tales of the Tennessee Vols: A Collection of the Greatest Vols Stories Ever Told* (Champaign, IL: Sports Publishing, 2002), 54; Martin, *Benching Jim Crow*, 238–39.

70. The University of Kentucky had already recruited two African American players for its freshman team in 1966, but their varsity team did not have Black players until the fall of 1967. For this reason, UT and Kentucky essentially desegregated their teams simultaneously; Interview, Theotis Robinson, October 7, 1992, OUHC, 1819–1997, AR.0015, Box 63, Folder 21, UTSC; Henderson, *Sidelined*, 170; Siler, *Tennessee's Dazzling Decade*, 68; Epling, "Seasons of Change," 1–13, 78.

71. Epling, "Seasons of Change," 111.

72. Ibid, 114.

73. "Desegregation at UT: The Beginnings," Sept. 21, 1989, University Historian's Vignettes, Box 1, Folder 20, UTSC.

74. "Conredge Holloway Ahead of his time," *Chattanooga Times Free Press*, February 19, 2011.

75. Siler, *Tennessee's Dazzling Decade*, 112.

76. Jay Greeson and Stephen Hargis, *Game of My Life: Memorable Stories of Volunteers Football* (Wilmington, DE: Sports Publishing, 2013), 21–31; Lane Demas, 3q [?]

77. "Dickey Receives A 5-Year Contract to Coach Florida," *New York Times*, January 1, 1970; "Dickey Signs Vols Aides," *New York Times*, January 5, 1970; Siler, *Tennessee's Dazzling Decade*, 72–73, 80–82.

78. Lovett, *Civil Rights Movement in Tennessee*, 401.

79. Distribution of Employees by EEO Category and Race Fall 2017, 2017–18 Fact Book, UT Office of Institutional Research and Assessment, 36, https://oira.utk.edu/wp-content/uploads/sites/66/2018/10/Archive-17_18-Fact-Book.pdf; Montgomery, Folmsbee, and Greene, *To Foster Knowledge*, 451n29.

80. Thompson, "'A Taste of Student Power,'" 86; Katherine Ballantyne, "'Students Are [Not] Slaves': 1960s Student Power Debates in Tennessee," *Journal of American Studies* 54, Issue 2 (May 2020): 302–4.

81. *Daily Beacon*, July 30, 1968; The Speaker Ban Controversy: A Statement of Facts and Principle by the Student Government Association, University of Tennessee, Hodges Library; Scott Frizzell, "Not Just a Matter of Black and White: The Nashville Riot of 1967," *Tennessee Historical Quarterly* 70, no. 1 (Spring 2011): 26–51; Benjamin Houston, *The Nashville Way: Racial Etiquette and the Struggle for Social Justice in a Southern City* (Athens: University of Georgia Press, 2012), 164–201.

82. *Hawkins County Post* (Rogersville, TN), June 27, 1968.

83. Speaker Ban Controversy.

84. Thompson, "'A Taste of Student Power,'" 85; Ballantyne, "'Students Are [Not] Slaves,'" 305–6, 315.

85. Ed Hooper, ed., *Knoxville in the Vietnam Era* (Chicago: Arcadia Publishing, 2008), 51.

86. Ballantyne, "'Students Are [Not] Slaves,'" 315; Fry, *The American South and the Vietnam War*, 285–322.

87. Thompson, "'A Taste of Student Power,'" 85; Ballantyne, "'Students Are [Not] Slaves,'" 318–20.

88. Fry, *The American South and the Vietnam War*, 298.

89. Leadbetter, *Big Orange*, 12–13,

90. *Daily Beacon*, September 25, 1968, quoted in Thompson, "'A Taste of Student Power,'" 85.

91. "Protest Stirs Ruckus at U-T," *Knoxville News Sentinel*, January 16, 1970; "Trustees-Please! Include Us, Too," clipping August 1, 1969, OUHC, 1819–1997, AR.0015, Box 23, Folder 13, UTSC.

92. Interview of Jack Reese by Milton Klein, January 14 and March 19, 1991, BWP; "Boling Rejects SGA Request," *Daily Beacon*, January 15, 1970, OUHC, 1819–1997, AR.0015, Box 23, Folder 13, UTSC.

93. "Statement for Student Disruption," January 15, 1970, OUHC, 1819–1997, AR.0015, Box 23, Folder 13, UTSC.

94. Clipping, "Sale of '22' Raffle Tickets Causes Disorder," April 25, 1970, OUHC, 1819–1997, AR.0015, Box 23, Folder 12, UTSC.

95. Randall E. King, "When Worlds Collide: Politics, Religion, and Media at the 1970 East Tennessee Billy Graham Crusade," *Journal of Church and State* 39, no. 2 (Spring 1997): 276–77; Leadbetter, *Big Orange*, 14–15.

96. Unprocessed notes, BWP. The Clarence Brown Theatre was constructed on what was then the west side of the UT campus during the tumult of 1970 thanks to an endowment from the eponymous Hollywood director and 1910 UT graduate. Brown had few connections to his alma mater after World War II, until the Volunteers came to Los Angeles to kick off the 1967 season against UCLA (UCLA, 20–16). Boling invited Brown to an attendant reception where a discussion ensued about donations after a slide show of scenes from campus. Reportedly touched by nostalgia, Brown agreed to an initial donation of $50,000 for the construction of a much-needed theatre space, and

he was on hand in Knoxville three years later for the cornerstone ceremony, standing alongside movie stars Jane Wyman and Claude Jarman (stars of Brown's 1946 cinematic adaptation of Marjorie Rawlings's novel *The Yearling*) 274–87, 330–31.

97. Notes, March 15, 2006, panel, BWP; Ballantyne, "'Students Are [Not] Slaves,'" 318–19.

98. King, "Worlds Collide," 277–79.

99. Protests and Progress: Nixon Visit Put Knoxville on National Stage," *Knoxville News Sentinel*, August 26, 2012.

100. "Statement from Chancellor Weaver," *Daily Beacon*, May 29, 1970, OUHC, 1819–1997, AR.0015, box 23, folder 21, UTSC; Rick Perlstein, *Nixonland: The Rise of a President and the Fracturing of America* (New York, Simon & Schuster, 2009), 500.

101. Perlstein, *Nixonland*, 500–3.

102. Lovett, *Civil Rights Movement in Tennessee*, 295.

103. Steven P. Miller, *Billy Graham and the Rise of the Republican South* (Philadelphia: University of Pennsylvania Press, 2009), 141–43; King, "Worlds Collide," 279–80; Wheeler, *Knoxville, Tennessee*, 145–46.

104. Quoted in Kevin M. Kruse, *One Nation Under God: How Corporate America Invented Christian America* (New York: Basic Books, 2015), 260.

105. "Smith, Nixon Discuss Main Goals," *Daily Beacon*, May 29, 1970, OUHC, 1819–1997," AR.0015, box 23, folder 21, UTSC.

106. Interview, Dr. Charles Reynolds, April 27, 1987, OUHC, 1819–1997, AR.0015, Box 63, Folder 22, UTSC; Wheeler, *Knoxville, Tennesseend*, 145–46; Perlstein, *Nixonland*, 500–3; Miller, *Billy Graham and the Republican South*, 141–143; Mark Boulton, *Failing Our Veterans: The G.I. Bill and the Vietnam Generation* (New York: New York University Press, 2014), 169.

107. Interview, Gus Hadorn, February 21, 2020.

108. Interview, Dr. Charles Reynolds, April 27, 1987, OUHC, 1819–1997, AR.0015, Box 63, Folder 22, UTSC

109. "32 Nixon Hecklers Held in Tennessee," *New York Times*, June 4, 1970; Thompson, "'A Taste of Student Power,'" 90–91.

110. Clipping, "The Truth Has Always Hurt," "OUHC, 1819–1997," AR.0015, box 23, folder 21, UTSC.

111. "Summary of Actions Taken by the Supreme Court," *New York Times*, January 22, 1974.

112. University of Tennessee, *The Volunteer*

113. Martin, *Benching Jim Crow*, xiii–xv; Leadbetter, *Big Orange*, 69.

114. "Sports People: Colleges; Tennessee Quits Club," *New York Times*, April 11, 1989; Martin, *Benching Jim Crow*, xiii–xv; Epling, "Seasons of Change," 131, 134–35.

115. "Attendance at 'Ulysses Called Poor," *Daily Beacon*, February 24, 1971, OUHC, 1819–1997," AR.0015, Box 23, folder 17, UTSC.

116. Thompson, "'A Taste of Student Power,'" 93.

117. Montgomery, Folmsbee, and Greene, *To Foster Knowledge*, 401. It is difficult to reckon whether this quote should be attributed to Montgomery or Greene (Folmsbee was deceased before this chapter of their book was completed).

118. Interview, Gus Hadorn, February 21, 2020

6. UT SEES THE FUTURE, 1970–2010

1. Calvin B. T. Lee, *The Campus Scene*, 23, 166.
2. Earl H. Zwingle to Leonard Raulston, May 7, 1968, OUHC, 1819–1997, AR.0015, Box 24, Folder 24, UTSC.
3. "UT's New Queen Had It In the Bag," *Kingsport Times*, November 20, 1970q.
4. Notes for March 15, 2006, panel, BWP
5. "'He That Beareth a Torch,'" *Daily Beacon*, May 2, 1967, OUHC, 1819–1997, AR.0015, Box 24, Folder 24, UTSC.
6. Milton Klein, "Historical Vignette," *Context*, April 26, 1990, OUHC, 1819–1997, AR.0015, Box 24, Folder 24, UTSC.
7. Amy McRary, "Taken for Granite," *Knoxville News Sentinel*, September 20, 1992, OUHC, 1819–1997, AR.0015, Box 24, Folder 24, UTSC; Klein, *Volunteer Moments*, 151–56.
8. Interview with Professor Rosalind Hackett, April 17, 2019.
9. Quoted in Anthony Badger, *Albert Gore, Sr.: A Political Life* (Philadelphia: University of Pennsylvania Press, 2018), 129–30. See also Banker, *Appalachians All*, 236–37.
10. (Nashville) *Tennessean*, February 25, 1982.
11. Banker, *Appalachians All*, 244q.
12. Unlabeled Notes, BWP.
13. Interview of Jack Reese by Milton Klein, January 14 and March 19, 1991, BWP 14.
    Interview with Professor Rosalind Hackett, April 17, 2019
15. Hugh Davis Graham and Nancy Diamond, *The Rise of American Research Universities: Elites and Challengers in the Postwar Era* (Baltimore: Johns Hopkins University Press, 1997), 52–58.
16. Inventory of State Appropriations Supporting Education for the Health Professions, FY 1971–72, 88.
17. "UT Trustees Delay Vote on Credits," (Nashville) *Tennessean*, October 20, 1984; "Surviving Semesters: How UT Did It," *AU Report*, Auburn University, Winter 1997, http://www.auburn.edu/administration/univrel/news/semesters.html
18. Longwith, *Light Upon a Hill*, 164–65.
19. Neel, *Accidental Dean*, 284–85.
20. Neel, *Accidental Dean*, 79–81.
21. David M. Gross and Sophfronia Scott, "Proceeding with Caution," *Time*, July 16, 1990, 58.
22. Gelley notes, BWP; Neel, *Accidental Dean*, 118–19, 140.
23. Dennis K. Mumby, *Communication and Power in Organizations: Discourse, Ideology, and Domination* (Norwood, NJ: Ablex Publishing, 1988), 91n10.
24. "Funding" notes, BWP.
25. OUHC, AR.0015, Box 38, folder 21, UTSC; Scott Jaschik, "Proposed 10% Budget Increase Becomes a 10% Cut at University of Tennessee," *Chronicle of Higher Education*, September 4, 1991, https://www.chronicle.com/article/Proposed-10-Budget-Increase/80607.
26. Monica Kast, "Former UT Chancellor, physicist John Quinn dies," *Knoxville News Sentinel*, October 9, 2018; Neel, *Accidental Dean*, 212.

27. William T. Snyder to Dr. Donald Eastman, December 7, 1992, Office of the Chancellor Records, AR.0541, box 1, folder December 1992, UTSC.

28. "Teacher Pay on Agenda for Reagan In Knoxville," *New York Times*, June 14, 1983.

29. Office of the Dean of Liberal Arts, "A New Curriculum for the College of Liberal Arts: Report from the Liberal Arts Committee on Curriculum Study and Reform, March 1972" (unpublished report), Hodges Library, University of Tennessee.

30. (Nashville) *Tennessean*, August 3, 1978q; Demetrius D. Richmond, "A Case Study of Two Exemplary Black Cultural Centers in Higher Education" (unpublished PhD diss., University of Tennessee, 2012), 17–18; Adjoa Aiyetoro, "Historic and Modern Social Movements for Reparations: The National Coalition for Reparations in America (N'COBRA) and its Antecedents," (unpublished PhD diss., University of Arkansas, 2010), 51.

31. Interview of Jack Reese by Milton Klein January 14 and March 19, 1991, William Bruce Wheeler Papers; (Nashville) *Tennessean*, January 23, 1980q; "Recruiting at UT Hurt by Blacks' Prosecution," (Nashville) *Tennessean*, January 31, 1980.

32. "UT Makes Dramatic Desegregation Progress: UT President," University of Tennessee Libraries, August 14, 1995, https://libguides.utk.edu/c.php?g=578432&p=6431189.

33. Clippings, OUHC, 1819–1997," AR.0015, Box 23, folder 21, UTSC.

34. "'No Hours' Established as Permanent Fixture," *Daily Beacon*, September 25, 1969, OUHC, 1819–1997," AR.0015, Box 23, folder 21, UTSC.

35. Clipping, February 11, 1969, OUHC, 1819–1997," AR.0015, Box 23, folder 21, UTSC.

36. "University Charges Women's Leaders," *Daily Beacon*, May 5, 1970, OUHC, 1819–1997," AR.0015, Box 23, folder 21, UTSC.

37. William T. Snyder to William Rawson, December 7, 1992, Office of the Chancellor Records, AR.0541, box 1, folder December 1992, UTSC; Interview of Jack Reese by Milton Klein January 14 and March 19, 1991, William Bruce Wheeler Papers; "It's about time: UT's Ayres Hall finally gets clocks," *Knoxville News-Sentinel*, June 28, 2010.

38. Materials on Desegregation Center, C. Glennon Rowell to Milton Klein, OUHC, 1819–1997, AR.0015, Box 23, Folder 6, UTSC.

39. BWP.

40. Sheryl Gay Stolberg, "Obama Taps Health Aide with Links to Industry," *New York Times*, March 2, 2009.

41. Interview with Professor Rosalind Hackett, April 17, 2019

42. Welch Suggs, *A Place on the Team: The Triumph and Tragedy of Title IX* (Princeton, NJ: Princeton University Press, 2005), 31, 47–48.

43. Pat Summitt with Sally Jenkins, *Sum It Up: 1,098 Wins, a Couple of Irrelevant Losses, and a Life in Perspective* (New York: Crown Archetype, 2013), 65.

44. Kloiber, "True Volunteers," 32, 36–37, 44, 64–70.

45. Suggs, *A Place on the Team*, 24–25, 47–48.

46. Summitt, *Sum It Up*, 143–44.

47. Kloiber, "True Volunteers," 70.

48. Bill Haltom and Amanda Swanson, *Full Court Press: How Pat Summitt, a High School Basketball Player, and a Legal Team Changed the Game* (Knoxville: University of Tennessee Press, 2018), 88, 90.

49. Summitt, *Sum It Up*, 121–22, 132–33.

50. Suggs, *A Place on the Team*, 62; John R. Thelin, "Good Sports? Historical Perspective on the Political Economy of Intercollegiate Athletics in the Era of Title IX, 1972–1997," *Journal of Higher Education* 71, no. 4 (July/August 2000): 396.

51. Summitt, *Sum It Up*, 111–14.

52. Haltom and Swanson, *Full Court Press*, 89–99, 125–26.

53. Summitt, *Sum It Up*, 131.

54. Summitt, *Sum It Up*, 132.

55. "Tennessee Player Tells of Coach Battle's Plight," *New York Times*, December 7, 1976.

56. Browning, *Third Saturday in October*, 290–313.

57. UT, "Summitt to Go for the Gold," *The Volunteer* (Knoxville: 1983), 151.

58. "Pat Summitt's Climb to 1,098 Wins," (Nashville) *Tennessean*, June 28, 2016.

59. *Centennial Alumni*, 14; Leadbetter, *Big Orange*, 67–68.

60. Suggs, *A Place on the Team*, 97–100.

61. Brad Wolverton, "Tennessee's Pat Summit [*sic*] is First Woman in College Athletics' $1-Million Club," *Chronicle of Higher Education*, June 2, 2006, https://www.chronicle.com/article/Tennessees-Pat-Summitt-Is/10438.

62. Pat Summitt with Sally Jenkins, *Raise the Roof: The Inspiring Story of the Tennessee Lady Vols' Undefeated 1997–1998 Season* (New York: Broadway Books, 1998), 27.

63. "Pat Summitt, Tennessee Basketball Coach Who Emboldened Women's Sports, Dies at 64," *New York Times*, June 28, 2016.

64. Summitt, *Sum It Up*, 209–210.

65. CBS News, "Tennessee Football Scandal," September 27, 1999, https://www.cbsnews.com/news/tennessee-football-scandal/.

66. Suggs, *A Place on the Team*, 100.

67. Kloiber, "True Volunteers," 11.

68. Philip A. Scheurer to Jack Reese and Howard Aldmon, September 27, 1973, Records of the Office of the Vice Chancellor for Administration and Student Affairs, AR.0411, Box 18, folder 1, UTSC; Thomas B. Scott to Kyle W. McDaniel, Jr., March 5, 1971, Records of the Office of the Vice Chancellor for Administration and Student Affairs, AR.0411, Box 18, folder 2, UTSC.

69. "Gay People's Alliance, Special Committee's Findings," accessed October 7, 2019, http://voicesoutloudproject.org/archive/items/show/65.

70. Ronald C. Leadbetter to Dr. Edward J. Boling, Mr. John C. Baugh, Dr. Joseph E. Johnson, Mr. Charles E. Smith, and Dr. Jack E. Reese, February 15, 1974, Records of the Office of the Vice Chancellor for Administration and Student Affairs, AR.0411, Box 18, folder 1, UTSC.

71. Beauchamp E. Brogan to Members of the Board of Trustees, November 3, 1980, Records of the Office of the Vice Chancellor for Administration and Student Affairs, AR.0411, Box 18, folder 2, UTSC.

72. Wheeler, *Knoxville Tennessee*, 157–166.

73. "Petro's, Strohaus and $1 cigarettes: 1982 World's Fair student staffers remember," *Shopper News*, May 9, 2019.

74. "The Desolate Legacy of Knoxville's World's Fair," *New York Times*, May 18, 1984.

75. William Bass and Jon Jefferson, *Death's Acre: Inside the Legendary Forensic Lab the Body Farm Where the Dead Do Tell Tales* (New York: Penguin, 2004); Mason White and Maya Przybylski, *On Farming* (Barcelona: ACTAR, 2010),195–197.

76. *Daily Beacon* clipping, November 17, 1982, OUHC, AR.0015, Box 38, folder 3, UTSC.

77. *Knoxville News Sentinel*, November 25, 2019; undated clipping, OUHC, AR.0015, Box 38, folder 3, UTSC.

78. Assorted Letters, OUHC, AR.0015, Box 38, folder 3, UTSC.

79. Graham and Nancy Diamond, *American Research*, 84–95.

80. Charles Dorn, *For the Common Good: A New History of Higher Education in America* (Ithaca, NY: Cornell University Press, 2017), 196.

81. Stanley Aronowitz, *The Knowledge Factory: Dismantling the Corporate University and Creating True Higher Learning* (New York: Beacon Press, 2000), 61.

82. OUHC, AR.0015, Box 38, folder 5, UTSC; Neel, *Accidental Dean*, 147–54.

83. OUHC, AR.0015, Box 38, folder 1, UTSC.

84. Neel, *Accidental Dean*, 206–207.

85. "UT Takeover Process Starts for Alexander," (Nashville) *Tennessean*, February 14, 1988; "Halt Alexander Appointment, Blanton Urges," (Nashville) *Tennessean*, January 19, 1988; OUHC, AR.0015, Box 38, folder 14, UTSC.

86. Neel, *Accidental Dean*, 28–29, 209–210q.

87. Notes, BWP; OUHC, AR.0015, Box 38, folder 22, UTSC; Neel, *Accidental Dean*, 28, 29, 214–217, 239, 262, 273.

88. "Tennesseans Dream of 'What Could Have Been' if Lamar Alexander Stayed on as UT President," *Knoxville News Sentinel*, January 3, 2021, https://www.knoxnews.com/story /news/politics/2021/01/03/senator-lamar-alexanders-time-ut-president-short-but -visionary/6338833002/?utm_campaign=snd-autopilot.

89. Clipping, John Clark, "UTK and Tennessee Eastman form Quality Partnership," *Context*, August 5, 1993q; "Landing Strategic Partnerships," *Connections* 20, no. 3 (Fall 1995): 19–20, AR.0015 Office of the University Historian, box 39, folder 17, UTSC.

90. Various clippings, AR.0015 Office of the University Historian, box 39, folder 18, UTSC.

91. Johann M. Neem, *What's the Point of College? Seeking Purpose in an Age of Reform* (Baltimore: Johns Hopkins University Press, 2019), 60–64.

92. Various clippings, AR.0015 Office of the University Historian, box 39, folders 13, 15, UTSC; Richard Wisniewski, afterword to *Reforming a College: The University of Tennessee Story* (New York: Peter Lang, 2000), 192–93.

93. Dianne Whitaker, "A New Faculty Member at a New College," in *Reforming a College: The University of Tennessee Story*, ed. Richard Wisniewski (New York: Peter Lang, 2000), 161.

94. Various letters, Office of the Chancellor Records, AR.0541, box 1, UTSC.

95. "Toward a Climate for Enhancing Diversity on the UTK Campus," OUHC, AR.0015, Box 39, folder 8, UTSC.

96. Faye V. Harrison, *Outsider Within: Reworking Anthropology in the Global Age* (Urbana, IL: University of Illinois Press, 2008), 273–274q.

97. John R. Thelin, *American Higher Education: Issues and Institutions* (New York: Taylor & Francis, 2017), 350–357.

98. William T. Snyder to Dr. Otto C. Kopp, December 7, 1992, Office of the Chancellor Records, AR.0541, box 1, folder labeled "December 1992, UTSC.

99. "An Unpleasant Excitement," *Knoxville News Sentinel*, August 27, 1992; "Majors Checks Out of Hospital," *Knoxville News Sentinel*, September 2, 1992; "UT Mulls Majors' Contract University Unsure of Future Course," *Knoxville News Sentinel*, November 12, 1992; "UT to Buy Out Majors," *Knoxville News Sentinel*, November 13, 1992; "Majors Confirms It's Over; UT Might Announce Fulmer By Dec. 1," *Knoxville News Sentinel*, November 14, 1992; "UT's Majors Rides Out a Winner; Vols Have No Trouble With 'Cats," *Knoxville News Sentinel*, November 22, 1992; "Nothing Was Wrong With UT Timing Of Coaching Change," *Knoxville News Sentinel*, November 22, 1992; Christopher J. Walsh, *Where Football Is King: A History of the SEC* (New York: Taylor Trade Publishing, 2006), 114.

100. Walsh, *Where Football Is King*, 114–15.

101. Thelin, *American Higher Education*, 36.

102. Clay Travis, *On Rocky Top: A Front-Row Seat to the End of an Era* (New York: It Books, 2009), 280–338.

103. Walsh, *Where Football Is King*, 42–48.

104. Smith, *Pay for Play*, 172–173, 274n30.

105. "ESPN Alleges UT Academic Fraud, Cover-Up—Dickey Says Players Are Out Until Probe Is Complete," *Knoxville News Sentinel*, September 27, 1999q; "Questions Arise on UT Academics," (Nashville) *Tennessean*, September 27, 1999.

106. "UT Under a Cloud—School Launches Probe into Alleged Plagiarism," *Knoxville News Sentinel*, September 28, 1999.

107. *Johnson City* (TN) *Press*, May 23, 2002.

108. William C. Dowling, *Confessions of a Spoilsport: My Life and Hard Times Fighting Sports Corruption at an Old Eastern University* (University Park, PA: Pennsylvania State University Press, 2007), 113–19; Peter Finley, Laura Finley, and Jeffrey Fountain, *Sports Scandals* (Westport: Greenwood Press, 2008), 105–7; Allen L. Sack, *Counterfeit Amateurs: An Athlete's Journey Through the Sixties to the Age of Academic Capitalism* (University Park, PA: Pennsylvania State Press, 2008), 155–56; Smith, *Pay for Play*, 184, 277n34; Welch Suggs, "U. of Tennessee Shortchanges Athletes Academically, Professor Charges," *Chronicle of Higher Education*, April 24, 2000, https://www.chronicle.com/article/U-of-Tennessee-Shortchanges/105167; CBS News, "Tennessee Football Scandal."" https://www.cbsnews.com/news/tennessee-football-scandal/

109. "What Happens After the Whistle Blows," *New York Times*, July 20, 2000.

110. "UT Prof Tells FBI Of Bugging, Break-Ins—Also Got Mail Threats, Bensel-Meyers Says," *Knoxville News Sentinel*, May 13, 2000; UT Prof Alleges Another Break-In—Bensel-Meyers Had Already Gone To FBI," *Knoxville News Sentinel*, May 16, 2000; Dowling, *Confessions of a Spoilsport*, 114–19.

111. "UT Professor Who Alleged Academic Fraud Resigns, (Nashville) *Tennessean*, May 28, 2003.

112. "UT Professor Who Sparked '99 Athletics Probe Resigns—Bensel-Meyers Will Teach in Colorado Next Fall," *Knoxville News Sentinel,* May 28, 2003; Robert D. Benford, "The College Sports Reform Movement: Reframing the 'Edutainment' Industry," *Sociological Quarterly* 48, no. 1 (Winter 2007): 14; Walsh, *Where Football Is King,* 46.

113. Robert Lipsyte, "Descent into March Madness," *The Nation,* April 2, 2007, https://www.thenation.com/article/archive/descent-march-madness/.

114. Leadbetter, *Big Orange,* 389–404.

115. Teri Del Rosso, Rebecca Ortiz, and Anne Osborne, "Put Me in Coach: Co-Building the Institutional Bias by Universities and Media in Sexual Misconduct Cases Involving Student-Athletes" in *Building Sexual Misconduct Cases against Powerful Men,* ed. Shing-Ling S. Chen, Zhoujun Joyce Chen, and Nicole Allaire (New York: Lexington Books, 2019), 88–93.

116. "Gilley's Vision for UT May See Revision," (Nashville) *Tennessean,* June 3, 2001.

117. Leadbetter, *Big Orange,* 52.

118. "UT Committee Approves Tuition Increase of 9%," (Nashville) *Tennessean,* June 19, 2003; "UT Veteran Fly Ending Term as Acting President," *Jackson* (TN) *Sun,* May 28, 2002; "UT President Sees Changes Ahead for School," *Johnson City* (TN) *Press,* September 10, 2002.

119. Thelin, *American Higher Education,* 36.

120. "Learn from History," (Memphis) *Commercial Appeal,* October 3, 2004.

121. "Shumaker Won't Face Prosecution—No Charges: Behavior Was 'Disappointing,' but Not Criminal," *Knoxville News Sentinel,* January 21, 2004.

122. "Power Struggle Ousts Crabtree," *Knoxville News Sentinel,* January 4, 2008; "Survey: U-T Ag Campus Backs Petersen," *Elizabethton* (TN) *Star,* February 14, 2008; "Korda: A Lesson Taught by John Petersen," *Knoxville News Sentinel,* February 23, 2009; Marjorie Valbrun, "Presidential Spouses Behaving Badly," *Inside Higher Education,* October 24, 2018, https://www.insidehighered.com/news/2018/10/24/controversial-spouses -college-presidents-can-hurt-image-president-and-university; Scott Jaschik, "Scrutiny for a Presidential Spouse," *Inside Higher Education,* December 1, 2008, https://www .insidehighered.com/news/2008/12/01/scrutiny-presidential-spouse; Leadbetter, *Big Orange,* 563.

123. "DiPietro Deserving of Support at UT's Helm," *Knoxville News Sentinel,* October 26, 2010; OUHC, AR.0015, box 39, folder 21, UTSC.

124. Jesse Fox Mayshark, "UT's New President Faces a Daunting Array of Issues," (Knoxville) *Metro Pulse,* January 19, 2011, OUHC, AR.0015, box 39, folder 21, UTSC.

125. "UT Ranks 44th in 2020 U.S. News and World Report Rankings," UT, September 9, 2019, https://news.utk.edu/2019/09/09/ut-ranks-44th-in-2020-u-s-news-and-world -report-rankings/.

126. "Joe DiPietro Elected 24th President of the University of Tennessee," *Knoxville News Sentinel,* October 26, 2010; OUHC, AR.0015, box 39, folder 21, UTSC.

EPILOGUE

1. Mark Nagi, *Decades of Dysfunction: The Road to Tennessee's Crazy Coaching Search* (Knoxville: Mean Streets Press, 2018), 329–32.

2. "UT Disbands Diversity Office, Eliminates Four Positions," *Knoxville News Sentinel*, May 20, 2016.

3. Colleen Flaherty, "'De-Tenure' Do-Over," *Inside Higher Education*, March 3, 2015, https://www.insidehighered.com/news/2015/03/03/u-tennessee-system-backtracks -de-tenure-language; "University of Tennessee Board Approves Controversial Tenure Changes," (Memphis) *Commercial Appeal*, March 23, 2018.

4. "Bill to Reduce UT Board of Trustees Membership Passes in Senate," *Knoxville News Sentinel*, March 26, 2018.

5. "A GOP State Lawmaker Said the U.S. Should 'Get Rid of' Colleges for Being 'Liberal Breeding Grounds,'" *Washington Post*, September 10, 2019.

6. Neem, *What's the Point of College?* 130.

7. Whitehead, "Southern Universities," 560.

8. Andy Holt, *Going Fishing,* 68–69.

BIBLIOGRAPHY

Acts of the State of Tennessee Passed at the General Assembly. Vol. 34. Nashville: S. C. Mercer, 1866.

Acts of the State of Tennessee, Passed at the Second Session of the Thirty-Fifth Assembly (1868–69). Nashville: S. C. Mercer, 1869.

Acts passed at the first session of the Twenty-third Tennessee General Assembly of the State of Tennessee, 1839–40. Nashville: J. George Harris, 1840.

Adamson, June N. "Few Black Voices Heard: The Black Community and the Desegregation Crisis in Clinton, Tennessee, 1956," *Tennessee Historical Quarterly* 53 (1994): 30–41.

Addis, Cameron. *Jefferson's Vision for Education: 1760–1845.* New York: Lang, 2003.

Aiyetoro, Adjoa. "Historic and Modern Social Movements for Reparations: The National Coalition for Reparations in America (N'COBRA) and its Antecedents." PhD diss., University of Arkansas, 2010.

Alexander, John Edminston. *Brief History of the Synod of Tennessee, from 1817 to 1887.* Philadelphia: MacCalla, 1890.

Allison, Clinton B. *Teachers for the South: Pedagogy and Educationists in the University of Tennessee, 1844–1995.* New York: Peter Lang, 1998.

———. "Training Dixie's Teachers: The University of Tennessee, a Case Study." In *Three Schools of Education: Approaches to Institutional History*, 9–10. SPE Monograph Series, 1984.

Amaker, Norman C. *Civil Rights and the Reagan Administration.* Washington, DC: Urban Institute Press, 1988.

Anderson, James D. *The Education of Blacks in the South, 1860–1935.* Chapel Hill: University of North Carolina Press, 2010.

Andrew, Rod, Jr. *Long Gray Lines: The Southern Military School Tradition, 1839–1915.* Chapel Hill: University of North Carolina Press, 2004.

Annual Report of the State Superintendent of Public Instruction for Tennessee. Nashville: Foster & Webb, 1899.

Aronowitz, Stanley. *The Knowledge Factory: Dismantling the Corporate University and Creating True Higher Learning.* New York: Beacon Press, 2000.

Atkins, James A. *The Age of Jim Crow*. New York: Vantage Press, 1964.

Atkins, Jonathan M. *Parties, Politics, and the Sectional Conflict in Tennessee, 1832–1861*. Knoxville: University of Tennessee Press, 1997.

Auburn University. "Surviving Semesters: How UT Did It." *AU Report*, Winter 1997. http://www.auburn.edu/administration/univrel/news/semesters.html.

Austin, Brad. "'College Would Be a Dead Old Dump Without It': Intercollegiate Athletics in East Tennessee during the Depression Era." *Journal of East Tennessee History* 69, Issue 1 (January 1997): 52–53.

Badger, Anthony. *Albert Gore, Sr.: A Political Life*. Philadelphia: University of Pennsylvania Press, 2018.

Bailey, Fred. "Oliver Perry Temple and the Struggle for Tennessee's Agricultural College." *Tennessee Historical Quarterly* 36, no. 1 (Spring 1977): 45.

Ballantyne, Katherine. "'Students Are [Not] Slaves': 1960s Student Power Debates in Tennessee." *Journal of American Studies* 54, Issue 2 (May 2020): 295–322.

Banker, Mark T. *Appalachians All: East Tennesseans and the Elusive History of an American Region*. Knoxville: University of Tennessee Press, 2010.

Barksdale, Kevin. *The Lost State of Franklin: America's First Secession*. University Press of Kentucky, 2009.

Barry, Marion, and Omar Tyree. *Mayor for Life: The Incredible Story of Marion Barry, Jr.* New York: Strebor Books, 2014.

Bass, William, and Jon Jefferson. *Death's Acre: Inside the Legendary Forensic Lab the Body Farm Where the Dead Do Tell Tales*. New York: Penguin, 2004.

Batteau, Allen. *The Invention of Appalachia*. Tucson: University of Arizona Press, 1990.

Bean, Betty. "A Consequential Man: Brown Ayres Remembers." Knox TN Today. November 14, 2018. https://www.knoxtntoday.com/a-consequential-man-brown-ayres-remembers/.

Benford, Robert D. "The College Sports Reform Movement: Reframing the 'Edutainment' Industry." *The Sociological Quarterly* 48, no. 1 (Winter 2007): 1–28.

Bergeron, Paul. *Antebellum Politics in Tennessee*. Lexington: University Press of Kentucky, 2015.

———, ed. *The Papers of Andrew Johnson*. Vol. 10, *February–July 1866*. Knoxville: University of Tennessee Press, 1992.

Biographical Record of the Alumni of Amherst College During Its First Half Century, 1821–1871. Amherst: J. E. Williams, 1883.

Boles, John B. *The South Through Time: A History of an American Region*, 3 vd ed., vol. 2. Upper Saddle River, NJ: Prentice Hall, 2004.

Bond, James E. *No Easy Walk to Freedom: Reconstruction and the Ratification of the Fourteenth Amendment*. Westport, CT: Praeger, 1997.

Boulton, Mark. *Failing Our Veterans: The G.I. Bill and the Vietnam Generation*. New York: New York University Press, 2014.

Brashear, Craig. "The Market Revolution and Party Preference in East Tennessee: Spatial Patterns of Partisanship in the 1840 Presidential Election." *Appalachian Journal* 25, no.1 (Fall 1997): 8–29.

Broughton, William Harold. *The Cleggs of Old Chatham: the Ancestry, Family, Descendants of Thomas A. Clegg & Bridget Polk: their kin & events of interest.* Charlotte, NC: Clegg Family Association, 1977.

Browning, Al. *Third Saturday in October: Tennessee versus Alabama.* Nashville: Rutledge Hill Press, 1987.

Bryan, Charles F., Jr. "A Gathering of Tories: The East Tennessee Convention of 1861." *Tennessee Historical Quarterly* 39, no. 1 (Spring 1980): 27–48.

Bucy, Carole Stanford. *Tennessee Through Time, the Later Years.* Layton, UT: Gibbs, Smith, 2007.

Burnside, Jacqueline. "A 'Delicate and Difficult Duty': Interracial Education at Maryville College, Tennessee, 1868–1901," *American Presbyterians* 72, no. 4 (Winter 1994): 235–38.

Burran, James A. "Labor Conflict in Urban Appalachia: The Knoxville Streetcar Strike of 1919." *Tennessee Historical Quarterly* 38, no. 1 (Spring 1979): 62–78.

Cain, S. A., and L. R. Hesler. "Harry Milliken Jennison, 1885–1940." *Journal of the Tennessee Academy of Science* 15, no. 2 (1940): 173–76.

Caldwell, J. W. "History of Knoxville, Tennessee." In *East Tennessee, Historical and Biographical.* Chattanooga: A.D. Smith, 1893.

Calloway, Colin G. *The American Revolution in Indian Country: Crisis and Diversity in Native American Communities.* Cambridge: Cambridge University Press, 1995.

Cance, Alexander Edmond. "The Legal Status of Religious Instruction in the Public Schools." Master's thesis, University of Wisconsin, 1906.

Cansler, Sarah. "Stamp Out This Awful Cancer: The Fear of Radicals, Atheists, and Modernism at the University of Tennessee in the 1920s." *Journal of East Tennessee History* 85 (2013): 64.

Carter, W. Burlette. "The Age of Innocence: The First 25 Years of The National Collegiate Athletic Association, 1906 to 1931." *Vanderbilt Journal of Entertainment and Technology Law* 8, no. 2 (Spring 2006): 225–29.

Catalogue of the Officers and Students of East Tennessee University, 1876–7. Knoxville: Whig & Chronicle, 1877.

CBS News. "Tennessee Football Scandal." September 27, 1999. https://www.cbsnews.com/news/tennessee-football-scandal/.

The Centennial Alumni of the University of Tennessee. Knoxville: Tennessee Alumnus, 2017.

Chambers, Crystal Renée. *Law and Social Justice in Higher Education.* New York: Taylor & Francis, 2016.

"College for Teachers in the University of Tennessee, A." *The Journal of Education* 56, no. 21 (November 27, 1902): 355.

Conkin, Paul. *Gone with the Ivy: A Biography of Vanderbilt University.* Knoxville: University of Tennessee Press, 1985.

———. *When All the Gods Trembled: Darwinism, Scopes, and American Intellectuals.* New York: Rowman & Littlefield, 1998.

Corlew, Robert Ewing, Stanley J. Folmsbee, and Enoch L. Mitchell, *Tennessee, A Short History.* 2nd ed. Knoxville: University of Tennessee Press, 1990.

Creekmore, Betsey B. *Tennessee: A Celebration of 200 Years of the University*. Cincinnati:
    Scripps Howard, 1994.
Croy, Homer. "Atheism Rampant in Our Schools: How Propaganda Works on the Youthful
    Mind." *World's Work* 54 (June 1927): 142–44.
Crutchfield Family Papers. Tennessee State Library and Archives, Nashville.
Davenport, Charles B. "The University of Tennessee and Professor Schaeffer." *Science* 58, no.
    1492 (August 3, 1923): 86.
Davenport, F. Garvin. "Scientific Interests in Kentucky and Tennessee, 1870–1890." *Journal of
    Southern History* 14, no. 4 (November 1948): 500–21.
Del Rosso, Teri, Rebecca Ortiz, and Anne Osborne. "Put Me in Coach: Co-Building the
    Institutional Bias by Universities and Media in Sexual Misconduct Cases Involving
    Student-Athletes." In *Building Sexual Misconduct Cases against Powerful Men*, edited
    by Shing-Ling S. Chen, Zhoujun Joyce Chen, and Nicole Allaire, 88–93. New York:
    Lexington Books, 2019.
Demas, Lane. *Integrating the Gridiron: Black Civil Rights and American College Football*. New
    Brunswick: Rutgers University Press, 2011.
Dennis, Michael. *Lessons in Progress: State Universities and Progressivism in the New South,
    1880–1920*. Urbana: University of Illinois Press, 2001.
Department of Mechanical, Aerospace, and Biomedical Engineering, University of Tennessee.
    "Did You Know? 9 Astronauts Are UTSI Alumni." October 2, 2014. https://mabe.utk
    .edu/did-you-know-10-current-and-former-astronauts-have-a-utsi-background/.
Dillon, Merton L. "Three Southern Antislavery Editors: The Myth of the Southern Anti-
    slavery Movement," *East Tennessee Historical Society's Publications* no. 42 (1970): 48–51.
———. *Ulrich Bonnell Phillips: Historian of the Old South*. Baton Rouge: Louisiana State
    University Press, 1985.
Dorchester, Daniel. *Christianity in the United States from the First Settlements down to the
    Present Time*. New York: Hunt & Eaton, 1889.
Dorn, Charles. *For the Common Good: A New History of Higher Education in America*. Ithaca,
    NY: Cornell University Press, 2017.
Dosser, Ralph, and Ann Wilson, *A History of the University of Tennessee Computing Center*.
    Knoxville: UTCC, 1992.
Dowling, William C. *Confessions of a Spoilsport: My Life and Hard Times Fighting Sports
    Corruption at an Old Eastern University*. University Park: Pennsylvania State University
    Press, 2007.
*Dr. Newton's Columns on the Position of the Old School Presbyterian Assembly on the Subject of
    Slavery*. Jackson, MS: Purdom, 1859.
Drake, Richard B. "Slavery and Antislavery in Appalachia." *Appalachian Heritage* 14, no. 1
    (Winter 1986): 25–33.
Dunaway, Wilma. *Women, Work and Family in the Antebellum Mountain South*. Cambridge:
    Cambridge University Press, 2008.
Dunkelman, Mark H. "Blood Marked Their Tracks: A Union Regiment's Hard March to the
    Relief of Knoxville in 1863." *Tennessee Historical Quarterly* 63, no. 1 (Spring 2004): 2–17.

Dunn, Durwood, ed. *An Abolitionist in the Appalachian South: Ezekiel Birdseye on Slavery, Capitalism, and Separate Statehood in East Tennessee, 1841–1846.* Knoxville: University of Tennessee Press, 1997.

———. *Cades Cove: The Life and Death of a Southern Appalachian Community, 1818–1937.* Knoxville: University of Tennessee Press, 1988.

Durham, Walter T. *Before Tennessee: The Southwest Territory, 1790–1796: A Narrative History of the Territory of the United States South of the River Ohio.* Piney Flats, TN: Rocky Mount Historical Association, 1990.

Dye, David H. "Trouble in the Glen: The Battle over Kentucky Lake Archaeology." In *Shovel Ready: Archaeology and Roosevelt's New Deal for America,* edited by Bernard K. Means. Tuscaloosa: University of Alabama Press, 2013.

East Tennessee Historical Society. *First Families of Tennessee: A Register of Early Settlers and Their Present-Day Descendants.* Knoxville: East Tennessee Historical Society, 2000.

Eaton, Clement. *The Mind of the Old South.* Baton Rouge: Louisiana State University Press, 1976.

Eaton, Rachel Caroline. *John Ross and the Cherokee Indians.* Menasha, WI: George Banta, 1914.

Effland, Anne B. "The Evolution of a Public Research System: The Economic Research Service and the Land-Grant Universities." In *Service as Mandate: How American Land-Grant Universities Shaped the Modern World, 1920–2015,* edited by Alan I. Marcus, 115–51. Tuscaloosa: University of Alabama Press, 2015.

Egerton, John. *Speak Now against the Day: The Generation before the Civil Rights Movement in the South.* Chapel Hill: University of North Carolina Press, 1994.

Elliott, Sam Davis. *Isham G. Harris of Tennessee: Confederate Governor and United States Senator.* Baton Rouge: Louisiana State University Press, 2010.

Epling, Robert Thomas. "Seasons of Change: Football Desegregation and the University of Tennessee and the Transformation of the Southeastern Conference, 1963–67." PhD diss., University of Tennessee, 1994.

Fass, Paula. *The Damned and the Beautiful: American Youth in the 1920s.* Oxford University Press, 1977.

Fifteenth Annual Report of the Directors of the American Education Society. Boston: Perkins & Marvin, 1831.

Finger, John R. *Tennessee Frontiers: Three Regions in Transition.* Bloomington: Indiana University Press, 2001.

Finley, Peter, Laura Finley, and Jeffrey Fountain. *Sports Scandals.* Westport, CT: Greenwood Press, 2008.

Fisher, Noel. "Definitions of Loyalty: Unionist Histories of the Civil War in East Tennessee." *Journal of East Tennessee History* 67 (1995): 58–88.

Flaherty, Colleen. "'De-Tenure' Do-Over." *Inside Higher Education,* March 3, 2015. https://www.insidehighered.com/news/2015/03/03/u-tennessee-system-backtracks-de-tenure-language.

Fleming, Cynthia Griggs "A Survey of the Beginnings of Tennessee's Black Colleges and Universities, 1865–1920." *Tennessee Historical Quarterly* 39, no. 2 (Summer 1980): 201–2.

———. "White Lunch Counters and Black Consciousness: The Story of the Knoxville Sit-ins." *Tennessee Historical Quarterly* 49, no. 1 (Spring 1990): 40–52.

Flynn, Daniel J. *The War on Football: Saving America's Game*. New York: Simon & Schuster, 2013.

Folmsbee, Stanley J. "The Early History of the University of Tennessee: An Address in Commemoration of its 175th Anniversary." *East Tennessee Historical Society's Publications* no. 42 (1970): 3–19.

———. "East Tennessee University, 1840–1879: Predecessor of the University of Tennessee." *University of Tennessee Record* 62, no. 3 (May 1959): 57.

Foner, Eric. *Reconstruction: America's Unfinished Revolution, 1863–1877*. New York: Harper & Row, 1988.

Ford, Lacy K., Jr. "Making the 'White Man's Country' White: Race, Slavery, and State-Building in the Jacksonian South," *Journal of the Early Republic* 19, no. 4 (Winter 1999): 713–37.

Franklin, John Hope. *The Militant South: 1800–1861*. Urbana: University of Illinois Press, 1956.

Fraser, Walter J., Jr. "Black Reconstructionists in Tennessee," *Tennessee Historical Quarterly* 34, no. 4 (Winter 1975): 362–82.

Frizzell, Scott. "Not Just a Matter of Black and White: The Nashville Riot of 1967." *Tennessee Historical Quarterly* 70, no. 1 (Spring 2011): 26–51.

Frost, Dan R. *Thinking Confederates: Academia and the Idea of Progress in the New South*. Knoxville: University of Tennessee Press, 2000.

Fry, Joseph A. *The American South and the Vietnam War: Belligerence, Protest, and Agony in Dixie*. Lexington: University Press of Kentucky, 2015.

Gaither, Gerald H., and James R. Montgomery, eds. "Letters of Samuel Henry Lockett: Professor and Commandant at the University of Tennessee." *The East Tennessee Historical Society's Publications* no. 42 (1970): 10–23.

Gambold, Anna Rosina, and John Gambold. *The Moravian Springplace Mission to the Cherokees: 1814–1821*. Lincoln: University of Nebraska Press, 2007.

Garner, James W., F. H. Hodder, Edward H. Kraus, H. A. Millis, Edward S. Thurston, and H. F. Goodrich. "Report on the University of Tennessee." *Bulletin of the American Association of University Professors* 10, no. 4 (April 1924): 21–68.

"Gay People's Alliance, Special Committee's Findings." Accessed October 7, 2019. http://voicesoutloudproject.org/archive/items/show/65.

Gelber, Scott. *The University and the People: Envisioning American Higher Education in an Era of Populist Protest*. Madison: University of Wisconsin Press, 2011.

Genovese, Elizabeth Fox, and Eugene Genovese. *The Mind of the Master Class: History and Faith in the Southern Slaveholders' Worldview*. Cambridge: Cambridge University Press, 2005.

Gildrie, Richard. "Tennessee in the American Revolution: A Reconsideration." In *Before the Volunteer State: New Thoughts on Early Tennessee, 1540–1800*, edited by Kristofer Ray, 109–30. Knoxville: University of Tennessee Press, 2014.

Gilmore, Glenda. "Which Southerners? Which Southern Historians? A Century of Southern History at Yale," *Yale Review* 99, no. 1 (January 2011): 236.

Glier, Ray. *How the SEC Became Goliath: The Making of College Football's Most Dominant Conference*. New York: Simon & Schuster, 2013.

Gold, David, and Catherine L Hobbs. *Educating the New Southern Woman: Speech, Writing, and Race at the Public Women's Colleges, 1884–1945.* Carbondale: Southern Illinois University Press, 2014.

Graf, Leroy P., and Ralph Haskins, eds. *The Papers of Andrew Johnson.* Vol. 3, *1858–1860.* Knoxville: University of Tennessee Press, 1972.

———. *The Papers of Andrew Johnson.* Vol. 10, *1862–1864.* Knoxville: University of Tennessee Press, 1983.

Graham, Don. "Remembering the Alamo: The Story of the Texas Revolution in Popular Culture," *Southwestern Historical Quarterly* 89, no. 1 (July 1985): 35–66.

Graham, Hugh Davis, and Nancy Diamond. *The Rise of American Research Universities: Elites and Challengers in the Postwar Era.* Baltimore: Johns Hopkins University Press, 1997.

Green, Fletcher M. *The Role of the Yankee in the Old South.* Athens: University of Georgia Press, 1972.

Greeson, Jay, and Stephen Hargis. *Game of My Life: Memorable Stories of Volunteers Football.* Wilmington, DE: Sports Publishing, 2013.

Grose, S. E. ed. *Botetourt County, Virginia, Heritage Book, 1770–2000.* Summersville, WV: Shirley Grose & Associates, 2001.

Gross, David M., and Sophfronia Scott. "Proceeding with Caution." *Time,* July 16, 1990.

Gwynne, S. C. *The Perfect Pass: American Genius and the Reinvention of Football.* New York: Simon & Schuster, 2017.

Haltom, Bill, and Amanda Swanson, *Full Court Press: How Pat Summitt, a High School Basketball Player, and a Legal Team Changed the Game,* Knoxville: University of Tennessee Press, 2018.

Hampton, Monte Harrell. *Storm of Words: Science, Religion, and Evolution in the Civil War Era.* Tuscaloosa: University of Alabama Press, 2014.

Hand-book of Politics for 1874, A: Being a Record of Important Political Actions, National and State, from July 15, 1872, to July 15, 1874. Washington, DC: Solomons & Chapman, 1874.

Hardy, William E. "'Fare well to all Radicals,': Redeeming Tennessee, 1869–1870." PhD diss., University of Tennessee, 2013.

Hargrove, Erwin C. *Prisoners of Myth: The Leadership of the Tennessee Valley Authority, 1933–1990.* Princeton, NJ: Princeton University Press, 1994.

Hargrove, Erwin C., and Paul Keith Conkin, *TVA: Fifty Years of Grass-Roots Bureaucracy.* Urbana: University of Illinois Press, 1983.

Harlow, Luke E. *Religion, Race, and the Making of Confederate Kentucky, 1830–1880.* Cambridge: Cambridge University Press, 2014.

Harrison, Faye V. *Outsider Within: Reworking Anthropology in the Global Age.* Urbana, IL: University of Illinois Press, 2008.

Hart, Freeman Hansford. *The Valley of Virginia in the American Revolution, 1763–1789.* Chapel Hill: University of North Carolina Press, 1942.

Hatch, Nathan O. *The Democratization of American Christianity.* New Haven: Yale University Press, 1989.

Henderson, Simon. *Sidelined: How American Sports Challenged the Black Freedom Struggle.* Lexington: University Press of Kentucky, 2013.

Henderson, William A. *East Tennessee: Historical and Biographical*. Chattanooga: A. D. Smith, 1893.

Hess, Earl J. *The Knoxville Campaign: Burnside and Longstreet in East Tennessee*. University of Tennessee Press, 2012.

———. *Lincoln Memorial University and the Shaping of Appalachia*. Knoxville: University of Tennessee Press, 2011.

Hobson, Fred. *Tell About the South: The Southern Rage to Explain*. Baton Rouge: Louisiana State University Press, 1983.

Hodges Library, University of Tennessee, Knoxville.

Hoffschwelle, Mary S. *Rebuilding the Southern Community: Reformers, Schools, and Homes in Tennessee, 1900–1930*. Knoxville: University of Tennessee Press, 1998.

Hofstadter, Richard. *Anti-Intellectualism in American Life*. New York: Vintage, 1966.

Hofstadter, Richard, and Walter P. Metzger. *The Development of Academic Freedom in the United States*. New York: Columbia University Press, 1955.

Holt, Andy. *Going Fishing*. Knoxville: University of Tennessee, 1981.

Holt, William L. "A Statistical Study of Smokers and Non-Smokers at the University of Tennessee." *Journal of the American Statistical Association* 18, no. 142 (June 1923): 766–72.

Hooper, Ed, ed. *Knoxville in the Vietnam Era*. Chicago: Arcadia Publishing, 2008.

Hopkins, Charles Howard. *History of the Y.M.C.A. in North America*. New York: Association Press, 1951.

Horn, Stanley F. *The Army of Tennessee*. 1941. Reprint, Wilmington, NC: Broadfoot, 1987.

———. "Thomas Jefferson on Lotteries and Education." *Tennessee Historical Quarterly* 3, no. 3 (September 1944): 273–74.

Hoskins Collection. University of Tennessee Special Collections.

Houston, Benjamin. *The Nashville Way: Racial Etiquette and the Struggle for Social Justice in a Southern City*. Athens: University of Georgia Press, 2012.

Howard, Patricia Brake. "Tennessee in War and Peace: The Impact of World War II on State Economic Trends." *Tennessee Historical Quarterly* 51, no. 1 (Spring 1992): 51–71.

Hsiung, David C. *Two Worlds in the Tennessee Mountains: Exploring the Origins of Appalachian Stereotypes*. Lexington: University Press of Kentucky, 1997.

Humes, Thomas William. *The Loyal Mountaineers of Tennessee*. Knoxville: Ogden Brothers, 1888.

Humes and Dabney Papers. University of Tennessee Special Collections.

Hymowitz, Theodore. "The History of the Soybean." In *Soybeans: Chemistry, Production, Processing, and Utilization*, edited by Lawrence A. Johnson, Pamela J. White, and Richard Galloway Elsevier, 1–31. Urbana, IL: AOCS Press, 2015.

Index to the Reports of the Committees of the Senate of the United States, for the Second Session of the Forty-Second Congress (1871–'72). Washington, DC: Government Printing Office, 1872.

Ingrassia, Brian M. *The Rise of Gridiron University: Higher Education's Uneasy Alliance with Big-Time Football*. Lawrence: University Press of Kansas, 2012.

Israel, Charles A. *Before Scopes: Evangelicalism, Education, and Evolution in Tennessee, 1870–1925*. Athens: University of Georgia Press, 2004.

Jaschik, Scott. "Proposed 10% Budget Increase Becomes a 10% Cut at University of Tennessee." *Chronicle of Higher Education*, September 4, 1991. https://www.chronicle.com/article/Proposed-10-Budget-Increase/80607.

———. "Scrutiny for a Presidential Spouse." *Inside Higher Education*, December 1, 2008. https://www.insidehighered.com/news/2008/12/01/scrutiny-presidential-spouse.

Johnson, Thomas Cary, ed., *The Life and Letters of Robert Lewis Dabney*. Richmond, VA: Whittet & Shepperson, 1903.

Journal of the House of Representatives of the Fiftieth General Assembly of the State of Tennessee. Nashville: Franc M. Paul, 1897.

Kantrowitz, Stephen. *Ben Tillman and the Reconstruction of White Supremacy*. Chapel Hill: University of North Carolina Press, 2000.

Karns, T. C. *History of the University of Tennessee*. Washington, DC: Government Printing Office, 1893.

Katznelson, Ira. *When Affirmative Action Was White: An Untold History of Racial Inequality in Twentieth-Century America*. New York: W. W. Norton, 2006.

Kennedy, David M. *Freedom from Fear: The American People in Depression and War, 1929–1945*. New York: Oxford University Press, 1999.

Kerber, Linda K. *Toward an Intellectual History of Women*. Chapel Hill: University of North Carolina Press, 1997.

Ketchersid, William L. "Major Campbell Wallace: Southern Railroad Leader." *Tennessee Historical Quarterly* 67, no. 2 (Summer 2008): 90–105.

Kincheloe, Joe. "The Battle for the Antebellum Southern Colleges: The Evangelicals vs. the Calvinists in Tennessee," *Journal of Thought* 18, no. 3 (Fall 1983): 119–33.

———. *Volunteer Moments: Vignettes of the History of the University of Tennessee, 1794–1994*. Knoxville: University of Tennessee, 1996.

King, Randall E. "When Worlds Collide: Politics, Religion, and Media at the 1970 East Tennessee Billy Graham Crusade." *Journal of Church and State* 39, no. 2 (Spring 1997): 273–95.

Klarman, Michael J. *Brown v. Board of Education and the Civil Rights Movement*. Oxford: Oxford University Press, 2007.

———. *From Jim Crow to Civil Rights: The Supreme Court and the Struggle for Racial Equality*. Oxford: Oxford University Press, 2006.

Klein, Milton. "Academic Freedom at UT: The Crisis Years." *Context*, March 3, 1995.

———. "Academic Freedom at UT: The McCarthy Era." *Journal of East Tennessee History* 69 (January 1997): 66–69.

Kloiber, Eric John. "True Volunteers: Women's Intercollegiate Athletics at the University of Tennessee, 1903 to 1976." Master's thesis, University of Tennessee, 1994.

Kluger, Richard. *Simple Justice: The History of Brown v. Board of Education and Black America's Struggle for Equality*. New York: Vintage, 2004.

Kruse, Kevin M. *One Nation Under God: How Corporate America Invented Christian America*. New York: Basic Books, 2015.

Lacy, Eric R. "Tennessee Teetotalism: Social Forces and the Politics of Progressivism." *Tennessee Historical Quarterly* 24 (1965): 219–41.

Laprade, W. T., John Kuiper, and Claiborne G. Latimer. "Academic Freedom and Tenure: University of Tennessee." *Bulletin of the American Association of University Professors* 25, no. 3 (June 1939): 310–19.

Larson, Edward J. *Summer of the Gods: The Scopes Trial and America's Continuing Debate over Science and Religion*. Cambridge: Harvard University Press, 1997.

Leab, Grace. "Tennessee Temperance Activities, 1870–1899," *East Tennessee Historical Society's Publications* 21 (1949): 52–68.

Leadbetter, Ron. *Big Orange, Black Storm Clouds and More: A History of the University of Tennessee*. Self-published, CreateSpace, 2015.

Lee, Calvin B. T. *The Campus Scene, 1900–1970: Changing Styles in Undergraduate Life*. New York: David McKay, 1970.

Lester, Connie L. *Up from the Mudsills of Hell: The Farmers' Alliance, Populism, and Progressive Agriculture in Tennessee, 1870–1915*. Athens: University of Georgia Press, 2006.

Lewis, Charles Lee. *Philander Priestly Claxton: Crusader for Public Education*. Knoxville: University of Tennessee Press, 1972.

Leyburn, James G. *The Scotch-Irish: A Social History*. Chapel Hill: University of North Carolina Press, 1962.

Lipsyte, Robert. "Descent into March Madness." *The Nation*, April 2, 2007. https://www .thenation.com/article/archive/descent-march-madness/.

Longwith, John. *Light Upon a Hill: The University at Chattanooga, 1886–1996*. University of Chattanooga, 2000.

Lopez, Diana Crisp. *Graduate Education at Tennessee: An Historical Perspective*. Knoxville: Graduate School, University of Tennessee, 1990.

Lovett, Bobby L. *The Civil Rights Movement in Tennessee: A Narrative History*. Knoxville: University of Tennessee, 2005.

MacArthur, William. *Knoxville, Crossroads of the New South*. Tulsa: Continental Heritage Press, 1982.

Marinucci, Kimberly "God, Darwin, and Loyalty in America: The University of Tennessee and the Great Professor Trial of 1923," *History of Intellectual Culture* 1, Issue 1 (January 2001): 1–15.

Marsden, George M. *The Soul of the American University: From Protestant Establishment to Established Nonbelief*. Oxford: Oxford University Press, 1994.

Martin, Charles H. *Benching Jim Crow: The Rise and Fall of the Color Line in Southern College Sports, 1890–1980*. Urbana: University of Illinois Press, 2010.

Mattingly, Thomas J., and Earl C. Hudson. *Smokey: The True Stories behind the University of Tennessee's Beloved Mascot*. Knoxville: University of Tennessee Press, 2013.

McCandless, Amy Thompson. "Maintaining the Spirit and Tone of Robust Manliness: The Battle against Coeducation at Southern Colleges and Universities, 1890–1940." *National Women's Studies Association Journal* 2, Issue 2 (Spring 1990): 199–216.

McCarthy, Cormac. *Suttree*. New York: Vintage, 1979.

McClure, Arthur F., James Riley Chrisman, and Perry Mock, *Education for Work: The Historical Evolution of Vocational and Distributive Education in America*. London: Associated University Presses, 1985.

McDonald, Michael J., and John Muldowny. *TVA and the Dispossessed: The Resettlement of Population in the Norris Dam Area.* Knoxville: University of Tennessee Press, 1982.

McKenzie, Robert Tracy. "Civil War and Socioeconomic Change in the Upper South: The Survival of Local Agricultural Elites in Tennessee, 1850–1870." In *Tennessee History: The Land, the People, and the Culture,* edited by Carroll Van West. Knoxville: University of Tennessee Press, 1998.

———. *Lincolnites and Rebels: A Divided Town in the American Civil War.* Oxford University Press, 2006.

McKinney, Gordon. *Southern Mountain Republicans: Politics and the Appalachian Community.* Chapel Hill: University of North Carolina Press, 1978.

McPherson, James M. *Battle Cry of Freedom: The Civil War Era.* New York: Ballantine, 1988.

McWhirter, Cameron. *Red Summer: The Summer of 1919 and the Awakening of Black America.* New York: Henry Holt, 2011.

"Memorial Address for Cooper Davis Schmitt delivered by George F. Mellen, May 29, 1911." *University of Tennessee Record* 14, no. 5 (August 1911): 17.

Mendoza, Alexander. *Confederate Struggle for Command: General James Longstreet and the First Corps in the West.* College Station: Texas A&M University Press, 2008.

Merriam, Lucius Salisbury. *Higher Education in Tennessee.* Washington, DC: Government Printing Office, 1893.

Merritt, Keri Leigh. *Masterless Men: Poor Whites and Slavery in the Antebellum South.* New York: Cambridge University Press, 2017.

Miller, Steven P. *Billy Graham and the Rise of the Republican South.* Philadelphia: University of Pennsylvania Press, 2009.

Mims, Edwin. *The South in the Building of the Nation: History of the Literary and Intellectual Life.* 1909. Reprint, Gretna, LA: Pelican, 2002.

Montgomery, James R. "John R. Neal and the University of Tennessee: A Five-Part Tragedy." *Tennessee Historical Quarterly* 38, no. 2 (Summer 1979): 214–34.

———. *Threshold of a New Day: The University of Tennessee, 1919–1946.* Knoxville: University of Tennessee Record, 1971.

———. *The University of Tennessee Builds for the 20th Century: A History of the University of Tennessee during the Administration of Brown Ayres, 1904–1919.* Knoxville: University of Tennessee Record, 1957.

———. *The Volunteer State Forges Its University: The University of Tennessee, 1887–1919.* Knoxville: University of Tennessee Record, 1966.

Montgomery, James R., Stanley J. Folmsbee, and Lee S. Greene. *To Foster Knowledge: A History of the University of Tennessee, 1794–1970.* Knoxville: University of Tennessee Press, 1984.

Moreno, Paul D. *The American State from the Civil War to the New Deal: The Twilight of Constitutionalism and the Triumph of Progressivism.* Cambridge: Cambridge University Press, 2013.

Morgan, Harcourt Alexander. Harcourt Alexander Morgan Papers. University of Tennessee Special Collections.

Morgan, Wiley L. "The University of Tennessee." *The T. P. A. Magazine: Official Organ of the Travelers' Protective Association of America,* 1920.

Morse, Josiah. "The University Commission on Southern Race Questions." *The South Atlantic Quarterly* 19, no. 2 (April 1920): 302–10.

Mumby, Dennis K. *Communication and Power in Organizations: Discourse, Ideology, and Domination*. Norwood, NJ: Ablex Publishing, 1988.

Munzer, Martha. *Valley of Vision*. New York: Alfred A. Knopf, 1969.

Myers, Christine D. *University Coeducation in the Victorian Era: Inclusion in the United States and the United Kingdom*. New York: Palgrave MacMillan, 2010.

Nagi, Mark. *Decades of Dysfunction: The Road to Tennessee's Crazy Coaching Search*. Knoxville: Mean Streets Press, 2018.

"National Affairs, Report Card." *Time*, September 19, 1955.

Neel, Warren. *The Accidental Dean*. Warren Neel, 2010.

Neely, Jack. "How Alumni Memorial Changed Knoxville." *Torchbearer*, June 21, 2019. https://torchbearer.utk.edu/2019/06/how-alumni-memorial-changed-knoxville/.

Neem, Johann M. *What's the Point of College? Seeking Purpose in an Age of Reform*. Baltimore: Johns Hopkins University Press, 2019.

Noe, Kenneth W. *Southwest Virginia's Railroad: Modernization and the Sectional Crisis in the Civil War Era*. Tuscaloosa: University of Alabama Press, 1994.

Nord, Warren A. *Religion & American Education: Rethinking a National Dilemma*. Chapel Hill: University of North Carolina Press, 1995.

Norrell, Robert J. *Up from History: The Life of Booker T. Washington*. Cambridge: Harvard University Press, 2009.

Norris, Geoffrey. *Rachmaninoff*. Oxford: Oxford University Press, 2000.

Norton, Herman Albert. *Religion in Tennessee, 1777–1945*. Knoxville: University of Tennessee Press, 1981.

Obituary for Capt. John M. Brooks. *Confederate Veteran Magazine* 30, no. 1 (January 1922): 111.

Office of the Chancellor Records. University of Tennessee Special Collections.

Office of the University Historian Collection. University of Tennessee Special Collections.

Ogren, Christine A. *The American State Normal School: "An instrument of Great Good."* New York: Palgrave MacMillan, 2005.

Oriard, Michael. *King Football: Sport and Spectacle in the Golden Age of Radio and Newsreels, Movies and Magazines, the Weekly and the Daily Press*. Chapel Hill: University of North Carolina Press, 2005.

———. *Reading Football: How the Popular Press Created an American Spectacle*. Chapel Hill: University of North Carolina Press, 1993.

O'Steen, Neal. "Pioneer Education in the Tennessee Country." *Tennessee Historical Quarterly* 35, no. 2 (Summer 1976): 199–219.

———. "The University of Tennessee: Evolution of a Campus." *Tennessee Historical Quarterly* 39, no. 3 (Fall 1980): 257–81.

Papers of Oliver Perry Temple. University of Tennessee Special Collections.

Patrick, James. *Architecture in Tennessee, 1768–1897*. Knoxville: University of Tennessee Press, 1981.

Payne, Weldon. *Web to the Stars: A History of the University of Tennessee Space Institute.* Dubuque, IA: Kendall-Hunt, 1992.

Perdue, Theda. *Cherokee Women: Gender and Culture Change, 1700–1835.* Lincoln: University of Nebraska Press, 1998.

Perlstein, Rick. *Nixonland: The Rise of a President and the Fracturing of America.* New York, Simon & Schuster, 2009.

Pollitt, Phoebe Ann. *African American and Cherokee Nurses in Appalachia: A History, 1900–1965.* Jefferson, NC: McFarland, 2016.

Posey, Walter Brownlow. *Frontier Mission: A History of Religion West of the Southern Appalachians to 1861.* Lexington: University Press of Kentucky, 1966.

Prather, H. Leon. *Resurgent Politics and Educational Progressivism in the New South, North Carolina, 1890–1913.* Cranbury, NJ: Fairleigh Dickinson University Press, 1979.

"President Thomas W. Humes." *The University of Tennessee Record* no. 5 (July 1898): 220–21.

Progress and Problems: A Time for Building (Central Report; Self Study). Knoxville: University of Tennessee Press, 1970.

Proudfoot, Merrill. *Diary of a Sit-In.* Urbana: University of Illinois Press, 1990.

Prude, James C. "William Gibbs McAdoo and the Democratic National Convention of 1924." *Journal of Southern History* 38 (November 1972): 621–28.

Purcell, Aaron. "'The Greatest Event Since the Civil War': Progressivism and the Summer School of the South at the University of Tennessee," *Journal of East Tennessee History* 76 (2004): 1–28.

———. *White Collar Radicals: TVA's Knoxville Fifteen, the New Deal, and the McCarthy Era.* Knoxville: University of Tennessee Press, 2009.

Raffel, Jeffrey A. *Historical Dictionary of School Segregation and Desegregation: The American Experience.* Westport: Greenwood Press, 1998.

Ratcliffe, Donald. "The Right to Vote and the Rise of Democracy, 1787–1828," *Journal of the Early Republic* 33 (Summer 2013): 219–54.

Ratner, Lormen. *Andrew Jackson and His Tennessee Lieutenants: A Study in Political Culture.* Westport, CT: Greenwood Press, 1997.

Read, Ira. "The Church College in Central Appalachia." In *Christianity in Appalachia: Profiles in Regional Pluralism,* edited by Bill J. Leonard. Knoxville: University of Tennessee Press, 1999.

Reid, Debra A. *Science as Service: Establishing and Reformulating American Land-Grant Universities, 1865–1930.* Tuscaloosa: University of Alabama Press, 2015.

Reisch, George A. *How the Cold War Transformed Philosophy of Science: To the Icy Slopes of Logic.* Cambridge: Cambridge University Press, 2005.

Reynolds, John S. *Reconstruction in South Carolina, 1865–1877.* Columbia, SC: State Publishers, 1905.

Richmond, Demetrius D. "A Case Study of Two Exemplary Black Cultural Centers in Higher Education." PhD diss., University of Tennessee, 2012.

Ring, Natalie J. *The Problem South: Region, Empire, and the New Liberal State, 1880–1930.* Athens: University of Georgia Press, 2012.

Robison, Daniel Merritt. *Bob Taylor and the Agrarian Revolt in Tennessee*. Chapel Hill: University of North Carolina Press, 1935.

Roblyer, Leslie F. "The Fight for Local Prohibition in Knoxville, Tennessee, 1907," *East Tennessee Historical Society's Publications* 26 (1954): 27–37.

Rohrbaugh, Malcolm J. *The Land Office Business: The Settlement and Administration of American Public Lands*. New York: Oxford University Press, 1968.

Romalis, Shelly. *Pistol Packin' Mama: Aunt Molly Jackson and the Politics of Folksong*. Urbana: University of Illinois Press, 1999.

Roper, John H. C. *Vann Woodward, Southerner*. Athens: University of Georgia Press, 1987.

Rothrock, Mary, ed. *The French Broad-Holston Country: A History of Knox County, Tennessee*. Knoxville: East Tennessee Historical Society, 1972.

Sack, Allen L. *Counterfeit Amateurs: An Athlete's Journey Through the Sixties to the Age of Academic Capitalism*. University Park: Pennsylvania State Press, 2008.

Sanford, Edward T. *Blount College and the University of Tennessee: An Historical Address Delivered Before the Alumni Association and Members of the University of Tennessee, by Edward T. Sanford, A. M., June 12th, 1894*. Knoxville: University of Tennessee, 1895.

Saunders, James Edmonds. *Early Settlers of Alabama, Part 1*. New Orleans: L. Graham & Son, 1899.

Savitt, Todd L. "Money versus Mission at an African-American Medical School: Knoxville College Medical Department, 1895–1900." *Bulletin of the History of Medicine* 75, no. 4 (Winter 2001): 680–716.

Scotch-Irish Congress. *The Scotch-Irish in America: Proceedings of the Scotch-Irish Congress*. Vol. 7. Nashville: Barbee & Smith, 1895.

Shannon, Samuel H. "Land-Grant College Legislation and Black Tennesseans: A Case Study in the Politics of Education." *History of Education Quarterly* 22, no. 2 (Summer 1982): 139–57.

Shapiro, Adam R. *Trying Biology: The Scopes Trial, Textbooks, and the Antievolution Movement in American Schools*. University of Chicago Press, 2013.

Sherrod, Alan. "Rachmaninoff's Last Performance." *Classical Journal* (blog). Updated February 13, 2013. https://classicaljournal.wordpress.com/2010/08/17/rachmaninoffs -last-performance/.

Siler, Tom. *Tennessee's Dazzling Decade, 1960–1970*. Knoxville: Hubert E. Hodge, 1970.

———. *The Volunteers*. Knoxville: Archer & Smith, 1950.

Smith, Frank J. "Robert Lewis Dabney." In *Religion and Politics in America: An Encyclopedia of Church and State in American Life*, 225–26. New York: ABC-CLIO, 2016.

Smith, John David. "Ulrich B. Phillips: Dunningite or Phillipsian Sui Generis?" In *The Dunning School: Historians, Race, and the Meaning of Reconstruction*, edited by John David Smith and J. Vincent Lowery. Lexington: University Press of Kentucky, 2013.

Smith, Ronald A. *Pay for Play: A History of Big-Time College Athletic Reform*. Urbana: University of Illinois Press, 2011.

Snipes, J. T., and Carl Darnell. "Non-Black Student Recruitment at Historical Black Colleges and Universities." In *Black Colleges Across the Diaspora: Global Perspectives on Race and*

Stratification in Postsecondary Education, edited by M. Christopher Brown II and T. Elon Dancy II, 49–67. Bingley, UK: Emerald Publishing, 2018.

Statute laws of the State of Tennessee of a general character: passed since the compilation of the statutes by Caruthers and Nicholson in 1836: and being a supplement to that work, 1847–1848. Nashville: James G. Shepard, 1848.

Stetar, Joseph M. "In Search of a Direction: Southern Higher Education after the Civil War," *History of Education Quarterly* 25, no. 3 (Autumn 1985): 341–67.

Stevens, Robert. *Legal Education in America from the 1850s to the 1980s*. Union, NJ: Lawbook Exchange, 2001.

Stokely, Jim. "The Roles of Wilma Dykeman." *Appalachian Heritage* 41, no. 2 (Spring 2013): 28–33.

Suggs, Welch. *A Place on the Team: The Triumph and Tragedy of Title IX*. Princeton, NJ: Princeton University Press, 2005.

———. "U. of Tennessee Shortchanges Athletes Academically, Professor Charges." *The Chronicle of Higher Education*, April 24, 2000. https://www.chronicle.com/article/U-of-Tennessee-Shortchanges/105167.

"Suit Filed against University of Tennessee." *The Crisis*, June 1936.

Summitt, Pat, with Sally Jenkins. *Raise the Roof: The Inspiring Story of the Tennessee Lady Vols' Undefeated 1997–1998 Season*. New York: Broadway Books, 1998.

———. *Sum It Up: 1,098 Wins, a Couple of Irrelevant Losses, and a Life in Perspective*. New York: Crown Archetype, 2013.

Sydnor, Charles. *The Development of Southern Sectionalism: 1819–1848*. Baton Rouge: Louisiana State University Press, 1966.

Taylor, Amy Murrell. *The Divided Family in Civil War America*. Chapel Hill: University of North Carolina Press, 2005.

Teichgraeber Richard F., III, *Building Culture: Studies in the Intellectual History of Industrializing America, 1867–1910*. Columbia: University of South Carolina Press, 2010.

Teloh, Mary H., and James Thweatt. "Tennessee Medical Imprints of the Nineteenth Century." *Tennessee Historical Quarterly* 53, no. 3 (Fall 1994): 208–17.

Temple, Oliver Perry. *East Tennessee and the Civil War*. Cincinnati: Robert Clarke, 1899.

———. *Notable Men of Tennessee: From 1833 to 1875, Their Times and Their Contemporaries*. New York: Cosmopolitan Press, 1912.

Tennessee Law Review 1, no. 1 (November 1922).

Thelin, John R. *American Higher Education: Issues and Institutions*. New York: Taylor & Francis, 2017.

———. "Good Sports? Historical Perspective on the Political Economy of Intercollegiate Athletics in the Era of Title IX, 1972–1997." *Journal of Higher Education* 71, no. 4 (July/August 2000): 391–410.

———. *A History of American Higher Education*. Baltimore: Johns Hopkins University Press, 2004.

Thompson, Ruth Anne. "'A Taste of Student Power': Protest at the University of Tennessee, 1964–1970." *Tennessee Historical Quarterly* 57, no. 1 (Spring/Summer 1998): 80–97.

Tindall, George B. "Southern Mythology." In *The South and the Sectional Image: The Sectional Theme Since Reconstruction*, edited by Dewey Grantham. New York: Harper & Row, 1967.

Toma, J. Douglas. *Football U.: Spectator Sports in the Life of the American University*. Ann Arbor: University of Michigan Press, 2003.

"'To Promote No Creed': Religion at the University of Tennessee." *Context*, November 1995.

Travis, Clay. *On Rocky Top: A Front-Row Seat to the End of an Era*. New York: It Books, 2009.

Turner, Martha L. "The Cause of the Union in East Tennessee." *Tennessee Historical Quarterly* 40, no. 4 (Winter 1981): 366–80.

Turpie, David. "From Broadway to Hollywood: The Image of the 1939 University of Tennessee Football Team and the Americanization of the South." *Journal of Sport History* 35, no. 1 (Spring 2008): 119–40.

"University Commission on Southern Race Questions, The." *Fisk University News* 9, no. 10 (June 1919): 12–16.

University of Tennessee. "Notable Woman Award 1998: Dr. Mary Douglas Ayres Ewell." Accessed July 1, 2018. http://web.utk.edu/~cfw/awards/notable_woman/winners/notable-1998.shtml.

University of Tennessee. "Summitt to Go for the Gold," *The Volunteer*. Knoxville: 1983.

———. "UT Ranks 44th in 2020 U.S. News and World Report Rankings," September 9, 2019, https://news.utk.edu/2019/09/09/ut-ranks-44th-in-2020-u-s-news-and-world-report-rankings/.

———. *The Volunteer*. Knoxville: 1950.

University of Tennessee Libraries. "UT Makes Dramatic Desegregation Progress: UT President." August 14, 1995. https://libguides.utk.edu/c.php?g=578432&p=6431189.

University of Tennessee Office of Institutional Research and Assessment. Distribution of Employees by EEO Category and Race Fall 2017, 2017–18 Fact Book. https://oira.utk.edu/wp-content/uploads/sites/66/2018/10/Archive-17_18-Fact-Book.pdf.

University of Tennessee President's Papers. University of Tennessee Special Collections.

University of Tennessee Record 74, Issue 6 (1971): 339.

University of Tennessee Special Collections. University of Tennessee Libraries.

Valbrun, Marjorie. "Presidential Spouses Behaving Badly." *Inside Higher Education*, October 24, 2018. https://www.insidehighered.com/news/2018/10/24/controversial-spouses-college-presidents-can-hurt-image-president-and-university.

Veysey, Laurence R. *The Emergence of the American University*. Chicago: University of Chicago Press, 1965.

Vick, Alison. "'We Are a Distinct and Peculiar People': Oliver Perry Temple and the Knoxville Industrial Association Address of 1869." *Journal of East Tennessee History* 84 (2012): 87–100.

Volunteer Leaders: A Bicentennial Directory of Some Notable Alumni of The University of Tennessee, Knoxville, 1794–1994. Knoxville: Office of the University Historian, 1995.

Vonnegut, Kurt. *Palm Sunday: An Autobiographical Collage*. New York: Random House, 2009.

Walsh, Christopher J. *Where Football Is King: A History of the SEC*. New York: Taylor Trade Publishing, 2006.

Watterson, John Sayle. *College Football: History, Spectacle, Controversy*. Baltimore: Johns Hopkins University Press, 2000.

West, Carroll Van. *Tennessee's Historical Landscapes: A Traveler's Guide.* Knoxville: University
of Tennessee Press, 1995.

West, Marvin. *Legends of the Tennessee Vols.* Champaign, IL: Sports Publishing, 2005.

———. *Tales of the Tennessee Vols: A Collection of the Greatest Vols Stories Ever Told.*
Champaign, IL: Sports Publishing, 2002.

Wheeler, William Bruce. *Knoxville, Tennessee: A Mountain City in the New South,* 3rd ed.
Knoxville: University of Tennessee Press, 2020.

———. William Bruce Wheeler Papers (BWP).

Whitaker, A. P. "The Public School System of Tennessee, 1834–1860." *Tennessee Historical
Magazine* 2, no. 1 (March 1916): 1–30.

Whitaker, Dianne. "A New Faculty Member at a New College." In *Reforming a College:
The University of Tennessee Story,* edited by Richard Wisniewski. New York: Peter
Lang, 2000.

White, Kate. "Knoxville's Old Educational Institutions." *Tennessee Historical Magazine* 8, no. 1
(April 1924): 3–6.

White, Mason, and Maya Przybylski. *On Farming.* Barcelona: ACTAR, 2010.

White, Moses. Papers. University of Tennessee Special Collections.

Whitehead, John S. "Southern Universities: Are They Rising?" *History of Education Quarterly*
25, no. 4 (Winter 1986): 553–68.

Wiebe, Robert H. *The Search for Order, 1877–1920.* New York: Hill & Wang, 1967.

Wilder, Craig Steven. *Ebony and Ivy: Race, Slavery, and the Troubled History of American
Universities.* New York: Bloomsbury Press, 2013.

Wilentz, Sean. *The Rise of American Democracy: Jefferson to Lincoln.* New York: W. W.
Norton, 2005.

Williamson, Joel. *The Crucible of Race: Black-White Relations in the American South since
Emancipation.* Oxford University Press, 1984.

Winn, Thomas H. "Liquor, Race, and Politics: Clarksville During the Progressive Period."
Tennessee Historical Quarterly 49 (1990): 207–17.

Wisniewski, Richard. Afterword to *Reforming a College: The University of Tennessee Story.*
New York: Peter Lang, 2000.

Wolfe, Margaret Ripley. "Bootleggers, Drummers, and National Defense: Sideshow to Reform
in Tennessee, 1915–1920," *East Tennessee Historical Society's Publications* 49 (1977): 77–92.

Wolverton, Brad. "Tennessee's Pat Summit [*sic*] is First Woman in College Athletics' $1-Million
Club." *Chronicle of Higher Education,* June 2, 2006. https://www.chronicle.com/article
/Tennessees-Pat-Summit-Is/10438.

Woodward, C. Vann. *Origins of the New South.* Baton Rouge: Louisiana State University
Press, 1981.

Young, Gwenda. *Clarence Brown: Hollywood's Forgotten Master.* Lexington: University Press
of Kentucky, 2018.

Zagumny, Lisa L. "Sit-Ins in Knoxville, Tennessee: A Case Study of Political Rhetoric." *Journal
of Negro History* 86, no. 1 (Winter 2001): 45–54.

Zellner, Bob, with Constance Curry. *The Wrong Side of Murder Creek: A White Southerner in
the Freedom Movement.* Montgomery: New South Books, 2008.

INDEX

Milles, Carl, 135

Mill Springs, Battle of, 21

Min, Nancy-Ann, 141

modernism, 70–71

Montgomery, Lou, 91

Morgan, Arthur, 77–78

Morgan, Harcourt: on academic freedom, 73–76; and farmers, 71; and "new frontier," 78, 95; president, appointment as, 66; and TVA, 77–78; and UT state funding, 91–92

Morrill Act (1862, federal), 26–29, 33. *See also* land-grant schools

Morrill Act, second (1890, federal), 43, 51, 61. *See also* land-grant schools

Mueller, A. D., 78

Napier, J. C., 62

Nashville Medical College, 65

National Alliance for College Athletic Reform, 158

National Association for the Advancement of Colored People, 102

National Collegiate Athletic Association (NCAA), 83, 143, 156–59

Neal, John R., 75, 77–78

New South, 43, 53

Newton, Kenneth, 128

Neyland, Robert, 85–91, 104, 118, 156, 158–59

Nicholson, Hunter, 29, 33, 38–39

Nixon, Richard, 127–30

Norman, Ralph, 128–30

Oak Ridge Associated Universities, 108

Oak Ridge Institute of Nuclear Studies, 108

Oak Ridge National Laboratories, 152

Obama, Barack, 146

Oberlin College, 6

Orange & White, 54, 74, 108

Parker, Paul, 86

Parker, William E., 6

Parsons, Howard, 101–2

Patterson, Joseph, 113

Payne, John K., 30–31

Peabody, George, 38

Pearlstein exhibit, 149–50

Peay, Austin, 74–75, 91

Peel, Brenda, 115

Perkins, Angie, 58

Peterson, John, 160–61

Phillips, Ulrich B., 60

Piper, James, 11

Plessy v. Ferguson (1896), 61–62

Polk, Leonidas, 51

Pollio, Howard, 131

Populist Party (People's Party), 48

Powell, Adam Clayton, 122

Presbyterian Church, 3–5, 12–14, 16

Princeton University, 4, 11, 57

Prohibition, 69–70

Quinn, John, 138–39

Rachmaninoff, Sergei, 97

radio, 85–86, 89–90

railroads, 16

Ramsey, James, 15

Randolph, Boots, 135

Ray, David, 124

Ray, Gloria, 144

Reagan, Ronald, 151

Reconstruction, 22–24, 34–35

Redemption, 29–33

Redmond, William, 111–12

Red Scare, 101–4

Red Summer, 67–68

Reese, Jack, 136, 139, 150

Reese, William, 13, 16

Reynolds, Charles, 128, 130

Ridge, John (Skah-tle-loh-skee), 6

Roane, Archibald, 4

Roberts, Kerry, 166

Robinson, Harvey, 118